*Phonological Acquisition
and Change*

Phonological Acquisition and Change

JOHN L. LOCKE

MGH Institute of Health Professions
Massachusetts General Hospital
Boston, Massachusetts
and
Department of Neurology
Harvard University Medical School
Boston, Massachusetts

With a Foreword by Michael Studdert-Kennedy

ACADEMIC PRESS   1983

A Subsidiary of Harcourt Brace Jovanovich, Publishers

New York   London
Paris   San Diego   San Francisco   São Paulo   Sydney   Tokyo   Toronto

ACADEMIC PRESS, INC.
111 Fifth Avenue, New York, New York 10003

United Kingdom Edition published by
ACADEMIC PRESS, INC. (LONDON) LTD.
24/28 Oval Road, London NW1 7DX

Library of Congress Cataloging in Publication Data

Locke, John L.
   Phonological acquisition and change.

   Includes index.
   1. Language acquisition. 2. Grammar, Comparative
and general--Phonology. 3. Linguistic change.
I. Title. [DNLM: 1. Speech--In infancy and childhood
2. Phonetics. 3. Language development. WS 105.5.C8
L814p]
P118.L62 1983   401'.9   83–2811
ISBN 0–12–454180–1

PRINTED IN THE UNITED STATES OF AMERICA

83 84 85 86 · 9 8 7 6 5 4 3 2 1

For Linda

Contents

Foreword

Interest in the biological foundations of language has revived during the past 25 years, spurred in large part by discoveries in generative linguistics. For if there is indeed a deep structure of language from which surface structure arises, and if the underlying forms of the deep structure are indeed *sui generis,* distinct from the underlying forms of meaning and thought (i.e., of general cognition), the conclusion that language is a biologically specialized faculty is hard to resist. If we now add the (dubious) proposition that the speech a child hears is too poor, too variable and degenerate, for the child to learn a language without some special purpose mechanism, we are led to posit an innate "language acquisition device." From here the path to a full-fledged revival of faculty psychology is direct. Language now becomes a "mental organ" or, if we prefer computer metaphors, a "module."

Yet even if we accept such metaphors, we will not advance our understanding of the biology of language until we set about dissecting the "mental organ." Neither the phylogeny nor the ontogeny of an organ is necessarily impenetrable. The structure and function of the heart, for example—and even, perhaps, its evolutionary history—can be illuminated by studying the biophysical principles to which it conforms and by tracing its embryological development.

Perhaps what we need, then, is an "embryology" of language. For the biologist, development (anatomical, physiological, and behavioral) is a continuous interaction between an acting organism and its environment, from the first divisions of the fertilized egg to death. Each stage in the process is an adaptive response of the organism to its present environment, but may also be seen, teleologically, as a necessary step in a developmental sequence. In studying language, anatomists and physiologists might begin with prenatal development of the vocal apparatus and lateralized regions of the brain. Such work is indeed going forward. Psychologists, on the other hand, will be likely to begin with the first postnatal evidence of behaviors that will be marshaled, in due course, for speaking.

Notice that this approach no longer concerns itself with "acquisition" of language. Language is not seen as an object, or even a skill, that lies outside the child and has somehow to be internalized. Rather, it is seen as a mode of action, implicit in the child's structure, that will automatically begin to function—as do heart and lungs—in a range of appropriate environments. The precise path of development is not preordained, since no animal structure specifies a unique function. The process is epigenetic, an accumulation of adaptive changes that may continue even in the adult, exposed to the accent, lexicon, and syntax of a new dialect. From this vantage, the adult's language is seen as emerging from the child's language rather than the child's as "acquired" from the adult. Of course, this is no more than a change of emphasis, but it is one that may prove fruitful in several areas of language study.

Consider, in the present context, phonology. The achievements of generative phonology have been possible because, despite the rejection of structuralism, the recasting of *langue* and *parole* as competence and performance was not, in fact, a revolutionary change of paradigm. The primacy of linguistic form over linguistic substance was still assumed—despite lip-service to "universal phonetics." Certainly, the assumption has proved its worth. It has enabled phonologists to shed the troublesome details of actual speech behavior and to isolate the sound forms, and "rules" for their combination, shared by members of a language community.

However, once we turn to the development of language—or even to the mundane activities of speaking and hearing—we can no longer dismiss the variability of speech, since this is precisely the stuff we have to work with. If we accept this fact, we need no longer view our task as one of wrestling with a paradox, namely, the incommensurability of speech with its underlying forms. Rather, we will see the task as one of tracing the development of those forms from their "embryological" precursors in the child.

How then are we to begin? A necessary preliminary is surely to establish the child's initial phonetic proclivities and to show that they survive (profoundly modified of course, as is all human behavior, by the biases of a particular cultural environment) in the adult. This is what John Locke has done in this book. He has compiled a massive recension of evidence on the phonetic biases shared by infants and by adult speakers of many languages. He shows that many of those preferences—ultimately, we may hope, all of them—can be rationalized in terms of physiological and aerodynamic constraints on vocal action. Finally, he indicates how infant preferences may be gradually modified by the language they are learning. Some preferences are maintained because they are also retained by adult speakers of the language, some are lost because they are not. Other preferences, more rarely, are maintained despite their loss by adult speakers, and so may come to mark the language—to the benefit, no doubt, of the child's descendants.

The notion that the phonetic proclivities of the child may become frozen into adult forms, thus contributing to language change, has been, as Locke shows, a recurrent speculation since the end of the nineteenth century, when evolutionary views of language were first explored. What surprised me and will, I believe, surprise other readers is how extensive the evidence on these matters is. I was particularly struck by the many studies that agree on the properties of infant babbling, on the continuity between babbling and speech, and on the developmental sequence of sound mastery, both across infants (including during the first year of life, the congenitally deaf) and across languages. Locke has done an enormous service in bringing together the detailed results of hundreds of studies. His bibliography comprises some 450 scattered items, ranging from nineteenth-century texts through obscure Master's theses of the 1940s and 1950s to current studies (including his own), many of them still in press.

But this monograph is very much more than an annotated bibliography. It is a critical, theoretically guided review and coordination of the literature. Many of the conjunctions are entirely surprising—for example, studies of Down's syndrome infants, inebriate speech and glossolalia—yet have unquestionable bearing on human phonetic proclivity. Moreover, Locke has often found more in the studies than the studies did themselves. He reanalyzes data, points to unnoticed regularities, computes new correlations, and sets the results in a larger frame where fresh implications come suddenly into view. Thus, studies, weak in isolation, take on new force when marshaled with others, tending to similar conclusions.

Much, of course, remains to be done, and the book has many hints and explicit suggestions for future research. For example, further studies of the developmental physiology of articulatory control and more shrewdly directed studies of infant perceptual capacity, taken with the few already done and discussed by Locke, may lead to more satisfactory definitions of the useful, but difficult, concepts, "ease of articulation" and "perceptual distinctiveness." These concepts, in turn, may throw light on the origins of phonological structure in perceptuomotor constraints. For this seems to be Locke's ultimate goal. What he has done here is to take a first, large step toward deriving phonology from phonetics, grounding the axiomatic primitives of linguistic description, and the "rules" for their combination, in the anatomy and physiology of the speaking animal.

In short, anyone who has been tempted to speculate that language may take form from its substance, rather than substance from its form, will find grist for his mill in this insightful and authoritative monograph.

MICHAEL STUDDERT-KENNEDY

Preface

This monograph reflects my belief that language acquisition can be understood—not merely described—and represents my view that phonological development and change are dynamic processes in which cognitive, biological, and social factors continuously interact throughout the life of human speakers. I am intrigued by the ways children learn, reinvent, analyze and manipulate sound categories. But to understand acquisition, I believe one needs also to understand what might be termed "ecophonology": childrens's inherent phonetic tendencies in relation to the everyday speech habits of the adults, older children, and peers in their environment.

The purpose of this monograph is to propose and to support several particular theories of phonological acquisition and change. In doing this, I present in the first chapter a comprehensive review of the published and unpublished literature on the babbling-to-speech transition. In order to evaluate the relative force of biological and environmental factors, I examine the vocalizations of children whose linguistic environments are different and of children whose awareness of their environment (or ability to learn about it) is lower than average. Some previously unpublished data are reported in this chapter and also in Chapter 2, where I examine developmental universals, the phonetic patterns common to children learning a variety of languages. In the second chapter I also delineate several stages of development and propose a phonetic and perceptual explanation of children's early phonological patterns.

The third chapter comprises an analysis of the speech pattern of adults, revealed in laboratory experiments, casual speech, brain damage, slips of the tongue, glossolalia, and the segment inventories of standard languages. Chapter 4 identifies the nonarbitrary nature of standard phonological systems and questions the implications of "naturalness" for acquisition, usage, and change. Chapter 5 explores the developmental consequences of an adult system that is represented by distortions and variability. In the final chapter, I present a cognitive and interactive model of children's speech errors, arguing that many errors are the result of system restructuring as well as vocal tract constraints.

I wrote this monograph to examine intensively a particular set of hypotheses, and I think of it primarily as a theoretical treatise and reference work. As such, it should be of value to those in language development, linguistics, speech–language pathology, psycholinguistics, and child development. Because of its extensive literature review, it will also be a useful supplement to a text for courses in language development and disorders.

Acknowledgments

I wrote this monograph at my roll-top desk, composing the first several drafts with the help of a good friend, L. C. Smith, my elderly typing machine. After that, I got some assistance from a number of scholars who took time from their productive lives to read and criticize earlier drafts of this monograph. There are two whose efforts particularly stand out: each read the entire manuscript in detail and suggested numerous improvements. One is Michael Smith of Western Carolina University, the other is Bruce Smith of Northwestern University. Each can take a bit of the credit for this monograph.

During the 1982 Linguistic Institute I was able to prevail upon a number of "captive" readers, and I wish to thank them as well. Chief among them was Wolfgang Dressler, who read and commented on the monograph from his European perspective, calling my attention to an impressive array of literature. I also wish to thank Ann Peters, whose comments on the constructions of formulas and other issues have strengthened this book. Jill de Villiers and Hugh Buckingham made a number of useful criticisms of the first two and the second two chapters, respectively. I also wish to thank Michael Studdert-Kennedy for his invaluable Institute course on "An approach to the biology of speech and language" and for expressing an interest in this project.

Others offering assistance were Carol Stoel-Gammon and Marilyn Vihman, who read and commented on the manuscript, Dan Dinnsen, who remarked helpfully on Chapters 3 and 4, and Florina Koopmans-van Beinum and Kristine Mackain, who made valuable criticisms of Chapter 1. I am pleased to have the opportunity to thank James Flege publicly for his interest in my work over the past 4 years. Jim has called my attention to relevant literature and has taught me a great deal about phonetics and phonetic learning through his own research and correspondence.

Many of the ideas expressed in this monograph were developed while I was on the staff of the Institute for Child Behavior and Development, University of Illinois. All the writing was done at the University of Maryland, where I received partial support for processing of the manuscript. I wish to thank Sandra Wood-ruff and Shirley Norton of the BSOS Computer Center for assisting me in using the prime word-processing system.

I have a great personal debt to Teresa Plevyak Kenney. Teresa efficiently typed and cheerfully retyped the entire manuscript onto a word processor, con-tributing to this project the typing experience of a legal secretary, the knowledge of a speech–language pathologist, and the service of a good and loyal friend.

Finally, I wish to thank my parents, Edward and Lillian Locke, for creating the loving and literate home that placed so many wonderful things within my reach.

Note on Style

In presenting my own data and examples, I have used the symbols of the International Phonetic Association. When reproducing the transcriptions of others, I have attempted to preserve the authors' original notations. Throughout this monograph, the word *change* is used in its most general sense, sometimes referring to discrepancies between adult and child forms, on other occasions referring to discrepancies between historical and present-day forms or between speakers' internally represented and overtly produced forms, or between their usual and accidental forms. That these various discrepancies are called by one name does not mean I think they are identical. Rather, I intend the word *change* in a neutral way, though I believe many changes ultimately will be understood in phonetic terms.

Let us now seek to understand how this undesigned trying of the articulate instrument passes into true significant articulation, how this speech-protoplasm develops into the organism that we call language.

—SULLY (1896, p. 138)

*Phonological Acquisition
and Change*

1

The Beginnings of Phonology in the Child

One cannot hope to understand the child's acquisition of any system of behaviors without observing the acquisitive process from the beginning. This requires that we determine when the child initially absorbs and analyzes that system, and accommodates to it in his own behavior. But in making such a determination we also must decide what behaviors will be taken as evidence of the child's acquisition.

Do we say a child has begun to acquire phonology when his vocal output is observed to be less like it was initially and more like that of his parents? If so, should we be bothered by the fact that—up to a point—this will occur for children who are born and raised deaf?

Shall we allow that aspects of a phonology may emerge without phonetic stimulation? Will we be comfortable with the definition of language that such a concession would seem to require? Does the environmental burden we presuppose for syntactic development fit with equal ease into our theory of phonological development?

If phonology begins with the child's first word—frequently the infamous *papa*—how are we to regard the fact that the fathers of the world, whatever their language, typically are called something very much like *papa?* When a child can blunder into a word, just how important is what we think of as ''learning''?

In the chronology of things, and in their dynamics, is there a difference between when the child begins actively to acquire an expressive phonology and when a primitive phonological system is first observable?

At the heart of any attempt to address such questions is the collected data on infant phonetic behavior, to be sure. I believe these data are really much more estensive than most scholars imagine, and I will begin to examine them in the succeeding pages. But just as crucial is our conception of what phonology is. If to have phonology a child must reveal a rigidly patterned system of segments, syllable shapes and stresses, phonotactic rules, and pitch contours—a system whose properties resemble those of the adult system, and are available to convey lexical meaning—then I feel certain that most children have phonology long before their first "true word" is evident. If to have acquired phonology the child's prelexical sound system must perceptibly change in the direction of the ambient system—in a way that could only be due to exposure—then I feel just as certain that a child's (expressive) phonological system may not be acquired until well after the appearance of his early words.

When Is the Beginning?

From my reading of the literature, there appear to be two conceptions of the significance—and the developmental onset—of phonology: Though these conceptions are in opposition to each other, I believe that both Jakobson's "prelinguistic" conception and Brown's "babbling drift" hypothesis are less than satisfying and are probably incorrect as to when phonological development begins.

Babbling as "Prelinguistic" Behavior

Jakobson (1941/1968) observed, or from the statements of Gregoire (1937, in Jakobson) was lead to believe, that babbling is characterized by "an astonishing quantity and diversity of sound productions . . . articulations which are never found within a single language or even a group of languages—consonants of any place of articulation, palatalized and rounded consonants, sibilants, affricates, clicks, complex vowels, diphthongs, etc. [p. 21]."

This statement seems to transmit an almost "helter-skelter" notion, that babbling is a "now you hear it, now you don't" dose of random oral-motor activity. Such an impression also was generated by Osgood (1953) who, during his time at Yale, recorded the vocal play of an infant in the first few months of life. Osgood heard in his young informant "all the speech sounds that the human vocal system can produce, including French vowels and trills, German umlaut and guttural sounds" and others that were difficult to classify (p. 684). Similarly, according to Bean (1932), "one cannot fail to hear all the vowels and consonants, diphthongs, aspirates, sub-vocals, nasals, German umlauts and tongue trills, French throaty trills and grunts, and even the Welsh *l* [p. 198]."

Such phonetic play on the part of the infant is, according to Jakobson, clearly "prelinguistic." For following the rich and varied and playful period which Jakobson described, "the child then loses nearly all of his ability to produce sounds in passing over from the prelanguage stage to the first acquisition of words, i.e., *to the first genuine stage of language* [p. 21; emphasis mine]."

This "loss of ability" which Jakobson spoke of was likewise surmised by Velten (1943), who observed that the infant's "ability to produce a multitude of speech sounds seems to vanish overnight [p. 281]." The division between "prelinguistic" and "linguistic" is temporal as well as functional, according to Velten, for "a period of complete silence sometimes intervenes between *the babbling stage and the acquisition of language* [p. 281, emphasis mine]." (In a later article, Jakobson, 1968, also referred explicitly to this period in which the child may be "totally mute.")

The legacy of the Jakobson–Velten era lies in several specific and empirical conjectures: babbling is highly varied phonetically, muteness separates babbling from the first words, and the infant loses phonetic ability in the babbling-to-speech transition. In a moment, we will see what the available data have to say about these assertions.

"Babbling Drift"

Though Roger Brown (1958) did not specifically allude to Jakobson's statements, he phrased several remarks that suggest an opposing position. Brown said, for instance, that "the most important thing about babbling [is] the fact that it drifts in the direction of the speech the infant hears [p. 199]." As Brown thought the occurrence of babbling was due to instinct, he invoked generalized secondary reinforcement as the psychological mechanism responsible for drift, the direction of which was determined by "the prevailing linguistic winds."

It is clear from Brown's remarks that he believed babbling would assert itself differently in different language environments. Note that it would not be necessary for the infant to produce words to prove that his phonological acquisition had begun—only for his phonetic values in babbling to become increasingly like those of his environment. There have been several attempts to test the drift hypothesis. There has also been a great deal of confusion about the yield of those efforts; shortly, I will examine both the reported studies and the subsequent misinterpretations.

The Infant's Phonetic Repertoire

If as Jakobson asserted, babbling is characterized by an "astonishing . . . diversity of sound productions," it would seem that a large number of sounds must have an evenly low frequency of occurrence. Surely we would not expect to find a small number of sounds with a high frequency of occurrence within and across infants.

Table 1.1 has the frequency of sounds approximating English consonants in the vocalization of infants reared in American English environments. The Irwin (1947) data are from 62 infants observed at 11–12 months of age; Column A displays these data in relative frequency (in percentages). The Fisichelli (1950) data are from 20 infants observed in two orphanages at 12 months. They are reported in Column B in percentages, as are the data in Column C, which represent my tabulations of Pierce and Hanna's (1974) records on 49 12-month-olds.

Both Irwin and Pierce and Hanna found [h] to be the most frequent consonant sound. It was the second most frequent sound in Fisichelli, possibly because some cases of aspiration were considered to be vegetative rather than phonetic. Note also that the incidence of [w] and [j] is higher in Fisichelli and in Pierce and Hanna than in Irwin. These differences may reflect a decision to classify such ambiguous sequences as [ua] and [ia] as glides rather than diphthongs.

Other than these (and a few other) minor discrepancies, the data from all three studies are remarkably tidy. They are unanimous in showing that among the more frequent 12 consonants (or "protoconsonants") are included all six of the stops, both glides, and two of the three nasals. Each of the voiced (or unaspi-

Table 1.1

Relative Frequency of English Consonant-like Sounds in the Babbling of 11–12-Month-Old American Infants[a]

	More frequent consonants				Less frequent consonants		
Sound	A[b]	B	C	Sound	A[b]	B	C
h	31.77	21.0	18.3	v	1.03	1.0	0
d	20.58	30.0	13.5	l	.96	1.0	1.6
b	9.79	5.0	10.0	θ	.85	0	.4
m	6.69	1.0	7.2	z	.56	0	0
t	4.34	0	3.6	f	.37	0	0.4
g	4.15	12.0	8.4	ʃ	.37	0	0
s	3.45	0	.4	ð	.34	0	0.8
w	3.39	17.0	8.4	ŋ	.33	1.0	3.2
n	2.65	1.0	4.4	ʒ	.10	0	0
k	2.12	1.0	6.3	r	.10	0	0
j	1.77	9.0	11.6	tʃ	0	0	0
p	1.63	0	1.6	dʒ	0	0	0
Totals	92.33	97.0	93.7		5.01	3.0	6.4

Source: Data taken from Locke (1980b).

[a]The three investigations represented are: A: Irwin (1947); B: Fisichelli (1950); C: Pierce and Hanna (1974).

[b]The A columns total less than 100% because the difference (2.66%) represents several sounds in Irwin's original tabulations that have no phonemic equivalent in American English phonology (e.g., [ʔ ç χ]).

Table 1.2
Percentage of Consonant- like Sounds across Three Breath-Group Positions in Infants' Vocalizations

Months	N	Initial	Medial	Final
1–2	61	60.7	37.9	1.5
3–4	79	51.5	44.3	4.2
5–6	74	49.6	45.5	4.9
7–8	63	48.4	44.1	7.5
9–10	61	49.7	40.4	10.0
11–12	61	46.8	40.9	12.3

Source: Derived from figures reported in Irwin (1951, Table 1).

rated) stops is more frequent than its voiceless (aspirated) cognate. The only contact fricative is [s], in Irwin. Among the 12 less frequent consonants are all other fricatives, both affricates, both liquids, and (for Irwin) the remaining (velar) nasal.

The outstanding feature of the data reported here is that the more frequent 12 consonants constitute about 95% of all the consonants heard in all three studies, with the less frequent ones amounting to approximately 5%. So it is not the case that many sounds are made a few times each; rather, a restricted subset of sounds accounts for most of the babbling. Both in Irwin and in Fisichelli the two top sounds sum at more than 50%! Rather than the random distribution that Jakobson's remarks prepared us for, it is clear instead that the infant has a segmental repertoire that is phonetically highly patterned and selective. This regularity is evident, additionally, at the syllabic level. Table 1.2 shows some data from Irwin (1951) on the distribution of consonant-like sounds across three breath-group positions in the babbling of infants during the first year of life. As a breath-group refers to a single exhalation, "Initial" corresponds approximately to utterance initial (therefore, presumably, to syllable initial) and "Final" corresponds to utterance final (therefore, presumably, to syllable final). It is probable that most of the medial consonants were syllable initial, but this cannot be ascertained from Irwin's data. It is clear that syllable-final consonants are extremely rare at 1–2 months, and that they rather steadily increased thereafter but even at 1 year are greatly dominated by syllable-initial forms.[1]

Were there non-English sounds in these infants' vocal play? There were some, and my own impression is that there might have been more if the listeners were themselves non-English, or more effectively oriented to non-English sounds and modes of symbolization. In Irwin, there was a 2.52% incidence of

---

[1]That the infant's sound making is segmentally and syllabically so restricted may implicate the power of anatomical constraints but it does not mean that *within such constraints* the infant is not actively and creatively exploring and deriving pleasure from his vocal activities (cf. Oller, 1981).

the phonemically non-English glottal stop, and a combined occurrence of [x] and [ç] of .14%. Fisichelli did not report non-English sounds. The data of Pierce and Hanna show that all subjects produced at least one glottal stop, and about 13 other non-English consonants appear in their transcriptions with some frequency: About 18.4% of the subjects produced at least one [β], 10.2% produced at least one [ɣ], 8.2% produced [x] and [bw], and 4.1% produced [dz] and [bβ].

Stockman, Woods, and Tishman (1981) observed four infants who were 7 to 21 months of age. My analysis of their data indicates that 19.01% of the sounds heard were phonemically non-English, including:

[ʔ]	15.32	[ts]	.09
[β]	1.65	[R]	.06
[x]	1.09	[dz]	.05
[λ]	.41	[ñ]	.03
[φ]	.29	[ɦ]	.02

After [ʔ], the next 11 sounds in frequency were among the 12 most frequent sounds in Irwin, comprising 91.48% of the English phones heard at 11–12 months. Though Stockman *et al.*'s infants were older than those in Table 1.1, there were still two English sounds not heard (/s, θ/).

The numerical data in Tables 1.1 and 1.2 also are supported by observations of individual children. Cruttenden (1970) reported that neither of his twin daughters ever produced [θ, ð, s, z, ʃ, ʒ] in their babbling; one never produced [f] or [v]. The most common consonants, according to Cruttenden, were [b, d, g, m, n, l]. The predominant syllabic shape was CV, often reduplicated. Cruttenden also noted some non-English sounds, classifiable mainly as bilabial, lateral, velar, or uvular fricatives or affricates. He commented, in summation, that "two claims often made for babbling seem not to be true (1) The children did not babble all the sounds of English. (2) The range of non-English sounds covered was not as wide as is usually implied [p. 112]."

At 15 months, Jessie Labov had not yet begun to produce recognizable words, but she babbled frequently and her parents (Labov & Labov, 1978) regularly transcribed her sound productions. Figure 1.1 shows the consonantal portion of Jessie's babbling repertoire at 15 months, with circles around the phones not yet in evidence. The figure shows that Jessie was mainly attracted to stops, nasals, and glides, with some exceptions, and was disinclined to produce many of the fricatives.

A rich source of information on infant phonetic production is the study of Oller, Wieman, Doyle, and Ross (1976). They analyzed the babbling of two groups of infants, one at 6–8 months and the other at 12–13 months. Rather than reporting segmental frequencies, Oller *et al.* analyzed infant sound production by featural class. For example, over 90% of the consonants produced by both groups were singletons rather than clusters (in Pierce and Hanna's data, 95% of

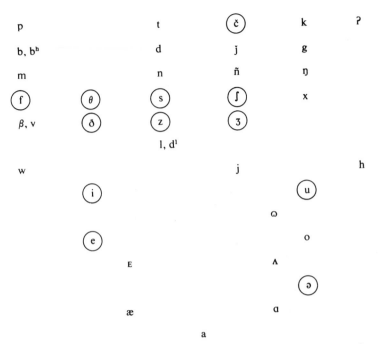

Figure 1.1. *Jessie's repertoire at 15 months. Circled phones are English segments not observed in Jessie's babbling [from Labov, W. & Labov, T. (1978). The phonetics of* cat *and* mama, Language, *54, 816–852; with permission from Linguistic Society of America].*

the consonants were singletons). The ratio of initial to final consonants was over three to one, supporting Cruttenden's observation of open syllable predominance. Unaspirated stops exceeded aspirated stops by a ratio of 49 to 1, coinciding with the greater frequency of [b, d, g] than [p, t, k] in the segmental counts of Table 1.1. In utterance-initial position, there were 149 stops, 9 fricatives, and 5 affricates. Prevocalically, glides exceeded liquids by a ratio of 4.4 to 1. Among the obstruent and nasal consonants, there were 351 apical sounds and just 83 with a dorsal contact.

These findings agree with my featural analyses of the segmental tabulations of Irwin, of Fisichelli, and of Pierce and Hanna; they also agree with the testimony of Cruttenden. And we would assert, as did Oller *et al.*, that "contrary to the position taken by Jakobson and many of his followers, babbling does appear to be governed by general restrictions of the human phonological capacity [p. 9]."

Is the Infant's Phonetic Repertoire Learned?

It is clear, then, that the infant has at his ready disposal a group of stops and nasals and glides, and is quite disinclined to utter fricatives and liquids and affricates. But why? Is this set of rather rigid "preferences" and "avoidances" the result of what he hears around him? We purposely selected the 11–12-month interval for our sampling of infants' phonetic production because of an interest in the babbling-to-speech transition; 12 months is commonly identified as the "age of first word" (Darley & Winitz, 1961). But what of the days and weeks before the first word—might not these barely prelexical infants have already learned something of the ambient system? Might not some of Roger Brown's "babbling drift" have already occurred?

Probably the most useful sound count available for American English is that of Mines, Hanson, and Shoup (1978). Their sample includes over 100,000 phones extracted from the conversations of speakers representing a variety of dialects and age groups. Moreover, the transcriptions are very narrow, that is, presented in allophonic detail. The frequency of the 12 most common (repertoire) sounds is 62.5% of all the consonants. This is some 30 percentage points less than is shown for the infants in Table 1.1. Conversely, the remaining sounds—only 5% for the infants—are nearly 40% for the adults. But clearly the infant figures are in the right direction, despite the differences in magnitude. And the infant does not yet have a fully formed set of neuromuscular routines to execute all the phonetic entities he might know about. So can we call this drift?

It is unnecessary to call it anything at this point. For one thing, we need first to rule out adult *perceptual drift,* the possibility that infants' "noises" derive their phonetic identity and frequency from the expectancies of listeners. These expectancies would be conditioned by the adult listeners' English experience. Goldstein (1980) has argued that precisely such frequency-based perceptual biases may operate in adults' perception of ambiguous syllables which, of course, infants' syllables are. Though Goldstein's frequency hypothesis was only weakly supported for CV syllables, which abound in babbling, I decided to perform a rank-order correlation between the English conversational frequency (from Mines *et al.,* 1978) and the Irwin (1947) babbling frequency of the identically transcribed sounds. The correlation was .45. A second and more directly relevant correlation was performed on the *word-initial* frequencies in Mines *et al.* and the Irwin data. This correlation was .61. These analyses—by themselves—suggest that adult perceptions of infant sounds may be moderately biased by linguistic experience. But recall that correlations do not imply the *direction* of a relationship between two variables. In my treatment of phonological universals in Chapter 3, I will entertain the epiphenomenal prospect that infant babbling and adult language frequencies are correlated because of their joint dependency on a third variable, the nature of the human vocal tract.

Other kinds of data are available on the babbling drift hypothesis. First, there are the phonetic patterns of infants reared in different linguistic environments (e.g., French, German, Hindi, etc.). Second, we have studies in which listeners tried to identify, or laboratory equipment was used to differentiate, such groups of infants. Third, there are the vocalizations of children born and reared deaf. Contrary to the claims of earlier writers, babbling in such children does not cease during the first year. Fourth, we know something of the babbling of children with Down's syndrome, who one might presume to be less proficient in phonetic *learning*. Finally, there are data on the neurological development of the infant, data that speak to the "drift capability" of the incompletely myelinated listener-speaker.

Babbling Cross-Linguistically

The large-scale efforts to quantify infant segmental production have been conducted by American investigators and tied to English. Consequently, we know far less about the babbling patterns of children reared in other-than-English environments. Do they have similar preferences and avoidances? Do they lean more toward the phonetic values of their home? According to Johnston (1896), the speech of babies "is strictly spontaneous, from within outwards; it is the same in babies of different lands, whose parents speak entirely different tongues [p. 502]."

Although present evidence permits no precise answer to such questions as these, it is possible to sketch a crude profile by consulting the diaries of linguists for (frequently their own) non-English children. Table 1.3 shows the occurrence of English or English-like (cf. Ladefoged, 1980) consonant segments in the babbling of infants reared in 14 non-English language environments. The order of the consonants was taken from the Irwin data in Table 1.1. Asterisks indicate that the corresponding sound was among those mentioned in the child's diary. The Afrikaans data are mine, and I will describe them in greater detail later in this chapter. The Mayan and Spanish data were reported by Huber (1970, p. 118); Blount (1970, Table 3), who did the Luo, and Omar (1973, pp. 38–39), who did Egyptian Arabic, are the other American analysts in the group. The Thai records were reported by Tuaycharoen (1977, p. 115), the Japanese by Nakazima (1962), the Chinese by Lin (1971, Table 2), the Slovenian by Kolarič (1959, p. 230), the Hindi by Srivastava (1974, pp. 112–113), the Dutch by Elbers (1980, Table 6), the Norwegian by Vanvik (1971); the German data were reported—though not gathered—by Meader and Muyskens (1950, Table 13); the Latvian data were supplied by Rūķe-Draviņa (personal communication, April 11, 1983), who studied the language development of several Latvian children from 5 months to 5 years (Rūķe-Draviņa, 1982). I have included Cruttenden's English data (1970) for purposes of comparison with the 14 non-English languages.

On the basis of the data in Table 1.3, it may be determined immediately that the consonantal repertoire of children reared in an English environment is like the repertoire of children reared in other environments. The representation of reper-

Table 1.3

Consonantal Babbling Repertoire in 15 Language Environments

Environment	Afrikaans	Mayan	Luo	Thai	Japanese	Hindi	Chinese	Slovenian	Dutch	Spanish	German	Arabic	Norwegian	Latvian	English
Infant N	1	2	2	2	6	1	1	2	1	2	4	3	1	—	2
Age in months	11–12	9	12	10–11	9–12	9–10	8–11	11	11	9	10–12	6–10	0–12	6–12	1–15
English repertoire															
h	*	*	*			*	*		*	*		*	*	*	*
d	*	*	*	*	*			*	*	*	*	*	*	*	*
b	*	*	*	*	*	*	*	*	*	*	*	*	*	*	*
m	*	*	*	*	*	*	*	*	*	*	*	*	*	*	*
t				*	*		*	*			*		*	*	
g	*		*		*	*	*	*	*	*			*		
s						*								*	*
w	*	*			*			*		*		*	*	*	*
n	*	*	*	*	*	*	*	*	*	*	*	*	*	*	*
k	*		*				*		*		*	*	*	*	*
j				*			*				*		*	*	
p	*	*		*	*	*	*	*		*	*		*	*	
Total	9	7	7	7	8	7	9	8	7	8	8	7	11	11	8
English nonrepertoire															
v	*											*	*		*
l			*										*	*	*
θ					*			*					*		
z															
f	*											*			
ʃ															*
ð									*						
ŋ			*				*						*		
3													*		
r	*										*				
tʃ															
dʒ															
Total	3	0	2	0	1	0	1	1	1	0	1	2	5	1	3

toire segments ranges from 51 to 91%, with a mean of 68%. The representation of nonrepertoire segments ranges from 0 to 42%, with a mean of 11%.

There are two repertoire segments common to all 15 environments, [m] and [b]. There are no repertoire segments that appear in none of the language environments. There are no nonrepertoire segments that occurred in all 15 environments, and 3 of these—[ʒ, tʃ, ʤ]—appeared in none of the language environments.

But what of the non-English sounds in these non-English children? And which of the English sounds are not in the language environment, hence—quite possibly—unrepresented in the mind or notational system of the listener? I determined the number of consonants that *could have been heard* if a native listener were expecting each of the sounds in his own system. The relative figures do not change greatly: 66% of the reperoire sounds that could occur in the language of the listener did occur in the babbling of the infant, and 12% of the nonrepertoire sounds that could occur in the listener's system did occur in the infant's babbling. This suggests that the greater frequency of repertoire sounds is not due to their abundance in the system—and expectancy in the mind—of the listener.

As in the case of English observers, there also is non-English testimony to support the statistical data. Murai (1964) states categorically that in the babbling of his Japanese infants "there are no fricative sounds." Elbers (1980) reported that in her Dutch infant's babbling "the total number of different types of babbles is astonishing small." Tuaycharoen (1979) observed that the babbling of her Thai subject was "restricted and systematic." Vanvik (1971), after having observed the babbling of his Norwegian daughter, Hilde, made the interesting comment that

> from much of the literature one may get the impression that in the babbling period the child produces all or almost all possible speech sounds. . . . I am not convinced that Hilde's repertoire was as great as that . . . Hilde obviously had sound preferences in the babbling period. She had favourite sounds and sound sequences which she would pronounce over and over again [p. 272].

Babbling Drift?

The data that have been cited imply the gloomiest of pictures where questions of "drifting" are concerned. For how likely is it that environmental differences would be reflected in the infant's babbling—even at 9–12 months—if his phonetic repertoire is very rigidly fixed and compressed? But Brown (1958) was nonspecific as to the phonetics of drift. He said nothing of *what* might drift. Our cross-linguistic analysis is of consonants, but what of vowels, syllable shapes, segmental sequences, tones, rhythms, patterns of stress?

Why expect that there would be drift? At first glance, there appear to be some excellent reasons; as the infant ages, he also seems to become increasingly aware of phonological categories in the language of his environment. These receptive changes appear to reflect *experience* (Eilers & Oller, 1982), in other words, some form of learning. One might think that for drift to occur, all the infant needs is a predisposition to imitate the sound patterns of others and a vocal tract good enough to do it, that is, to express his receptive categories in a way observers can distinguish from infants with different environmental histories.

But why should we be confident that the infant's vocal tract is sufficient to express *what he knows that other babies do not,* when he could not possibly express *all that he knows?* And how can we be certain that what is unique to the phonological system of the parents is unique, as well, to the *phonetic* stimulation of the child? MacKain (1982; MacKain & Stern, 1982) has argued that differences between two languages at the phonemic level may not exist, or exist as dramatically, at the phonetic level. She points to the futility of "contrasting" the VOT perception of English-exposed babies with that of infants exposed to Spanish (Eilers, Gavin, & Wilson, 1979; Lasky, Syrdal-Lasky, & Klein, 1975) or Kikuyu (Streeter, 1974)—languages that have voicing lead phonemically—when English has voicing lead phonetically (see pp. 106–107). MacKain also raised what appears to be the critical question in perceptual development, as well as in babbling drift: What is the difference between exposure and experience? To claim that sound contrasts are "experienced" and

that such experience enhances sensitivity to the perceptual cues that separate phonetic categories for adults of that community, we must attribute to the infant the processes by which such experience could affect subsequent discrimination performance. That linguistic experience has such an effect presupposes that infants have accomplished at least all of the following: 1) segmented the speech stream into discrete units, 2) recognized that the sounds to be contrasted vary along some underlying perceptual continuum(s), 3) ignored covarying redundant information, 4) identified variations along certain continuum(s) as perceptually equivalent (perceptual constancy), 5) recognized that these instances along the continuum(s) separate into contrasting categories, 6) recognized that these instances have occurred before (such that current experience is identified with previous experience), and 7) accounted for the frequency with which such instances have occurred. [This quote is reprinted from MacKain, K. S. (1982). Assessing the role of experience on infants' speech discrimintion. *Journal of Child Language,* 9, pp. 534–535; with permission from Cambridge University Press.]

If infants from two language communities have not had radically different phonetic exposure, and could not effectively experience even that which was different, why would one expect their babbling values to distinguish them? How, before speaking actually begins, can one assess the role of experience?

One possibility is that we could look at the loss or relinquishment of phonetic categories as the infant determines they have no functional role or, less cognitively, receives no environmental "reminders" of their existence. Here the vocal tract's capabilities are not called into question and the prospects for a sort of "negative drift" seem less theoretically encumbered. According to this logic, an infant whose target language has no /p/, for example, will be heard to make fewer and fewer [p]-like sounds as he gets older. This *selective loss* may be a partial way out of our empirical difficulties, and I discuss it in some detail later (pp. 87–92).

Another possibility for the study of drift is to look for—that is, to listen for—shifts in phonetic values that are defensibly under the infant's motor control. It is generally believed that vocalic distinctions occur receptively much earlier than consonant distinctions (Shvachkin, 1948/1973; Garnica, 1973), and that infants have greater control of loudness, pitch, and duration than of articulatory movements. If this logic were accepted, studies of environmental influence would include analyses of changing intonation. But only one of the studies reporting positive evidence for prelexical drift dealt explicitly with intonation. It was reported in scant detail and has been regarded—in my judgment—with far too little skepticism.

THE RUTH WEIR STUDY

In 1966, Ruth Weir presented at a conference some research she had done with Eleanor Maccoby on the babbling of infants reared in different linguistic environments. In work she clearly defined as a pilot study, Weir found that she and Maccoby were "usually" able to tell the pitch patterns of a Chinese infant, at 6–8 months of age, from those of an American and two Arabic infants of the same age. Weir and Maccoby "were unable readily to distinguish the two Arabic babies from the American one [p. 155]."

On the strength of these findings (or impressions), Weir and Maccoby had proceeded with a more ambitious study. At the time of the report, subjects had been selected: five children being reared in monolingual Chinese homes and an equal number growing up in homes in which American English or Russian was spoken. Recordings were to be made every month from 5 or 6 months to 18 months. But in her description, Weir clearly indicates that the study had only just begun, and that thus far only one or two recordings had been made of three Chinese, one Russian, and one American infant. She reported:

> Based on this *scant evidence,* I will *dare* to make a few general statements. One Chinese infant, recorded first at five-and-one-half and then at six-and-one-half months, shows in the second recording a very different pattern from the Russian and American infants. The utterances produced by the Chinese baby are usually monosyllabic and only vocalic, with much tonal variation over individual vowels. A neutral single vowel with various pitches is also typical of another six-month-old

Chinese infant, as well as of a still different seven-month-old one. The Russian and American babies, at six and seven months, show little pitch variation over individual syllables; they usually have a CV (consonant–vowel) syllable, often reduplicated or repeated at intervals several times, with stress patterns occurring occasionally and intonation patterns usually over a number of syllables. *If these general initial impressions can be substantiated,* with the additional evidence of ease of segmentation . . . we must ask ourselves how or when pitch and intonation patterns are acquired. [This quote is reprinted from Weir, R. W. (1966). *Some questions on the child's learning of phonology.* In F. Smith & G. A. Miller (Eds.), *The genesis of language.* Cambridge, Mass.: MIT Press, Copyright 1966 by MIT Press; p. 156; emphasis mine.]

It is clear from Weir's actual remarks that she, in essence, had no empirical findings. Nevertheless, many scholars persist in referring to the Weir "study" as evidence in support of the babble drift hypothesis. It also is clear that if there were reliable differences among infants, they might represent dissimilarities in *babbling stage* rather than *language environment.* In Koopmans-van Beinum and van der Stelt's (1981) study of 50 Dutch infants, at around 7 months there was an abrupt diminution in tonal variations and a marked increase in reduplicated syllable patterns (termed "canonical babbling" by Oller, 1980). From Weir's description, it appears that her Russian and American infants had already experienced this diminution at the time of observation. However, Weir says nothing of reduplicated syllable production in the Chinese infants, who were mostly recorded prior to 7 months. In short, Weir's Chinese infants may have been more tonal than the others because of their precanonical stage, not because of anything special about their linguistic environment. The individual difference data in Koopmans-van Beinum and van der Stelt suggest that the Chinese infants may have become *less tonal* a few days or weeks after their vocalizations were recorded.

Weir's remarks were originally made at a conference, and in the discussion period that ensued, Ira Hirsh referred to a study by Tervoort, a phonetician and teacher of the deaf in the Netherlands, who reported that his Dutch college students

could distinguish the babbling, from six months onward, of Dutch from non-Dutch. The languages involved were all nontonal. Tervoort later performed the same experiment with similar recordings in the United States and found that his American students could distinguish between the American and non-American samples but not among the non-American. [This quote is reprinted from Smith, F. & Miller, G. A. (1966). *The genesis of language.* Cambridge, Mass.: MIT Press; Copyright 1966 by MIT Press; p. 169.]

Though Tervoort never reported his study, a summary of his findings in Dinger and Blom (1973) fails to support Hirsh's description. Mehler (1971) claims to have heard "clear differences in intonation" between 6-month-olds reared in Argentina and in the United States. I have been unable to locate a fuller description or confirming report of Mehler's impressions. Bever (1971) has stated that at Haskins Laboratories it was learned "that at 8 or 9 months there begins to be a noticeable differentiation in the infant's vocalization of plosives, that is he starts to follow the regularities in his native language [p. 163]." I have not been able to find any report of this, either. However, I do know that Weir's claims have been subjected to scrutiny in several studies, one by Atkinson, MacWhinney, and Stoel (1968).

ATKINSON, MacWHINNEY, AND STOEL

Atkinson, MacWhinney, and Stoel (1968) used the Weir and Maccoby tape recordings to perform a more thorough analysis than the original investigators had done. They selected acoustically clear samples of vocal play from infants in each of the language environments (Chinese, English, and Russian) with three age levels within each language community (6–7½ months; 10½–11 months; 16–17 months). A first tape contained six samples from each of the three languages for use in an 18-item identification procedure. A second tape was prepared for use in a discrimination procedure. It contained babbling "pairs" in which, for example, a 10-sec sample of Chinese vocal play was paired with a 10-sec sample of Russian vocal play, Russian with English, and so on. Comparisons were from the 6–7½-month group or the 16–17 month group.

There were two groups of listeners. For the identification procedure, both groups were to decide whether individual samples were English or non-English. In the discrimination test, one group of listeners was told that the infants came from Chinese, English, and Russian environments. Both groups were to decide whether the paired samples came from the same linguistic community or from two different linguistic communities.

The overall performance on the identification test was 43% which—*it was said*—did not differ significantly from chance performance. The overall score on the discrimination procedure was 49%, which also *was said to be* (and undoubtedly would have been) nonsignificant. The authors reported that "adults can neither identify babbling infants raised in different language communities. . . . nor judge whether two samples from infants at a given age. . . . are from the same or different language communities [p. 6]." However, Atkinson *et al.* did observe that judges' responses were not random, and that their consistency could be traced to certain phonetic parameters, such as syllable shape, tonal patterns, and segment characteristics. As a consequence, the authors reopened the original question by stating that "with training" intercommunity differences might be detectable. They concluded with the comment that "our study simply questions the findings of Weir and Tervoort, it makes no attempt to resolve the initial problem: what is the nature of the relationship between an infant's babbling and the language he is going to acquire [p. 6]."

The study of Atkinson *et al.* (1968) was not without procedural difficulties, and two of them were noticed by Olney and Scholnick (1976). First, they questioned whether the judges were good enough to make the discriminations that had been requested of them. Second, Olney and Scholnick pointed out that the older infants in Atkinson *et al.* might not have vocalized differently from the younger ones, in which case there would be no reason to expect increasing discriminability with age.

Olney and Scholnick obtained tape recordings of two infants, one Chinese (Cantonese) and one American, at 6, 12, and 18 months. At each age, they prepared, by splicing, two 15-sec taped samples of vocalization per infant. There were, then, 12 samples in all. In their first experiment, Olney and Scholnick paired various samples *within* infants to see if listeners could identify the 6-, 12-, and 18-month samples. The judges were two groups of introductory psychology students, one for each of the two infants. Both groups were able to make these "age" identifications, doing especially well on the 6–18-month contrast. On the assumption that the judges were making appropriately fine distinctions, many of them were asked to serve in a second experiment. In the second experiment, vocalization pairs were constructed within and between infants at each of the three ages. Thus, at 6 months there were Chinese–Chinese, Chinese–English, English–English, and English–Chinese pairings, and likewise for 12 and 18 months. Listeners were to identify both "languages" in each pair. A sensitive d' analysis showed that discriminability at none of the ages differed significantly from chance.

The authors' closing remarks are reminiscent of the final statements of Atkinson *et al.* Olney and Scholnick first summarized their major finding, that naive adults failed "to differentiate the linguistic community of vocalizations within a given age level." Then, they observed that "there are many limitations to the data and to the generalizations which can be drawn from them. There may indeed be differences between the two language samples, but the differences may not have been perceived by judges untrained in phonetic transcription and unacquainted with Chinese [p. 151]." They also commented that their splicing techniques might have disrupted prosodic cues, which would figure importantly into comparisons between a tonal and a nontonal language.

Dinger and Blom (1973) recorded two American and two Dutch infants approximately every 3 weeks from 7 to 18 months. A 90-sec babbling "monologue'' was selected from each infant's recordings at about 33, 43, 53, 62, and 70 weeks. The 20 monologues (5 per infant) were played in random order to 50 American and 50 Dutch women, who were to identify as Dutch or American the baby producing each monologue. Analysis of listeners' judgments revealed accuracy scores of 48, 46, 57, 64, and 68% for the five sampling intervals. The first two of these scores are below chance, so there was no evidence for linguistic differentiation at or before 10 months. However, the latter three scores significantly exceeded chance, indicating that by 13 months listeners were able to detect the linguistic background of the infants. Unfortunately, by this age there might have been a few recognizable words mixed in with the babbling, making it difficult to determine whether there was any *prelexical differentiation.*

NAKAZIMA

Nakazima (1962) tape recorded the vocal play of several Japanese and American infants, three of them old enough (7–10 months) to conceivably be influenced by their difference linguistic environments. Nakazima's analysis was completely subjective; there were no quantifications, no listener judgments. But Nakazima remarked that he ''did not observe any meaningful differences between articulations of Japanese and Americans [p. 38].'' He indicated that the environment does have a clear influence, but not until about 1 year, and the examples he supplied are Japanese and English *words.*

PRESTON, YENI-KOMSHIAN, STARK, AND PORT

Preston, Yeni-Komshian, Stark, and Port (1969) studied the voice onset times of infants reared in Lebanese Arabic or English homes, with samples taken at about 12 months. As the VOT of initial stops differs in English and Arabic, this afforded an excellent opportunity to study in a more objective way the influence of an infant's phonetic environment on his own vocal output. Speakers of Lebanese Arabic were known to produce /d/ with a voicing *lead* and /t/ with a short *lag*. By contrast, speakers of English were thought to produce /d/ with a short lag and /t/ with a long lag (though see Smith, 1978a).

In order to reveal their separate linguistic experience, of course, the Arabic and English infants would have to have had the motor control necessary to execute such VOT values as they were able to detect. Whatever the reason, the findings were negative. The VOT values of all the infants' apical stops were in the 0–30 msec (short-lag) range, regardless of the linguistic environment of the infant.

ENSTROM

The findings of Preston *et al.* (1969) on apical stops in Lebanese Arabic and American English infants were compared—as part of a larger study by Enstrom

(1982)—to apical stops in Swiss German infants. First, it is necessary to understand certain aspects of Swiss German. According to Enstrom and Spörri-Bütler's (1981) study of Swiss German adults, word-initial stops of phonemically different voicing do not seem to be distinguishable on the basis of VOT values, which overlap considerably. However, Swiss German speakers do reveal a fairly regular articulatory progression. Labial stops are the most voiced with a mean VOT of 4.63 msec, followed by apicals (14.74 msec) and velars (26.74 msec).

Enstrom (1982) in his study of infants, made monthly recordings of eight Swiss German infants from 9 to 12 months of age. All eight infants came from environments in which only the Zürich dialect of Swiss German was spoken. In the recordings, Enstrom located 314 syllable-initial stops of labial, apical, or velar articulation and spectrographically determined the VOT of each stop. The values ranged from 0 to 30 msec, falling within the same short-lag category that had been observed in Swiss German adults. There was also an articulatory progression of voicing values. Labial stops had a mean VOT of 10.10 msec, apical stops had a mean VOT of 11.20 msec, and velar stops had the least voicing with a mean VOT of 17.37 msec. As one might guess from this pattern, Enstrom found more cases of voicing *lead* for labials than for apical and velar stops.

Enstrom saw little difference between the apical VOTs of Swiss German infants at 12 months and the apical values of Lebanese Arabic and American infants reported in Preston *et al.* (1969). In all three populations the VOTs fell predominantly in the 0–30 msec range. Enstrom concluded that ''the forces of nature rather than nurture determine manner of infant apical stop production [p. 47].'' The forces of nature, for Enstrom, are physiological constraints; the coordination of articulatory and laryngeal timing. Since there was no evidence in his study that apical values had been learned, Enstrom concluded that the place pattern in infants' stop voicing was also not the result of learning. It is significant in relation to what will be said later about maintenance (pp. 85–86) that this pattern of infant vocalization may persist in becoming a property of standard phonology.

EADY

In his master's thesis at the University of Ottawa (1980), Stephen Eady recorded and analyzed instrumentally the intonation patterns of infants reared in Cantonese and English environments. As Cantonese and English differ sharply in their use and nonuse of lexical tones, and as infants appear to have some control of pitch, this appears to be a very reasonable way to test the hypothesis of Crystal (1973, 1975) that ''the productive use of a language's prosodic patterns, especially its intonation, develops at round seven months [1975, p. 83].''

At each of three age levels, the Cantonese and American infants differed. However, they differed *differently* at each level. At 6 months, the significant variable was the range of fundamental frequency. At 9 months they differed as to the number of fundamental frequency fluctuations per utterance. At 11 months, the only differentiating variable was the duration of utterances. If the Cantonese infants were drifting toward a separate set of values than the American infants, and vice versa, each group would presumably become more different at each sampling interval along the same set of phonetic continua. As this did not happen, Eady regarded his findings as essentially negative, and Crystal's hypothesis as disconfirmed.

TUAYCHAROEN

In her doctoral dissertation, Tuaycharoen (1977) described the segmental and tonal changes in a Thai infant from 3 to 18 months. Though she followed only one infant, she did have access to the tonal classifications that had been made on children reared in nontonal environments. In a later report (1979), Tuaycharoen observed that "the characteristics of the vocalizations in the early babbling stages of the child in this study are not different from those of children in nontonal environments reported so far in the literature. Thus at the babbling stage, it may be difficult to distinguish children with different language backgrounds solely on the basis of vocalizations [p. 274]."

HUBER

Huber (1970) tape recorded five infants at the age of 9 months. Two came from homes in which only Mayan was spoken; two came from homes in which both Spanish and Mayan were spoken; one child came from an English-speaking home. For the most part the children were found to have a common repertoire of speech segments. Where there were differences, they formed no particular pattern. For example, the English child might have had a Yucatec sound and a Yucatec infant might have had a Spanish sound. Though she did not complete intonation and syllable analyses, on the basis of her segmental comparisons Huber was disposed to "argue little environmental influence and much individual variation in the vocalization of the nine-month babbling period [p. 119]."

OLLER AND EILERS

Huber's (1970) negative findings with regard to Spanish and English were confirmed in a rigorous investigation of similar language environments conducted by Oller and Eilers (1982). Oller and Eilers tape recorded eight infants being reared in monolingual Spanish homes and an equal number from monolingual English homes. Subjects were 11–14 months of age at the time of the study, with an average age of 12 months. Oller and Eilers performed careful analyses of the phonetic play of their subjects, reporting segment frequencies for the vowels and detailing the featural, syllabic, and phonotactic characteristics of the consonants. A portion of their consonantal data are shown here in Table 1.4. As in Oller *et al.*'s (1976) study of infants reared in English homes, the table reveals that *both* English and Spanish babies "preferred" singletons over clusters, initial over final consonants, initial plosives over fricatives and affricates, final fricatives and affricates over plosive, unaspirated over aspirated initial plosives, final voiceless obstruents over final voiced obstruents, prevocalic glides over liquids, and apical over dorsal obstruents. None of the differences between subject groups were significant statistically.

According to contrastive analysis of Miami-Cuban Spanish and American English, on what phonetic characteristics might the infants in Oller and Eilers's study have differed? Even the two (standard) languages, after all, might not be statistically different on each of the categories tabulated. The answer is instructive. One might expect, from the differing structures of English and Spanish, to find among Spanish infants fewer final consonants relative to initial ones, fewer clusters relative to singletons, more stops relative to fricatives, a lower ratio of voiced to voiceless final consonants. What one observes, however, is that both groups are so disinclined to produce final consonants at all, much less of the voiced type, and so disinclined to produce clusters and fricatives, that there may have been too little *opportunity* (or motoric wherewithal) for the inherent differences in Spanish and English structures to be revealed. What is instructive about this is a methodological problem of the most interesting theoretical proportions. It may be precisely where any two randomly selected languages differ that any two groups of infants are the most likely to be the same! Indeed, we will see

Table 1.4

Characteristics of the Consonant-like Sounds of Oller and Eilers's (1982) Spanish and English Infants

	Mean percentage of first type observed	
	Spanish	English
Singleton consonant versus consonant cluster	93.6	89.4
Initial versus final consonant	66.8	69.3
Initial plosive versus fricative or affricate	89.6	88.8
Final fricative or affricate versus final plosive	47.4	39.4
Unaspirated initial plosive versus aspirated initial plosive	89.0	93.9
Voiceless final obstruent versus voiced final obstruent	91.4	96.8
Prevocalic glide versus liquid	92.6	97.4
Apical versus dorsal obstruent	59.1	77.5

Source: Oller, D. K., & Ellers, R. E. (1982). Similarity of babbling in Spanish- and English-learning babies. *Journal of Child Language, 9,* 571, with permission from Cambridge University Press.

later that there is a positive relationship between the number of *children* that say a sound correctly and the number of *languages* that contain an equivalent of that sound. And it will be seen as harmonious that ''languages'' (i.e., adult speakers) have been the most likely to stumble upon and to make use of the sounds that are the easiest or most natural for humans, *including* children.

At this writing, Oller and Eilers (personal communication) are analyzing the same data via the potentially more powerful method in which adults label taped samples as Spanish or English. This procedure is not impaired by transcriptional constraints, nor is it limited to segmental and syllabic elements, so it will be interesting to see how this ongoing research is consumated.

BOYSSON-BARDIES

In a study by Boysson-Bardies (1981), a small amount of data is available on three infants at 8 and at 10 months who were being reared in different language environments. Many of the customery procedural details are lacking, and it is difficult to determine whether the 8- and 10-month-olds were actually the same or different subjects. At each age level, eight 15-sec vocalization samples from a French infant were paired with samples of equal duration from an Arabic and a Chinese baby. These vocalization pairs were played to 40 adults, who were to identify the French baby. Where an average of four pairs correct would be expected under a null hypothesis, Boysson-Bardies's listeners apparently averaged about six pairs correct for the French–Arabic pairs at both ages. However, the listeners averaged fewer than six correct for the 8-month-old French–Chinese samples, and they heavily misidentified the Chinese baby as French at 10 months. Though her results seem ambiguous, Boysson-Bardies apparently interpreted her French–Arabic data as supporting a phonetic drift hypothesis. She concluded, however, that ''the productions of 8 and 10 month babblers have . . . basic similarities across languages corresponding to common neuromuscular constraints and to the fact that adult languages have common perceptual cues. These similarities show up in the fact that common intonation patterns and phonetic preferences are found across language backgrounds for given ages [pp. 7–8].'' Incidentally, according to Boysson-Bardies, the consonants in her sample consisted mainly of stops, many with aspirate release; there also was a voiced pharyngeal fricative.

LOCKE

I tape recorded the babbling of Ian, a South African child, from his eleventh month through his eighteenth month of life. Though during this period Ian lived in Illinois, the only language spoken in the home was Afrikaans, the native language of his parents and 6-year-old brother. The analysis of Ian's pattern is, to my knowledge, the only one on a hearing infant that shows segment frequencies by syllable position. Ian's data, therefore, are valuable merely in what they suggest about the nature of babbling. However, a comparison of Ian's profile with that of infants reared in English homes is revealing in a different way. As outlined in what follows, it tells us something about the methodological problems encountered in performing a cross-linguistic analysis of any kind.

The consonant system of Afrikaans with respect to that of English is as follows (the Afrikaans inventory is drawn from Pienaar & Hooper, 1948):

Afrikaans only segments
/x/: voiceless velar fricative
/r/: rolled, with one flap initially and two flaps intervocalically
/ɦ/: voiced glottal fricative
/c/: unaspirated voiceless palatal stop
Shared English variants
/p, t, k/: unaspirated
/b, d, g/: no occurrence finally
/f, v/: no /v/ word finally
/s, l, m, n, ŋ/: as in English
/ʃ/: less lip rounding than in English
/j/: more friction than in English
/tʃ/: as in English
Absent (English only) segments
/w/, /ə/, /ð/, /z/, /r/, /h/, /ʒ/, and /ʤ/

If Ian has "drifted," as his chronological age surely suggests that he should have (by the end of the study he had acquired, possibly, about half a dozen words), we would expect more "Afrikaans only" than "English only" sounds. Ian's data appear in Table 1.5. It is immediately obvious from this tabulation that Ian was very attracted to [d]s and [b]s, less so to the other stops and nasals. As in previous studies of English-reared infants, Ian had a fairly high frequency of [h]-like productions; unlike the other studies his incidence of [r] is fairly high. Sounds in English not found in Ian's repertoire are [ə, ʃ, ʒ] and, as usual, the affricates [tʃ] and [ʤ]. There was one non-English sound [x], which occurred twice in syllable-final position.

Table 1.5 clearly indicates the predominance of syllable-initial sounds, which amount to 88% of all singletons. The most frequent final consonant is, not surprisingly, a sound both back and voiceless, [k]. After that sound, the frequency of final consonants falls off rapidly, with a mixture of stops, nasals, fricatives, and liquids that suggests no pattern as conspicuous as that of the initial segments.

There were 21 initial and 3 final consonant clusters, together accounting for just 3.2% of the total. Except for two initial affricates, [dz] and [gɣ], all clusters were stop + approximant [r, l, j, w] sequences.

Table 1.5
Consonants in the Babbling of an Infant Reared in an Afrikaans Environment, Sampled at 11–18 Months[a]

Syllable initial		Syllable final		Total		Percentage
d	160	k	32	d	163	22.1
b	115	m	18	b	119	16.2
g	88	t	11	g	89	12.1
m	57	s	8	m	75	10.2
t	52	b	4	k	70	9.5
k	38	l	4	t	63	8.6
h	38	d	3	h	39	5.3
r	31	n	3	r	31	4.2
j	20	g	1	j	21	2.9
p	17	h	1	p	18	2.4
l	10	j	1	l	14	1.9
n	9	p	1	n	12	1.6
s	4	f	1	s	12	1.6
ð	4	ŋ	1	ð	4	.5
f	1		89	f	2	.3
v	1			v	1	.1
w	1			w	1	.1
z	1			z	1	.1
	647			ŋ	1	.1
					736	99.8

[a]One other sound, [x], occurred twice in syllable-final position. I omitted it to facilitate certain cross-linguistic comparisons. I am indebted to Laura Kapp for obtaining the recordings of Ian, and to Bonnie Shapiro for preparing the transcriptions.

Does Ian's pattern show him to have been drifting, in Brown's (1958) terms, in the direction "of the prevailing linguistic winds"? If he were in perfect conformity with the rules of Afrikaans, Ian would not say [b, d, g] in final position, though he does to a limited extent. If Ian's pattern never violated the structural requirements of Afrikaans, he would not produce [p, t, k] with aspiration, but he did. And Ian would not be expected to produce the alien [w, ð, z, r, h], yet he did produce those sounds.

On the other hand, Ian did produce a large number of sounds that occur in both Afrikaans and English, and one that occurs only in Afrikaans, [x]. So the question, when properly put, is whether Ian's pattern is *more like* Afrikaans than English. To answer that, we need English data. It is obvious that we cannot successfully compare Ian to a *group* of English-exposed babies, for it is rare that an individual fits perfectly the profile of the population from which he was drawn. Instead, we should ask if Ian is less like an English infant than are other English infants, since we have more English than Afrikaans data.

Table 1.6 shows the consonantal frequencies of the individual 12-month-olds in Fisichelli's (1950) study. Ian's most common consonants were [d], [b], [g], in

Table 1.6

Consonant Repertoire of Individual Subjects Reared in Monolingual English Environments, Sampled at 12 Months[a]

Subject no.	p	b	m	w	v	t	d	n	z	ʒ	l	r	j	k	g	ŋ	h	ΣX
1		12		11			64	8			4		9		62	7	17	194
2		21	1	22	3	1	1		1				6		13	1	33	103
3		2		3									1				117	123
4	1	2		26			3				7		34				19	92
5		1	2	41			30						4				15	93
6		1	4	11	2	1	83	6					1		9		18	136
7				37	4		46					1		8	61		4	166
8		2		15		1	41		1	1			4				32	97
9	1	29	4	24			92		1	1			48		15	7	3	225
10		2		6			66						4		11		38	127
11		6	1	5	1		3						2	13	27	4	20	82
12		1		5			3						3		4		6	22
13				14												2	5	21
14		3		1			10						28				3	45
15		1	1	52			33		1				11		4		11	114
16							4										13	17
17		7		9	1		33						2		8			60
18	1	1		12			18						3		2		2	39
19		1		5			5								5		4	20
20		1		1			1						4				12	19
ΣX	3	93	13	300	11	3	536	14	4	2	11	1	169	21	221	21	372	1795

Source: From Fisichelli (1950, pp. 106–108).

[a]The following seven sounds were not recorded: [f, θ, ð, s, ʃ, tʃ, dʒ].

that order. In Table 1.6 one can locate one American infant who shows this pattern somewhat convincingly (Subject 9) and four others with very mild effects (Subjects 4, 5, 8, and 14). One also can locate a [b] > [g] > [d] pattern (Subject 2), and a [g] > [d] > [b] (Subjects 7 and 12), a [d] > [g] > [b] (Subjects 1, 6, 10, 15, 17, and 18), and a [g] > [b] > [d] (Subject 1). The only permutation of these three sounds not represented in Fisichelli's 20 subjects is [b] > [d] > [g]. As the statistics of the group favored [d] (536) over [g] (221) and [b] (93), it is not surprising that more subjects had this pattern (6) than any other pattern. But the *majority*—14 out of 20—did not have the "group" pattern!

The lesson in this is that if infants reared within a single language community have a variety of phonetic preferences, we cannot expect to complete a cross-linguistic study of consonant segments unless either the number of subjects or the size of the babbling sample is very large indeed!

BOYSSON-BARDIES, SAGART, AND BACRI

The "late babbling" of a French child, Sebastien, was described in a report by Boysson-Bardies, Sagart, and Bacri (1981). Sebastien was 18–20-months-old at the time of the observations. In fact, he was speaking ("some words or expressions could be distinguished"), though for the most part unintelligibly. His sample was elicited by procedures customarily used with child *speakers:* Sebastien was shown pictures and toys and *asked "Qu' est-ce qu'il y a?"* ("What is happening?") or *"Qu' est-ce que tu fais?"* ("What are you doing?").

In the analysis of his phonetic repertoire it appeared that Sebastien's conso-nantal frequencies corresponded more closely to those of conversational French than to English and Thai. It was concluded, therefore, that phonetic acquisition had occurred "during the babbling stage."

Sebastien's phonetic accomplishments, if they were real, should not be con-fused with babbling drift in the way we have used the term here. By the authors' own account, Sebastien was speaking French. That it was mostly unintelligible does not make it babbling, the accepted definitions of which typically convey its "premeaningful" sense (cf. Smith & Oller, 1981). It would be incorrect, there-fore, to accept Boysson-Bardies *et al.*'s study as evidence for babbling drift. As intelligibility can be harmed purely through the misassignment of segments, that Sebastien was unintelligible carries no implications for his segment inventory, and I am not surprised that it was French-like.

OLLER AND SMITH

Though Oller and Smith (1977) was not a cross-linguistic investigation, their methodology might be useful in the conduct of such studies, and I shall describe the procedures and results. Oller and Smith observed that there are languages, including English, Russian, German, and Swedish, in which the vowels in final syllables are lengthened considerably relative to nonfinal vowels. There are also, they commented, languages such as Finnish, Estonian, and Japanese that do not have a particularly strong difference of this sort. This suggests that final-syllable-lengthening effects are learned, and might be observable in infant babbling if babbling reflects phonetic learning.

Oller and Smith selected six infants, from 8 to 12 months of age, who (I presume) were being reared in monolingual English homes. From 7 to 40 reduplicated utterances were recorded per subject, utterances which ranged from two to six syllables in length. Oller and Smith measured the duration of vowels in final and nonfinal syllables in this infant group and also in a control group of native English adults.

When both the voiced and voiceless (breathy) portions of each vowel were measured, the adults had final-syllable vowel durations of about 233 msec and nonfinal vowel durations of about 143 msec. The ratio of final to nonfinal durations was about 1.6 to 1. The infants had final vowel durations of about 265 msec and nonfinal vowel durations of about 243 msec. The ratio was about 1.1 to 1, which fell significantly short of the adult ratio.

As this study involved a restricted age range and only one linguistic environment, the phonetic effects of learning could not have been neatly isolated. Nevertheless, it is interesting that there was little or no evidence of adultlike values in these soon-to-be-talking children. The highest final-to-nonfinal ratios (1.23:1 and 1.24:1) were displayed by two of the three 8-month-olds, the youngest subjects in the study! But reduplications are fairly easy to record, and one assumes vowel durations may reliably be controlled by the infant and quantified by the analyst, so cross-linguistic studies of this sort may prove to be enlightening.

Ironically, in a later study Laufer (1980) observed final lengthening effects in four American-reared children *prior to 6 months* of age. Laufer was unable to account for this apparent disagreement with Oller and Smith, though she identified a number of procedural and analytical differences between the two studies.

Babbling as an Auditory Experience

The cross-linguistic studies of babbling seem to have found no appreciable evidence in support of the babbling drift hypothesis. Of course the logic of the cross-linguistic study still is attractive in that it allows for a determination of the consonantal repertoire of babbling when the environmental values, and their proportions and systemic significance, are varied. Presumably, phonetic constancy in the face of such variation is a form of evidence that babbling patterns are determined by child-internal factors. But precisely what sort of "factors"?

Are infants, whose perceptual systems are progressing during the several stages of vocal development, attracted to certain *auditory* patterns? We know that infants are aware of their own voices (Cullen, Fargo, Chase, & Baker, 1968); do they enjoy hearing themselves reproduce the patterns they find pleasing in their environment, or those that are entirely of their own invention? Merely knowing the auditory patterns to which an infant was exposed would not help us to decide this one. But another kind of data would: the phonetic repertoire not of infants exposed to a variety of sound combinations, but of infants exposed to no sounds, usefully or at all.

The Babbling of Deafness

It has become increasingly common to identify hearing loss soon after birth, and to supply the hard-of-hearing infant with strong amplification immediately. But 30 and 40 years ago the situation was very different: There were no effective hearing tests for infants, and typically young children were not tested. As a consequence, it was not uncommon for a child to reach the age of 5 or 6 before it was determined that he *might* have a hearing loss.

During the 1940s and 1950s, four separate studies were done on the babbling of deaf children, and they show impressive facts about the sound production of *homo sapiens* when not under—and with no prior history of being under—the control or influence of various patterns of environmental stimulation.

To those who have read Lenneberg, the "babbling of deaf *children*" may be an anomalous phrase, for his writings (1964, p. 120; 1967, pp. 139–140) imply that vocalization declines in the deaf child at about 6 months. By 11 or 12 months, there would be nothing left to analyze. But the fact is that deaf children begin to babble and continue babbling throughout their early childhood, at *least* until the age of 6 *years*. At that age, articulatory development in the hearing child is nearly complete, so we might suppose that babbling in the 6-year-old deaf child is patterned by a fairly well-developed vocal tract. As we look at the phonetic output of these children, it will be interesting to see whether and how it differs from the less neuromotorically advanced hearing infants.

THE STUDY OF MISS JEAN SYKES

Long before the Irwin studies of hearing infants, and with essentially no helpful literature of any kind, Miss Jean Sykes did a study at the Clarke School for the Deaf, for her master's thesis at Smith College. Her investigation was conducted with keen attention to detail, and it is, therefore, a rich source of information about deaf children's babbling and the human's vocal potentials and preferences. In 1940, Sykes reported her work in an issue of *Psychological Monographs*. As it is a critical study, I will describe much of it here.

Subjects. The subjects were 14 beginning students at Clarke School whose ages ranged from 3:10 to 6:10. These children were divided, on the basis of hearing tests administered by school personnel, into a hard-of-hearing and a profoundly deaf group. Though decibel and frequency values were not reported, Sykes did say that the vocalizations of the hard-of-hearing children *could* have been influenced by their hearing. She judged that the profoundly deaf children "probably never experienced sound to a degree that would have affected their vocalizations [p. 107]." The hard-of-hearing group ranged in age from 4:8 to 6:9 with a mean of 5:7. The profoundly deaf group ranged in age from 3:10 to 6:10 with a mean of 5:1.

Observation. Each child was observed for 16–17 hours, both individually and in small groups. Sykes performed all of her analysis on live speech. Her transcription was necessarily broad, and she disregarded non-English sounds. Table 1.7 shows the absolute consonantal frequencies by syllable position and their overall frequency in percentages. There were only six consonant clusters in all, with five coming from one child (i.e., 12 of the 14 children produced singletons *only*).

There are some fascinating regularities embedded in the data contained in Table 1.7. Some 93% of the consonants occurred in syllable-initial position, much as we saw earlier in hearing infants. Apparently the VC structure is not any more attractive or spontaneously achievable at 6 years than it is at 6 months.

As with the hearing infants, there is a preference for voiced (unaspirated) over voiceless (aspirated) stops, with [b, d, g] exceeding [p, t, k]. There also is a marked and regular front–middle–back pattern:

[b] 493	[d] 81	[g] 68
[p] 48	[t] 20	[k] 10
[m] 288	[n] 58	[ŋ] 4

and a general preference for voiced (unaspirated) stops over nasals and voiceless stops. All three of those categories and glides exceeded the fricatives and affricates. The table shows, and Sykes specifically stated, that [z, ʃ, ʒ, ʤ, hw] never occurred.

Many sounds never occur in final position; only two that do are voiced obstruents (for 13%). Fricatives are somewhat more likely to occur in final position (20% of their total) than are stops (2% of their total).

There are several other regularities, which I will allow the reader to discover for himself. But what of the comparison with the hearing infant? Is the patterning basically the same? If one looks back at the data of all three groups in Table 1.1, it is apparent that the main differences involve noticeable increases in the relative frequency of [m, b], which have moved to the top of the list, and some increase

Table 1.7
Consonantal Frequencies in the Babbling of 3–6-Year-Old Deaf Children

Consonant	Syllable initial	Syllable final	Total	Percentage
b	483	10	493	35.0
m	184	44	288	16.2
j	128	0	128	9.1
d	81	0	81	5.8
h	75	0	75	5.3
w	69	0	69	4.9
g	68	0	68	4.8
l	61	4	65	4.6
n	47	11	58	4.1
p	41	7	48	3.4
t	20	0	20	1.4
f	15	3	18	1.3
θ	5	13	18	1.3
k	9	1	10	.7
ð	6	3	9	.6
v	8	0	8	.6
r	5	0	5	.4
ŋ	1	3	4	.3
s	1	0	1	.1
tʃ	1	0	1	.1
z	0	0	0	0
ʃ	0	0	0	0
ʒ	0	0	0	0
hw	0	0	0	0
dʒ	0	0	0	0
Σ X	1308	99	1407	100.0

Source: From data reported in Sykes (1940, Table 5).

in [l]. Otherwise, the "song" of the deaf child is very much like that of the hearing infant. In fact, the consonant sounds in Sykes' deaf children's repertoires constitute 88–97% of the consonant repertoires of hearing infants at 12 months.

As there were two gross levels of hearing sensitivity (hard-of-hearing and profoundly deaf) it is possible to determine whether the babbling frequencies seen here might have been environmentally induced to any degree. Sykes anticipated this point, and tabulated babbling frequencies separately for the two groups, as shown in Table 1.8.

It is apparent from Table 1.8 that the profoundly deaf made more [m]s and [g]s than the hard-of-hearing children. In the case of [m] one would be tempted to suggest that where the role of audition is less, the contribution of vision may be more, causing a highly visible sound such as [m] to be more frequent. Certainly the lip movements of adults are highly reproduceable by infants, even at 2–3 weeks of age (Meltzoff & Moore, 1977). And there is evidence that at 4–5 months infants are aware of discrepancies between speech sounds and visi-

Table 1.8

Consonantal Frequencies in the Babbling of Hard-of-Hearing and Profoundly Deaf 3–6-Year-Old Children

Consonant	Hard-of-hearing	Profoundly deaf
b	33.50	36.37
m	5.67	25.12
j	8.00	9.75
d	11.33	1.62
h	3.83	5.12
w	7.16	3.25
g	2.83	6.37
l	5.16	4.25
n	6.67	2.75
p	4.17	4.12
f	3.33	.50
t	2.33	.62
θ	3.00	0
k	1.83	.62
ð	.50	.12
v	.16	.62
r	.50	.12
ŋ	.16	.04
s	.33	0
tʃ	.16	0
	101.62	101.36

Source: From Sykes (1940, Table 6).

ble speech movements (Kuhl & Meltzoff, 1982; this intermodal processing capability may even be traced to the left cerebral hemisphere according to Mac-Kain, Studdert-Kennedy, Spieker, & Stern, 1983). But in light of this how do we explain the greater frequency of the relatively nonvisible [g] and the lack of an increase for [w], [p], and [f]?

I also am doubtful that the greater visibility of labial sounds is a factor because of the reported babblings of blind–deaf children. In 1929, McCarthy described briefly a 10-year-old girl who was born both deaf and blind, and who babbled infrequently. She was observed for an hour a day for 3 months, and her vocal output was recorded by phonetically oriented listeners. McCarthy observed as follows:

> In general she uses monosyllables, which are often preceded by an aspirate *h* and followed by rather muted consonants of doubtful phonetic notation. . . . The aspirate *h* frequently begins an utterance, and a rather prolonged *mmm* sound, and a soft *r* sound are favorite endings when the final sound is not muted. A favorite monosyllable is *mmm*. . . . In addition to these initial and final sounds, *b* and *d* are the most frequent consonants. . . . Other sounds which have been noted in her repertoire, but which are not as habitual as those already mentioned, are *w, v,* voiced and unvoiced *th, y* and a sort of guttural grunt [pp. 482–483].

As we have seen, the [h, m, b, d] sounds also are frequently babbled by hearing infants and deaf children. Of course, such anecdotes on blind children do not show that vision plays *no* role in sighted children. But they do suggest that it is *unnecessary* to assume that deaf children imitate visualized lip movements in order to explain their increased affinity for [m]. I think, instead; that the increase in [m] might more appropriately be thought of as a maturational event (cf. pp. 36–38). If so, it makes sense to examine the development of consonantal production patterns in the deaf starting with infancy.

The Development of Babbling in the Deaf

LENNEBERG, REBELSKY, AND NICHOLS:
THE FIRST THREE MONTHS

Though they undertook no phonetic analysis, Lenneberg, Rebelsky, and Nichols (1965) investigated the crying and emergent cooing of 16 hearing infants born to deaf (6) or to hearing (10) parents. The former group is of interest because, except for one infant, they could hear their own voices but not the voices of their parents, who communicated primarily in sign. One of the six infants in this group was later found to be deaf himself. During their first 3 months of life, weekly tape recordings were made in the home. All tapes were analyzed quantitatively and qualitatively.

Lenneberg *et al.* observed no difference between the two groups of infants in either their crying or their cooing behavior, and concluded that "cooing responses are *not contingent upon specific, acoustic* stimuli [p. 34; their emphasis]."

MAVILYA: THREE TO SIX MONTHS

Probably the youngest deaf infants on which phonetic data were systematically collected were those in Mavilya's dissertation study (1969). Mavilya located three infants who had been born deaf, and whose deafness had in infancy been diagnosed via conventional audiometric routines. Two of the children came from families in which older siblings had hearing impairment or in which the parents were deaf. In the third case, the mother apparently had had rubella and/or diabetes.

The infants were 12, 14, and 15 weeks of age at the start of the study. Mavilya tape recorded each of the infants one half-hour per week for 12 weeks. Consequently, the age range of the study is 12–26 weeks. From the data reported in Mavilya's dissertation, I have calculated the relative frequency of the consonants in her deaf infants' vocalization by two approximate age periods, 3–4 months and 5–6 months. The data are shown in Table 1.9.

The consonantal repertoire at 3–4 months is limited to a half dozen segments,

Table 1.9
Repertoire of Consonant-like Sounds in Deaf Infants at 3–4 and 5–6 Months

	3–4 Months		5–6 Months	
	N	%	N	%
g	101	76.5	52	8.7
h	10	7.6	1	.2
k	9	6.8	3	.5
b	5	3.8	20	3.4
d	4	3.0	454	76.3
w	3	2.3	3	.5
t	0	0	50	8.4
m	0	0	6	1.0
j	0	0	2	.3
n	0	0	2	.3
ŋ	0	0	2	.3
	132	100.0	595	99.9

Source: From data reported in Mavilya (1969, Appendix L).

with [g] the overwhelming favorite. There is a pronounced shift from velars to alveolars in the 5–6-month-olds. Considering [d, t] versus [g, k], the percentage of the velars at 3–4 months is 96.4; at 5–6 months the alveolars are 90.6%. Later in the chapter we will look at some analogous figures for hearing infants.

Table 1.9 indicates that the consonantal repertoire in very young deaf infants in general favors the same sounds preferred by the older hearing infants. And the deaf infants in Mavilya's study never produced any fricatives (except the dubious [h]) or affricates or liquids. Their entire repertoire is thus made up of stops and nasals and glides.

FORT: TWO YEARS

What changes might occur in the babbling of deaf children immediately after 6 months is unknown, for the next point at which systematic data are available is 2 years. In her master's thesis, Fort (1955) described the babbling repertoire of 16 deaf or partially deaf children ranging in age from 2 to 2:10. Fourteen of the 16 subjects had what would now be called "high risk" birth or developmental histories (there were three cases of maternal rubella, one case of child measles, and one case of child meningitis; there were two cases in which the mother had Rh negative blood while the father had Rh positive; there were four premature births). Several of the children had attempted a hearing aid briefly, but none had received any formal preschool training of any kind. Fort tape recorded each child for 30 min in three different play situations.

There were 1759 consonant productions overall; Table 1.10 shows the consonantal repertoire in relative frequency. It is apparent from the table that there is a

Table 1.10
Consonantal Segments in the Babbling of Deaf Children at 2 Years of Age

Segment	Percentage	Segment	Percentage
m	70.56	n	1.49
d	9.03	t	.74
b	7.45	p	.68
h	3.69	l	.23
w	3.24	k	.06
j	1.59	ʃ	.06

Source: From Fort (1955, Table 10).

decided preference for [m], with [d] and [b] as very distant second and third choices. With these three sounds making up over 87%, there is very little room left for anything else. The fricatives (except for [h]), affricates, and liquids sum at .29.

From Mavilya's 6-month-olds to Fort's 2-year-olds, we can now see an impressive increase in [m] from "barely occurring" to "totally dominating."

NEAS: THREE TO FOUR YEARS

Also in a master's thesis at Kansas, Neas (1953) studied the babbling of 15 3–4-year-olds whose auditory assessment showed them to be deaf. The children were of average intelligence and none had attended preschool for more than 1 year. Neas tape recorded each child for 75 min in five different free play situations. In all, there were 2309 consonants recorded.

Table 1.11 shows the consonantal frequencies. The more frequent consonants are [b], [d], and [m], in that order, making up over 81% of the total. By comparing the values for these 3–4-year-olds with those for the 2-year-olds in Table 1.10, it can be seen that except for the diminution of [m], every consonant

Table 1.11
Consonantal Segments in the Babbling of Deaf Children at 3 and 4 Years of Age

Segment	Percentage	Segment	Percentage
b	35.29	t	.86
d	27.45	k	.86
m	18.75	v	.47
n	6.03	l	.43
h	3.98	r	.38
w	3.98	s	.34
j	2.42	θ	.12
p	1.86	ʃ	.12
g	.95		

Source: From Neas (1953, Table 7).

occurring in the 3–4-year-olds is *increased*. With increasing age there is, then, both internal shifting and a tendency toward expansion. The 5–6-year-olds had 76% [d], the 2-year-olds 70% [m], and now in the 3- and 4-year-olds there is 35% [b], with a reduction in the frequency of [d] and [m], and increases in many of the others. Notable is the low frequency of the fricatives and liquids (none exceeds half a percent) and the continued absence of the affricates.

CARR: FIVE YEARS

Carr (1953) observed 48 deaf-born 5-year-olds upon their admission to the Iowa School for the Deaf. None had received formal speech instruction prior to their enrollment in the school and their participation in Carr's study. During the investigation the children were given no speech training in the classroom. Carr discovered, as had Neas, that at least three children needed to be present for sufficient vocalization to take place (with fewer children there was less interactive play and less vocalization).

In live-voice transcription Carr collected 5609 consonant sounds. Carr's reliability was established by comparing her transcriptions with those of a separate observer-transcriber. The separate observer-transcriber was Orvis Irwin, who also codirected this study as Carr's master's thesis. Table 1.12 shows the consonant frequencies as calculated by Carr. It may be seen that [b], [m], and [p] are the more frequent sounds, constituting 44% of all consonant-like sounds. Except for [ŋ], [z], and the affricates, all sounds have *some* frequency of occurrence, though the fricatives still are generally low.

Rather than constrict, the babbling of deaf children appears to elaborate, to become more complex. The most frequent consonant for the 5-year-olds is [b], as it was for the 3- and 4-year-olds, but it has declined from 35% to 20%. Some

Table 1.12
Consonantal Segments in the Babbling of Deaf Children at 5 Years of Age

Segment	Percentage	Segment	Percentage
b	20.48	t	2.64
m	12.19	s	2.01
p	11.36	k	1.57
h	10.47	ʃ	.87
w	9.13	v	.82
f	8.35	g	.66
d	6.79	θ	.61
j	4.69	r	.20
l	3.16	ð	.19
n	2.71	ʒ	.04

Source: From Carr (1953, Table 3).

interesting phonetic relationships also appear to be developing. For example, the ratio of [b] to [p] is 1.80 to 1; the ratio of [d] to [t] is 2.57 to 1; the ratio of [g] to [k] is .42 to 1. The "strength" of /b/ over /p/ but of /k/ over /g/ is something we will see again and again in this monograph, whether the data under review are oscillographic measurements of adult speech, adult slips of the tongue, phonological universals, or child errors.

SUMMARY: BIRTH TO SIX

In our earlier discussion of babbling drift in the normally hearing infant, I suggested that a certain amount of drift might be expected to occur regardless of whether the infant was in contact with and learning about his environment. And in the deafness data we have the opportunity to identify more precisely the nature of such extraenvironmental changes as might occur, and the schedule under which they do occur. As there was no appreciable evidence of fricatives, affricates, and liquids at any of the sampling intervals, we can focus our attention on the place changes among the stops and nasals.

Table 1.13 shows the relative frequency of bilabial ([p, b, m]), alveolar ([t, d, n]), and velar ([k, g, ŋ]) sounds from 3–4 months to 5 years. In calculating these figures, I have determined the percentage of the 12 segments that is represented by each set of three. Beginning with the 3- and 4-month-olds of Mavilya (1969), we see again the dominance of velar sounds, which gives way to the alveolars at 5–6 months. The data at 2 years (Fort, 1955) show a shift away from the alveolars—which, nevertheless, still exceed the velars—and toward the bilabials. This bilabial dominance persists at 3–4 years (Neas, 1953) and at 5 years (Carr, 1953).

The data suggest, then, that at some time between 6 months and 2 years, alveolars are surpassed by bilabials. Fortunately, some data from Smith and Oller (1981) show precisely when that shift takes place. It begins at 11–12 months and is complete by 15–18 months.

Table 1.13
Relative Frequency of Bilabial, Alveolar, and Velar Segments in the Vocalizations of Deaf Infants and Children

	Months		Years		
	3–4	5–6	2	3–4	5
Bilabial	4.2	4.4	87.4	60.7	75.4
Alveolar	3.4	85.9	12.5	37.3	20.8
Velar	92.4	9.7	.1	2.0	3.8
	100.0	100.0	100.0	100.0	100.0

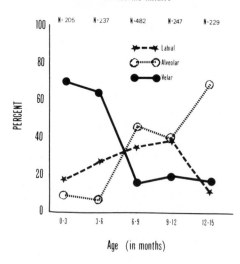

Figure 1.2. Place of articulation of consonant sounds in the vocalization of normal infants (from Smith & Oller, 1981).

SMITH: FIVE MONTHS TO TWO-AND-A-HALF YEARS

Bruce Smith, in longitudinal studies, followed normally hearing infants from soon after birth to about 15 months (Smith & Oller, 1981), and hearing-impaired infants from about 5 months to about 2½ years (Smith, 1982). Smith sampled the babbling of these infants in sessions of a half-hour or more at 3-month intervals. He performed segmental analyses and reported his data by categories of articulatory place. The analyses of normally hearing infants are shown in Figure 1.2. One can see an initial preference for velar sounds,[2] also observed by Mavilya (1969) in deaf infants at 3–4 months. This velar predominance declines slightly at 3–6 months and more sharply at 6–9 months. Then and thereafter (according to this particular figure), alveolars exceed velars. The decline of velar sounds in favor of their alveolar cognates also has been observed in non-English hearing populations as well as in English deaf children. Koopmans-van Beinum and van der Stelt (1980) report that Dutch infants demonstrate a predominance of velar movements at 6–9 weeks and a preference for tongue tip movements at 20–26 weeks (or about 6 months).

Smith and Oller's data show that labials—in the normally hearing infants— increase slightly over the developmental course, and then decline to a frequency less than that of the velars. Alveolars first dominate labials at 6–9 months. In

---

[2]In Smith (1982), as well as in Smith and Oller (1981), the "velar" category includes all postalveolar sounds, even if palatal, pharyngeal, or glottal.

Irwin (1948), alveolars are first seen to dominate labials in the 9–10-month interval, which essentially agrees with Smith and Oller. But unlike Smith and Oller, Irwin gamely continued to sample "babbling" until 29–30 months. At no time following the "alveolar take-over" at 9–10 months did the labials ever regain any of the ground lost to the alveolars. But these infants could *hear*, presumably they had long before 30 months begun to *talk*. They were undoubtedly influenced by the segmental frequencies or phonological function of the sounds in their environment. And in that English environment, alveolars (across word positions) would greatly have exceeded bilabials and velars (Mines *et al.*, 1978).

But what *would* have happened had English not come along and "perverted" (what I take to be) the mostly phonetic child? Would he not have stumbled upon the labials eventually anyway, as the deafness data of Fort (1955), Neas (1953), Carr (1953), and Sykes (1940) suggest? Figure 1.3 shows Smith's (1982) analyses of his hearing-impaired subjects. It is important to notice that the sampling intervals extend to 42 months, or about 3½ years). But the hearing infants were last sampled at 12–15 months. At that point—in Figure 1.2—it is apparent that alveolars exceed labials. But in the hearing impaired, at the very next (15–18 months) interval, the labials are dominant and remain so through the final sampling at 39–42 months. Stark (1972) observed two deaf infants at this same age

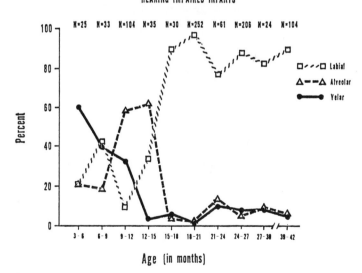

Figure 1.3. Place of articulation of consonant sounds in the vocalization of hearing-impaired infants (from Smith, 1982).

(about 18–19 months) who also produced more labial than tongue-front or tongue-back "frication sounds." From Stark's data (her Table 20-I), I calculated that 80% of their frication sounds were labial, 18% tongue-front, and 2% tongue-back. Stark's hearing infants preferred tongue-front articulations, which is not surprising since they were observed at 5 and 9 months, when deaf infants also have a clear alveolar preference. One might suppose, from these data, that environmental influence begins *before* the child's internal program has been fully executed, and that acquisition in the normal child masks the free and complete expression of the child's biological code.

Child-Internal Variations

So far, to weigh the relative contribution of environmental and constitutional factors, I have looked at babbling patterns when the environment was varied. Whether the baby was exposed to English or to some 14 other languages, he seemed to produce pretty much the same set of consonant-like sounds. Even where differences were observed, they were slight, and could as well have been due to the differing biases of native listeners, individual differences among infants, or to variations in sample size. We then looked at cross-linguistic studies in which the babbling of infants reared in different linguistic environments was more directly compared, and again saw little perceptual or instrumental differentiation. Finally, in comparing the babbling patterns of hearing and hearing-impaired infants, we continued to see a single phonetic repertoire in both populations. Even relocations among the stops were *within* the repertoire.

Of course, another logic exists. One could attempt to locate infants who are exposed to the same linguistic environment as other infants, but whose ability to respond to that environment is different. Obviously, it would be necessary that such a population babble freely so one could determine whether an environmental influence is present. Children with Down's syndrome apparently meet all three conditions.

The Babbling of Down's Babies

Down's syndrome can be identified at birth and usually is associated with mental retardation (though it may not be severe). It is therefore possible to study babbling in the retarded from birth onward. Now it may be that the phonetic learning required for babbling drift is so little that mildly or moderately retarded infants would be able to drift. But, since Down's children characteristically experience speech articulation difficulties in early childhood (Schlanger & Gottsleben, 1957), one might suppose their phonetic learning capability is reduced and—therefore—that their inclination or their ability to echo their linguistic environment in infancy also may be reduced.

Dodd (1972) studied the babbling of 10 normally developing and 10 Down's infants at 9–13 months of age. She calculated the number, range, and duration of consonants and vowels in each infant's vocal play. The Down's and normal infants did not differ significantly on any of these variables. With respect to babbling, Dodd concluded that the reason for the similarity between the two groups "is that the behaviour is not learned."

Smith and Oller's (1981) study, in addition to normal infants, also included 10 Down's babies. These infants were tested every 3 months from birth, or soon after, to 18–21 months. Figure 1.4 shows the pattern of labial, alveolar, and velar consonants produced by the Down's babies. It was very much like that of the normally developing children, whose data were previously presented in Figure 1.2. In each population, in early babbling there is a marked preference for velar articulations which, following the 3–6-month interval, gives way to alveolar and labial articulations. At 12–15 months, alveolar consonants predominate in both groups. Patterns of vocalic productions also were highly similar.

Since Down's infants are limited in their ability to respond to environmental stimulation, one might regard the (similar) patterns in normal children as evidence that babbling, in Smith and Oller's words, is not "a largely learned behavior [p. 50]." The corollary of this would seem to be that the phonetic composition of babbling is shaped primarily by internal factors, as yet unspec-

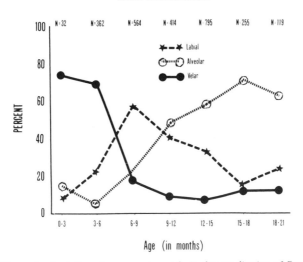

Figure 1.4. Place of articulation of consonant sounds in the vocalization of Down's syndrome infants (from Smith & Oller, 1981).

ified. Though I may exceed my authority by saying so, words like "biological" naturally come to mind, though merely invoking such terms does nothing further toward explaining the phenomena.

Keeping such points in mind, there are two other broad domains we have not yet explored. One is the sensory, motor, and cognitive systems of the infant at the age of babbling. Are they of such integrity and function as to allow the operations that appear to be required for babbling drift? Drift, one might suppose, demands that the infant hear others and himself, store auditory patterns, infer their articulatory source and neuromotor commands, and so forth. In the most elementary terms, the infant's ear must speak to his tongue, and vice versa. On the basis of what we know of the infant's neurology, are these operations all possible? In a moment, we will examine such evidence as we have.

The second broad domain also involves the infant's available "hardware." But instead of asking whether the infant could perform all the operations pertinent to phonetic learning, I will ask how—*other than through learning*—might we motivate the same phonetic repertoire? Showing that the infant's phonetic pattern is not traceable to the environment or due to learning is one thing. It is quite another to ask: if not due to imitation, then to what? First I will look at the neurological evidence to see if phonetic learning ought to be possible during the first years of life, and to see whether the available neurological evidence is theoretically useful.

The Nervous System of a Babbler

To reproduce ambient sounds one might think that the infant's analysis of those sounds must be accurate to a degree, and that the analysis must be transmittable to a motor command center and convertible into the appropriate articulatory correlates. When the articulatory activity yields an acoustic product different from the target pattern, one might suppose further that there must be a provision for the detection of this by the infant, and for subsequent self-correction. This would seem to require that the relevant circuitry be effectively in place and functioning at the time the behavioral operations are carried out. Neurologically, this means that the cortical networks responsible for auditory analysis (Wernicke's area) and speech–motor output (Broca's area) probably must be sufficiently developed that reasonably faithful transmission can occur. Presumably, these operations would require an effective set of interconnections between the analytical and output areas (arcuate fasciculus).

It should be obvious that to locate the relevant histological evidence it is necessary to decide first whether these neural routings are indispensable to phonetic learning in the infant. I am not sure they are. Our "common sense" constructions of what *needs* to take place may be different from what—in reality—*does* take place.

Let us examine an analogy. Recent research shows that in early infancy babies can imitate facial expressions. This, we imagine, is made possible by the "fact" that infants can see and analyze accurately what they see. The visual analysis is transmitted to a motor command center that "knows" which facial muscles to activate to achieve a replication of the original expressions. The motor command center has this knowledge because in the past, one supposes, the infant has seen his own face in a mirror and thereby learned which muscles need to be innervated to achieve each of the visible facial patterns.

Now let us examine such studies as are available to see if facial gestures are only imitable by those infants who have had copious time in front of a mirror. Meltzoff and Moore (1977) studied infants between 12 and 21 days of age to determine their ability to imitate various facial and manual gestures. The facial gestures included tongue and lip protrusion, and mouth opening, and the manual gesture involved sequential finger movement. Under highly controlled conditions, Meltzoff and Moore found that infants imitated the adult gestures, both during and following exposure to them, even though the infants could not see their own faces. They also report imitation in a 60-*minute*-"old" infant, which suggests that such activity does not require that the baby ever have seen his own face in the past (as does the discrimination of facial expressions by infants at 36 hours, reported in Field, Woodson, Greenberg, & Cohen, 1982). How, then, does the infant know what to do when a particular gesture is displayed, or that he is reproducing the gesture that he sees? Meltzoff and Moore concluded that "the imitative responses observed are . . . mediated by an abstract representatonal system," and that "the ability to use intermodal equivalences is an innate ability of humans [p. 78]."

A second experiment by Meltzoff (Meltzoff & Borton, 1979) showed that infants possess, to a striking degree, the capacity for intermodal matching. Meltzoff and Borton were curious to know whether infants would be more likely to *visually* recognize an object if their only previous experience with that object had been *tactile* (or, more properly, kinesthetic). They used an experimental procedure that resembles the visual habituation paradigm (Fagan, 1970) and methods for assessing oral stereognosis (Locke, 1968).

Meltzoff and Borton designed two rubber pacifiers, one with a smooth bulb and one with a knobby bulb. There were two groups of 32 infants, with a mean age of 29 days. One group was presented with the smooth bulb and allowed to explore it with their tongue and lips for 90 sec. They were not allowed to see the pacifier. Then the two shapes were displayed, one to the left, and the other to the right of the infant. A second experimenter—completely ignorant of the tactile stimulus—determined the direction and duration of the infants' gaze. The other group was given the knobby pacifier and the procedure was repeated. Meltzoff and Borton found that the majority of the infants in each group looked longer at the "matching" object than at the other one.

I think in Meltzoff's experiments there are caveats for the study of the neurological prerequisites of phonetic learning. Do infants need to hear themselves in order to replicate adult auditory patterns? Extrapolating from Meltzoff and Moore, one might expect that infants could produce articulations to match certain sound patterns without having heard their own vocalizations before, an assessment with which Meltzoff agrees (personal communication, October 1981). Obviously, the appropriate experiments need to be done before this matter can be resolved. In the meanwhile, it may be difficult to reliably judge the requisite neurology, including the need of a working tongue-to-ear transmission system.

Neurology in the Interim

Lacking an understanding of the cognitive and neural routings necessary to phonetic learning, what is it we do know regarding the nervous system of the babbler? What is known of the auditory and motor and linking structures? The histological evidence is that these structures are only partially myelinated during the first year of life (Milner, 1976; Whitaker, 1976). But if an infant's echoic curcuitry is partially myelinated, we are inclined to ask how myelinated need it be for low level phonetic accommodations? Is partial myelination enough for partial matching? To this, unfortunately, we have no satisfactory answer. Apparently partial myelination is sufficient to *some* level of function. According to Crelin (1973), "unmyelinated neurons have a long latency, are slow-firing, and fatigue early [p. 24]," which only seems to deny them *perfect* function. But whether infants possess the capability of *perfect* function seems quite irrelevant to the larger question at hand: whether an infant *could* express *some* of his (receptive) phonetic learning before he—according to the present literature— seems to.

Can Physiological Factors Explain the Infant's Phonetic Pattern?

If the specific "sutff" of babbling—the [d]s and the [m]s and the [j]s—are not inspired by the specific stimulation of the infant's environment, we apparently need to look *within* the child in any attempt to explain the phonetic patterning evident in babbling. Consideration of the nervous system has advanced our cause very little, and we are left with questions such as what it means for an infant to "prefer" alveolar stops. Does the infant say them because he likes the sound images? Apparently not, for the deaf produce alveolar stops in great abundance. Does an alveolar preference mean that the infant likes the feeling of apical–alveolar contact? Koopmans-van Beinum has indicated (personal communication) that infants may display speechlike movements *silently* perhaps a week or more prior to their first systematic execution audibly. But then why does oral-motor activity so universally become audible many months in advance of lexical communication? To say that certain movements are—as some have (e.g., Lewis, 1936, pp. 31–35)—associated with sucking or swallowing is not an explanation, and may even be inaccurate (Netsell, 1981). If the infant can (because he does) say both [d] and [g], why does he say more of one than the other? Why more [d] than [t]?

Babbling Explicanda

Before we examine the state of the literature in developmental physiology, it would be helpful if we could agree on just what it is that needs to be explained, and what it is we expect a literature review to accomplish. At first glance, this latter question seems, I suppose, fairly straightforward. We want the literature to show the neural and muscular bases for the articulatory movements *one associates* with specific phones. But this gets sticky right away, for we speak of "back sounds" and "bilabial sounds" when we intend, probably, to refer to sound patterns associated with back and bilabial *movements*. An opening caveat is that sounds are not isomorphic with movements in the infant any more than they are in the adult.

But beyond this initial timidity, one expects to find that where [t]s and [d]s abound there is some physiological milestone which implicates upward movements of the tongue tip. A first approximation to such a phonetic–physiological matrix was achieved by Kent (1980a). It is shown in Table 1.14. The matrix seems to work, more or less, with respect to Oller's (1980) broad stages of *vocal* development. Can a similar matrix be achieved for a segment hierarchy such as Irwin's?

It was seen in Table 1.1 that [h] was the most or next most common sound in the three studies consulted. McCarthy (1952) attributed the predominance of [h] to the aspiration that attends breathing, pointing out that the letter *h* derives from a Greek word which, she said, means "rough breathing." This seems reasonable enough, though it becomes necessary to account for individual differences in "rough breathing" (cf. Table 1.6).

That infants breathe also seems not to be much of an explanation. Infants breathe, but they also gulp, swallow, cough, and sneeze; our challenge here is to find out why they can make the movements that may resemble speech articulations.

If one moves down the list from [h] one immediately encounters, at least in

Table 1.14
Parallels between Phonetic and Vocal Tract Development

Age of infant	Phonetic development	Related anatomy and physiology
0–1 month Phonation stage	Nasalized vowels	Nasal breathing and nasalized vocalization because of engagement of larynx and nasopharynx; tongue has mostly back-and-forth motions and nearly fills the oral cavity.
2–3 months GOOing stage	Nasalized vowels plus g/k	Some change in shape of oral cavity and an increase in mobility of tongue
4–6 months Expansion stage	Normal vowels	Increased separation of oral and nasal cavities, so that nonnasal vowels are readily produced
	Raspberry (labial)	The necessary air pressure in the mouth can be developed because of disengagement of the larynx from the nasopharynx.
	Squeal and growl	Contrasts in vocal pitch are heightened perhaps because descent of larynx into the neck makes the vocal folds more vulnerable to forces of supralaryngeal muscles.
	Yelling	Better coordination of respiratory system and larynx permits loud voice.
	Marginal bubble	Alternation of full opening and closure of vocal tract are enhanced by larynx–nasopharynx disengagement.

Source: Kent, R. D. (1980a). Articulatory and acoustic perspectives on speech development. In A. P. Reilly (Ed.), *The communication game: Perspectives on the development of speech, language, and non-verbal communication skills.* Johnson & Johnson Baby Products Company Pediatric Round Table Series, Skillman, New Jersey; with permission from Johnson & Johnson Baby Products Company.

the 11–12-month-olds, [d]s and [b]s and [m]s and assorted other stops, nasals, and glides. In general, studies agree that [d] exceeds the bilabials (and most everything else), so perhaps we can take this "explicandum" as the starting point of a physiological explanation.

Why [d]?

It may be recalled that alveolars are not the first consonant-like sounds to appear in babbling. Glottal and velar stops are earlier, their dominance unchallenged over the first few months of life (cf. Table 1.13; Figure 1.2). As the infant approaches 6–7 months, the "back" sounds decline. The ascendancy of [d] relative go [g] is shown in Table 1.15, which summarizes data from Irwin (1947), Fisichelli (1950), and Kroehbiel (1940). According to my analyses of Irwin's data, the subordination of [g] to [d] occurs between the samples taken at 5–6 months and 7–8 months. Data reported in Krehbiel's longitudinal study of 15 infants show a marked decline of [g] relative to [d] between 4 and 6 months (other data in her study show that [g] occurs proportionately more often in crying than in noncrying vocalization). Among Fisichelli's infants, the shift occurred between 6 and 9 months. All three studies agree that the supremacy of [d] is achieved soon after 6 months, with [d] later reaching an occurrence of about 80%.

Earlier speculation as to why [d] becomes so prominent in infant babbling had a quasi-environmental tone. Lewis (1936), and Gregoire (1933) before him, both pointed to the infant's postural orientation as a factor. The young infant frequently is supine, a position in which gravity may pull the back of the tongue closer to the soft palate. Indeed, Fisichelli (1950) commented quite innocently that her "children in the 6 and 9 months age groups were placed in a crib, since institutionalized infants of this age characteristically remain in a supine position in their cribs for the greater part of the day. Children in the 12, 15 and 18-months age groups, however, were tested in either a high chair or play pen [pp. 25–26]." The importance of this is that many of the sounds made while the infant is on his back may be perceived as [g]-like or [k]-like purely through the passive force of gravity. When the infant sits erect or stands, this passive force ought then to minimize velar articulation.

Several years ago Oller and Gavin (in Oller, 1981) set out to test the body position hypothesis by tabulating the proportion of velar ("gooing") sounds produced by infants when supine and upright. Thirty infants were observed at 1–4 months of age, when velar sounds predominate. Analyses of the 10 most cooperative infants revealed no more "goo" sounds in the supine than in the upright position (in fact, there were slightly fewer). Though Oller pointed to various methodological problems, the data seemed to justify the conclusion that gravity appears "to have little, if any, effect on proportion of gooing sounds produced [p. 89]."

With disconfirmation of the body position hypothesis, there remain several

Table 1.15
The Increasing Dominance of [d] *over* [g] *in the Vocalizations of American English Infants*

				Irwin					
	1–2	3–4	5–6	7–8	9–10	11–12	13–14	15–16	17–18
d	0	2.64	2.06	6.46	15.73	20.58	19.42	20.04	20.56
g	2.79	11.73	7.46	5.43	4.12	4.15	4.91	5.55	5.17
%d	0	18.37	21.64	54.33	79.24	83.22	79.82	78.31	79.91

	Krehbiel			Fisichelli				
	4	5	6	6	9	12	15	18
d	19	7	32	57	353	536	675	2064
g	106	69	36	124	170	221	192	265
%d	15.2	9.2	47.0	31.5	67.5	70.8	77.9	88.6

Source: From data reported in Irwin (1947), Fisichelli (1950), and Krehbiel (1940) by months of age.

structural possibilities to be considered, one pertaining to the abundance of velar sounds, the other to the relative scarcity of alveolar sounds. According to Crelin (1973), the oral cavity of the neonate "is only a potential one when the mouth is closed because the tongue comes into contact with the gums (gingivae) laterally and with the roof of the mouth above [p. 27]." Presumably, these conditions invite the perception of velar phones. The shift from velars to alveolars would be precipitated by (a) the descent of the posterior region of the tongue into the developing pharyngeal cavity, decreasing the probability of dorsovelar contact; and (b) the infant's active mandibular closures, permitting passive lingual approximations of the tongue tip or blade to the alveolar area.

The paucity of alveolars could be related to structural factors of a different sort. Fletcher and Daly (1974) measured sublingual growth in 50 children from 1 to 5 months of age. They observed particularly sharp increases in the length of the lingual frenulum, which from other work (Fletcher & Meldrum, 1968) is known to be related to articulatory performance in general, and may be correlated with tongue tip elevation and protrusion in particular. Whether there is a discontinuity in frenular growth at around 6 months is not known.

There are, of course, a variety of other movement patterns that need to be explained. But an inspection of the present literature on the infant's developing vocal tract provides little in the way of specific answers. Returning to Crelin's (1973) description of the newborn oral cavity,

> The hard palate is short, wide, and only slightly arched at birth, whereas it is deeply arched both anteroposteriorly and transversely in the adult. . . the tongue of the newborn infant is relatively short and broad. . . the entire surface of the newborn tongue is within the oral cavity. . . the posterior third of the tongue descend[s] into the neck after birth to become part of the anterior wall of the pharynx. The descent begins gradually during the first year after birth and is essentially completed by the fourth or fifth year of age. . . the newborn infant is an obligate nose breather [pp. 27–28].

Such statements inspire speculation. They suggest, for example, that the velar "preference" may actually be an anatomical necessity; the palate is so low that lingual contact is difficult to avoid. But why the infant's affinity for [d] over [b] or [f]? Crelin (personal communication, October 5, 1981) has himself indicated that "as far as the vocal tract anatomy is concerned an infant can make all three of the above sounds when he can make the d-like sound," adding that he could only guess that the infant's preferences were "the result of the maturation of the neuromuscular mechanisms." Of course, there still is a difference between what an infant "can" do and what he might, for physiological or anatomical reasons, "prefer" to do.

One could devote considerable time to a physiological explanation for [d], so we should not be optimistic that we will soon discover an "internal" basis for the child's evident preference for stops, singletons, and open syllables over fricatives, clusters, and final obstruents.[3] But the work must begin if there is to emerge an explanation of the phonological patterns of children and the phonetic movement patterns of infants. Perhaps the best paradigm for such a beginning would be, as Kent (1980b) suggested, the young child's "learning of generalized spatio-temporal schemata for articulatory movements [p. 6; see also Kent, 1981]."

Training Studies

If pursued with sufficient rigor, there is a mode of inquiry that could indicate whether environmental influence is plausible at certain ages. This is the vocal or phonetic training study which, for the most part, has been neglected.

Recall that in the case of cross-linguistic studies such as we have reviewed earlier, nature has provided two groups of children with different patterns of phonetic stimulation. The patterns differ not according to the dictates of an experimenter, but according to factors outside his control. Consequently, comparisons of language environments are influenced, to a degree, by pragmatic constraints on the research. These may include the fact that the experimenter lives in Montreal or Miami, does or does not have a travel grant, and so forth. In the ideal case, the researcher selects the patterns of stimulation based on normative studies of vocal tract development (cf. Oller, 1980) showing that certain *motor* patterns—as would be necessary to reproduce particular *auditory* patterns—can be expected at certain chronological ages. Then, the investigator would select two languages that systematically manipulate the auditory patterns in question and see if there is a difference in the infants' patterns of vocalization.

One can also, perhaps with a somewhat freer hand in the design of things, select several patterns of vocalization and present them systematically and differentially as stimulus patterns to several groups of infants, allowing the infants' domestic stimulation to continue as it naturally would. One might manipulate intonation or fundamental frequency, segmental or syllabic configurations, voice quality, and so forth. Presumably, one's selection of phonetic parameters would be compatible with the infants' vocal capabilities, their perceptual prowess less likely to be in question (but also a factor to be considered).

Though a pair of psychologists once spent 3 years attempting to teach a chimpanzee to speak English words (cf. Hayes, 1951), I know of few cases

---

[3]Indeed, there are data that complicate, if not contradict, both structural and body position accounts of articulatory place preferences. In naturalistic studies of Dutch infants (Elbers, 1982; Koopmans-van Beinum & van der Stelt, 1981), place preferences have been observed to shift as infants began and progressed into new stages of babbling. For example, back articulations declined in favor of more anterior ones, which in turn yielded somewhat to back sounds at the onset of a subsequent stage of babbling.

where even an hour was devoted to training the human infant to reproduce simple sound patterns.

In her book on child development, Charlotte Bühler (1930) described her developmental screening test, which at 6 months contains an imitation item. To be considered normal in his development, the baby had to repeat "re–re–re" after the examiner. Bühler does not say how she determined that noncompliance would indicate delay.

Piaget (1962) indicated that at about 4 months of age, infants systematically and deliberately imitate sounds if the sounds already are familiar. This was confirmed in the investigation of Uzgiris and Hunt (1975), and quite incidentally in a study of speech perception by Kuhl and Meltzoff (1982). In their second experiment, 18–20-week-old infants were presented with two films of a female speaker saying /a/ or /i/ at 3-sec intervals. On one side of a screen the vowel heard and seen were identical, on the other side the infant heard the /a/ vowel but saw the talker producing /i/, or vice versa. Kuhl and Meltzoff were interested in determining whether the infants would look longer at the matching case (they did), but the authors also observed that some infants

> produced sounds that resembled the adult female's vowels. They seemed to be 'imitating' the female talker, 'taking turns' by alternating their vocalizations with hers . . . such vocal productions suggest that infants are directing their articulators to achieve auditory targets that they hear another produce, in other words, that they are capable of vocal imitation. [This quote is reprinted from Kuhl, P. K., & Meltzoff, A. N. (1982). The bimodal perception of speech in infancy. *Science, 218*, p. 1140. Copyright 1982 by the American Association for the Advancement of Science.]

In Kessen, Levine, and Wendrich (1979), 23 infants of 3–6 months were observed for their ability to vocally imitate different pitches, whether produced vocally or with a pitchpipe. The notes to be imitated were D, F, and A above middle C. Trained musicians were used to judge from tape recordings the incidence of pitch matches by the infants. Kessen *et al.* found that infants were reliably able to match the pitches presented. The authors speculated that the infant has "a congenital readiness to respond to pitched tones which is then adaptively modified to his experience of sounds in the first years of life [p. 99]."

There also have been negative results. In a confusing study by Webster (1969), four 6-month-olds were given several sessions of controlled stimulation in which they heard a 5-min tape either of a vowel series ([ɛ, e, a, i, o, u]) or of CV syllables ([ka, ba, da, ga, ma, wa]). Recordings were made of the infants' vocalization before and during the stimulation periods. Webster's results suggested that there might have been a differential effect of the different patterns of stimulation. However, the effect was not one of enhancement, as one might expect, but of suppression. That is, when exposed to consonantal stimulation the infants' vowel/consonant ratio went up, when exposed to vocalic stimulation their vowel/consonant ratio went down. Webster attributed this counterintuitive finding to "satiation."

It is obvious that environmental patterns ultimately have an enhancing function, but only after protracted periods of stimulation. It is hoped that appropriate research will soon be conducted to determine how soon such stimulation may take hold, and how much of it there effectively *needs* to be. In this remark I am reminded of a statement by Bateman (1917). It was about the child's first word, but could just as well have fit the "first imitations" I have been discussing.

> The sudden advent of the first word . . . is similar to other creations of like nature. At one moment something *is not* and at the next moment it *is* and we do not know what miracle fills the infinitesimal gap. Perhaps what happens in that fraction of time is something quite simple and the miracle is really worked out in the long preparation [p. 396].

2

Is Infant Babbling
Related to Child Speech?

Is infant babbling related to child speech? It should be obvious that one cannot begin to answer a question such as this without first examining the characteristics of infant babbling and their origins, as was done in Chapter 1. But what is "child speech" and what is meant by "related"?

First, we should understand that the issue is not whether early infant babbling is related to late child phonology. Early infant babbling (birth to 6 months) is not closely related to—in fact, in many ways is quite disparate from—late infant babbling (9–12 months). And many of the child's first utterances are rendered in ways not intimately like those in the more advanced stages of language acquisition. What we must ask, then, is whether late infant babbling is related to early child speech.

Second, it may be necessary to temporarily set aside the word *related*, at least with respect to its operational implications, and in a more elementary fashion speak in terms of observable *similarities*. If we find that late infant babbling is very similar to early child speech we may suspect a functional relationship between the two, and we may then probe its physiological or cognitive dynamics as a second step.

Third, I am not asking—as many before me have—whether babbling constitutes some form of "practice" for speaking, in which the infant learns associations between auditory-speech patterns and motor-speech movements (Kent, 1982; Mattingly, 1976). It is clear that infants are aware of their own voices (Cullen *et al.*, 1968), but it also is clear from the deafness studies that such awareness is not, cannot be, the raison d'etre for babbling. And it is apparent that if babbling is helpful in learning to talk, it surely is insufficient, for the Down's infants babble well and speak poorly. But beyond this it would be hard to go at present. And I am not sure of the theoretical value of exploring babbling from such a perspective.

Evidence of Continuity

What I prefer to ask is whether the infant at 9 or 10 months, who is soon to be talking, will take into that activity something that he already *has* and has been *doing*. Is there any sense in which early speech is the *continuation* of anything, whether that thing lies in a linguistic, psychological, social, or sensorimotor domain? If there are such continuations, they must surely be indexed by observable *continuities*, some temporal, some substantive.

Temporal Continuity

Jakobson (1941/1968) and Velten (1943) believed, as we saw earlier, that babbling and speech were clearly separated in time. And, if there is a temporal discontinuity—a "complete silence," in Velten's terms—between babbling and speech, it is a small step to the assumption of functional independence. It is, therefore, important to determine whether such a temporal discontinuity actually exists. If babbling and speech are related, would not the former blend smoothly and continuously, almost imperceptibly, into the latter?

Beyond that of Jakobson and of Velton, I have been able to find no testimony that babbling and speech are temporally discontinuous. On the other hand, I have located several accounts to the contrary. In his study of the acquisition of Luo, Blount (1969) observed that "babbling behavior continued to be exhibited during the early one-word utterance stage [p. 82]." Labov and Labov (1978) commented that their daughter Jessie "did not stop babbling when she began to use words [p. 833]." In the development of his daughter Hildegard, Leopold (1947) observed that "during the later months, 0;9–1;3 . . . babbling and speaking overlapped [p. 155]." Having studied longitudinally a Thai child, Tuaycharoen (1979) concluded that "there is a gradual transition from babbling to speech [p. 274]." Olmsted (1971) noted that his investigation of phonological development, beginning at 15 months, was complicated by the fact that the younger subjects "tended to relapse toward babbling on occasion [p. 53]." That babbling and speech overlap in the infant-child, is stated convincingly by Elbers (1980), based on observations of her Dutch son:

> When jargon babbling appeared I stopped recording . . . I had an implicit naive idea that, now that jargon appeared, repetitive babbling would be over. This,

however, was not the case. Two types of babbling now were to be observed; incomprehensible jargon and comprehensible repetitions. When the first words appeared there were three types of "babbling"; meaningful babbles, jargon, and repetitions [p. 12].

Substantive Continuity: The Earliest Phonology

Based on the testimony of these investigators, it appears that babbling typically continues during the child's initial attempts to speak, and in many cases goes some months beyond. But what is it that continues? Are we talking only about the persistence of vocalization, in very general terms? Or is the infant's segmental repertoire, as previously patterned, also continued? If the infant continues to babble particular consonant sounds preferentially, is he not also more likely to produce those sounds, whether called for or not, in speaking? The answer to this latter question may tell us a great deal about the relatedness of babbling and speech.

Anecdotal Evidence

Some of the evidence on substantive continuity exists in the form of anecdotal accounts where the linguist may also be the subject's parent. Elbers (1982) said that in her Dutch son, "repetitive babbling not only seemed to be the starting point for jargon babbling but for the first words as well. Babbles from the repetitive babbling repertoire could be used as words (i.e., they could acquire meaning) or as a springboard towards the gradual approximation of adult word forms [p. 60]."

Rūķe-Draviņa (1965) followed the phonological development of two Czech and two Latvian children. She noticed a similarity between the presence or absence of certain sounds in babbling and in speaking:

Quite early in the speech of small children one comes across the bilabial /p/-sound. . . . This sound occurred quite often in the case of both the Latvian children during the babbling stage. . . . The rolled apical /r/, on the other hand, was never registered during the first two years of life, neither in the case of the Czech children nor in that of the Latvian children, not even during the babbling period . . . [p. 61].

Cruttenden (1970) observed that in the babbling of his twin daughters, as they neared the "first words" stage,

syllables with [b] [d] [g] [m] [n] [l] account for a large part of the data. . . . Vowels of the [æ] [a] [ə] type predominated throughout the babbling period. . . . During the first three months of [the first words] stage the consonant sounds were predominately [b] [d] [g] [m] [n] while vowels were still predominately around [æ] [a] [ə] [pp. 114–115].

Thus Cruttenden observed one repertoire, used both in babbling and speaking. This seems also to be true of the Labovs (Labov & Labov, 1978), who commented that "in formulating her first words, Jessie had at least [her babbling] inventory . . . to draw on [p. 819]." In the numerous productions of *cat* and *mama* for which Jessie was famous, the Labovs observed a babbling– speaking relatedness, such that "the sounds used to form cat and mama were included in the set of sounds that Jessie used in babbling [p. 819]." In fact, they commented more generally that "Jessie's phonological inventory was only a small subset of her babbling inventory . . . phonological development was hardly an independent process [p. 849]."

Vanvik's (1971) Norwegian daughter, at the end of her first year of life, had a fairly well-defined babbling inventory. From Vanvik's annual summaries, it is apparent that the content of his daughter's speech was linked to the content of her babbling:

Year 1: At the end of the first year (i.e., the babbling inventory): "The lacking sounds are the retroflex [ʈ ɖ ɳ ɭ], the roll [r], and the fricatives [f ʃ ç] [p. 282]."

Year 2: At the end of the second year (i.e., the speaking inventory): "no new sounds are noted. . . . [ʈ ɖ ɳ ɭ r f ʃ ç] are still lacking . . . [p. 290]."

Year 3: At the end of the third year: "the following sounds were still lacking: [ʈ ɖ ɳ ɭ (ɾ) ʃ ç] [p. 302]," that is, the retroflex sounds and the palato-alveolar and palatal fricative.

Year 4: At the end of the fourth year: "the retroflex sounds and [ʃ] have developed. . . . The only phoneme lacking at the end of the fourth year is /ç/ [pp. 302–303]."

Perhaps the most detailed description of the transition from babbling to speech—and the last that I shall reproduce here—is due to Leopold (1947), who traced his daughter's development from birth to 2 years. His description of Hildegard's [d] productions was rich in detail.

The voiced dental stop *d* occurred much earlier than *t*. As an accidental sound it was heard as early as the cooing phase, E 0;1. In babbling, *d* was the first consonant approaching precise articulation, 0;6, three months before *t*. At 0;7–8 it was the most frequent consonant combined with vowels. At E 0;8 it yielded in frequency to *b* but continued without interruption into the speaking stage. It was contained in the first demonstrative interjections, *there* 0;10, *da* B 1;0, and in other primitive words. *t* competed with it to a limited extent from E 0;9, but the position of *d* was much stronger. Of the total vocabulary of the two years (377 words), 66 words began with *d*, nearly as many as with *b* (71). If we add those beginning with *t* (11), we find 77 beginning with a dental stop as against 79 beginning with a bilabial stop, nearly the same number . . . [pp. 168–169].

The anecdotal evidence suggests that a segmental repertoire is available to the child as he begins to speak, the same one he displayed in his most recent babbling. From this repertoire come the segments the child needs to produce words. This is not to say there are *no* segments in babbling that are not heard in the child's lexical attempts, and vice versa. In fact, Leopold (1947) gives several examples of babbling–speaking asymmetries (cf. pp. 162–186). I also agree with Labov and Labov (1978) who, having noticed that Jessie produced [d]s in both babbling and talking, commented that "babbling with [d] in an optimal, unmarked reduplicating syllable is not the same as programming a [d] into a specific syllabic position, integrated with a specific target vowel [p. 838]." Rather, what I am asserting is that if a segment is frequent in the prelexical babbling of an infant, it is *available to be programmed* into a lexical unit.

What is required, ideally, are longitudinal studies of small groups of children from 8 or 9 months to, perhaps, 18 or 24 months. Fortunately, two studies of this type have been reported, and I will describe the pertinent findings here.

Longitudinal Studies of Small Groups

Vihman, Macken, Miller, and Simmons (1981) followed the phonetic development of 10 children for 7 months beginning at 9 months of age. Their report includes an analysis of 6 of the children, whose vocalizations—and, later, words—were recorded in weekly home sessions. Detailed phonetic transcriptions were prepared, and consonant productions were categorized by place and manner of articulation in words and nonwords. The data were then examined according to the child's lexical stage. In Stage 1, only babbled "nonwords" were evident. In Stage 2, one to three words were used spontaneously within a recording session. In Stage 3, there were four or more spontaneous words. The data from all succeeding sessions were classified as occurring in Stage 4.

In their analysis of these data, Vihman *et al.* observed "differences across the subjects and across time in the use of the various consonantal place categories, but overall similarity in the word and non-word curves for any given subject [pp. 14–15 of the manuscript]." Inspection of their data does indeed indicate that labials and dentals generally exceed velars and palatals, and that word and nonword curves for any given articulatory place tend to parallel each other. However, a close examination reveals that, for all six of the children, both in Stage 3 and Stage 4 the relative incidence of labial consonants in *words* exceeded that in *nonwords,* whereas the opposite was true of dental consonants, which were less abundant in words than in nonword productions.

Since the Vihman *et al.* (1981) report, the analysis of 2 more of the original group of 10 children has been completed, and their data were sent to me by Marilyn Vihman. For the two additional children, the labial word–dental nonword pattern did not hold in Stage 3, but was evident in Stage 4. Taking the data as a whole, then, it can be said that all 8 children showed the labial word–dental nonword profile in those sessions in which the most words were used. These trends are in the right (ambient) direction, for word-initial /b, m/ exceed /d, n/ both in lexical (Moser, 1969) and in conversational frequency (Mines *et al.*, 1978).

It will be exciting to read Vihman *et al.*'s full report when it is available, and probably no additional generalizations should be attempted in the meanwhile. But preliminary analyses do suggest that at some time between 11 or 12 months and 15 or 16 months the children of Vihman *et al.* began, in targeting for words, to display different phonetic frequencies than they revealed in their babbling. Note that questions of vocal tract and perceptual development are irrelevant here, for the comparison is not between the young babbler and the older speaker, but between words and nonwords in *the same child at the same time.* If the results can be verified, it seems to follow that environmental effects may first be evident when the child begins freely to produce words, even if the words are not easily identifiable.

In relation to Jakobson's assertion that a "silent period" sometimes comes between babbling and speech, Vihman *et al.* commented that they "did not find such a period in any of the ten children [p. 15]." In relation to Jakobson's assertion that sounds change in some way when the child goes from babbling to speaking, Vihman *et al.* stated that "virtually everything we have seen goes against that view [p. 16]."

Stoel-Gammon and Cooper (1981) analyzed the utterances of three children, beginning in the late babbling period, 1 month prior to their first identifiable word (10;0–11;2), and ending with their acquisition of 50 words (16;2–19;0). Table 2.1 shows for each child the consonants occurring in babbling, in words, and in both babbling and words. All three children carried [b, d, m] into speaking; [n, s, h] were each carried in two out of three cases. As the second column indicates, a few non-English sounds [ř, β, x] dropped out—or were (appropriately) rejected—at this point. The final column shows that some sounds made their first appearance in words, including—ironically—the non-English [β] of

Table 2.1

Consonants Occurring with a Frequency of 1% or More in Babbling and in Two or More Words at the End of the Study

	Babbling and words	Babbling only	Words only
Daniel	b d m n s w	ř ð x j	p g ʔ β z ʒ tʃ
Sarah	b d m n l h	g β ř j	t k s w
Will	b d m t s z h	j w ʃ	g ʔ β ts tθ pw fw

Source: From Stoel-Gammon & Cooper (1981, Table 2).

Daniel and Will, and a variety of marginal and incorrectly used sounds and sequences such as [g, ʒ, ts, tθ, pw, fw]. Stoel-Gammon and Cooper commented that

> to some extent . . . the sounds a child uses in babbling are the same as those used in early meaningful speech. For each subject, over half the phones in the babbling sample also occurred in the production of real words. . . . Sarah was the only subject to produce [l] in the prelinguistic period and was also the only one to use it in meaningful speech. Conversely, Will was the only subject not to use [n] in his babbling and the only one who did not use it in at least two of his first 50 words [p. 7].

Incidentally, 10 English sounds were almost nonexistent in the babbling of Daniel, Sarah, and Will. Occurring less than 1% of the time were [p, f, v, θ, tʃ, ʤ, ʒ, ŋ, k, r], a disproportionate representation of fricatives and affricates.

The Course of Early Development

Recently, there have been several "phone tree" studies of child phonology. In the construction of phone trees, spontaneous utterances are obtained from children who are just beginning to talk. In the analysis, phonological categories are established for the initial sampling interval, and as the child's system expands over the succeeding weeks and months, the division, addition, loss, and reallocation of categories is plotted in treelike fashion. By their very nature, phone tree studies are required to begin with the child's first words, and therefore they are a valuable source of data on the early phonology part of the late babbling–early phonology comparison I spoke of previously.

Among the more interesting of the published phone tree studies are those of Ferguson and Farwell (1975) and Shibamoto and Olmsted (1978). A cross-sectional study by Leonard, Newhoff, and Mesalam (1980) also is useful in the present context as it documents a stage in the early development not of 2 or 3 children, but of 10. These children's ages ranged from 1:4 to 1:10, and their expressive vocabularies held about 50 words at the time segmental analyses were done.

Leonard *et al.* obtained a spontaneous sample of 140–250 utterances per subject. Words were defined as phonetic forms having consistency in accompanying action or reference. Phone classes were established on a phonological rather than a lexical basis. For example, if words beginning with /m/, /b/, and /p/ were all rendered as [b], a single [b] phone class was identified. If /d/ words were sometimes [d] and sometimes [g], the phone class was [d ~ g]. Figure 2.1 shows the phone classes of each of Leonard *et al.*'s 10 subjects prior to any treelike expression of systemic elaboration. The phone classes are spatially organized approximately by place of articulation.

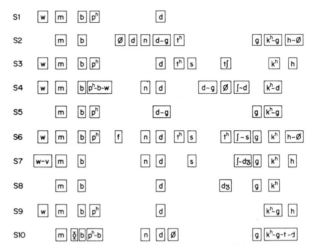

Figure 2.1. The word-initial phone classes for the 10 subjects in Leonard et al. [From Leonard, L. B., Newhoff, M., & Mesalam, L. (1980). Individual differences in early child phonology. Applied Psycholinguistics, 1, 7–30; with permission from Cambridge University Press.]

It is apparent from Figure 2.1 that the earliest phonological systems of children are dominated by segments classified as stops, nasals, and glides, with a modicum of fricatives and affricates. There are no liquids. As the figure represents *words,* it represents—even by Jakobson's definition—phonological *systems.* And yet the segment inventories look very little different from the babbling patterns we have examined for children just slightly older (the 2-year-old deaf) or younger (the 1-year-old hearing) groups.

Prather, Hedrick, and Kern (1975) used photographs of familiar objects to elicit naming, and obtained word-initial and word-final consonant productions from 20 normal children (cross-sectionally) at each 4-month interval from 24 to 48 months. The data from this study are useful for three reasons. First, the observations began with fairly young children. Second, the data came from an elicitation procedure, which means that the children could not control the data base to the extent that avoidance techniques and vocabulary factors permit in studies of spontaneous speech (cf. Olmsted, 1971). Third, Prather has provided me with a copy of the raw data, including all the specific substitutions and omissions observed in initial and final word positions. My continuity analyses are based on these raw data.

Figure 2.2 shows the mean percentage correct production of sounds within ("High frequency") or without ("Low frequency") the consonantal babbling repertoire at 11–12 months (cf. Table 1.1). It shows, for example, that the average accuracy of 24-month-olds for repertoire sounds was 81%, as compared to an average accuracy of 35% for nonrepertoire sounds. At the next sampling

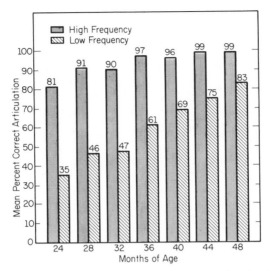

Figure 2.2. *Mean percentage of correct articulation of consonants in the infant babbling repertoire (high frequency) and outside the infant babbling repertoire (low frequency) by children from 24 to 48 months of age (figure taken from Locke, 1980b).*

interval, 28 months, the repertoire sounds are produced at an average 91% accuracy, and nonrepertoire sounds have jumped from 35 to 46% correct.

As the repertoire sounds are produced with considerable accuracy *from the beginning,* there is little room for additional improvement. But the accuracy of nonrepertoire sounds very steadily increases at each sampling interval. At 4 years they have finally achieved a level of performance similar to that of the repertoire segments as produced at the very beginning. Across the seven sampling intervals, the accuracy difference between repertoire and nonrepertoire segments declines from 46%, at 24 months, to 45, 43, 36, 27, 24, and, at the final interval, 16%.

The broader age range sampled by Templin (1957) supports Figure 2.2 and shows that the repertoire–nonrepertoire discrepancy persists until development is complete. The following are data calculated from Templin's annual samplings and are given as percentages of sounds said correctly:

	3	4	5	6	7	8
Repertoire	84	93	92	97	98	99
Nonrepertoire	46	66	74	84	92	96
Difference	38	27	18	13	6	3

If my interpretations are generally correct, there are several corollaries. First, there must be a relationship between babbling frequency and *intrusion* frequency in children's substitutions (there is a hint of this in the extended quotation from Leopold given earlier). Second, since we saw earlier that the babbling repertoire was universal, it ought to be the case that children's developmental progression in phonology is similar across languages. Third, it must be possible to predict, with reasonable accuracy, the developmental speech patterns of young children from a knowledge of their individual babbling profiles. And if the corollaries are valid, there must indeed be a huge biological component in phonology that manifests itself in the phonetic patterns of all humans, whether their system is developing, disintegrating, changing, or merely in use.

Babbling Frequency and Children's Substitutions

Earlier, I reproduced Leopold's description of his daughter's [d] and [t] productions as they occurred first in babbling and later in speaking. Leopold (1947) also observed that

> Since *d* was much more frequent than *t*, the list of consonants for which it served as a substitute is much longer. In addition to the instances in which it rendered standard *d* (also *dr, dR, ʤ*), it took the place of *t* (also *tr, tR, ts, tʃ; st, ʃt, str*), *ð, θ* (also *θr*), *g* (also *gl*), and *k* (also *kr, kR, skr*), that is to say, it stood for voiced and voiceless dental and palatal-velar stops and for both dental fricatives [pp. 168–169].

It is interesting that Leopold saw a connection between babbling frequency and phonological *utility,* as his use of the word "since" seems to imply. Figure 2.3 shows some additional data produced by the Prather *et al.* (1975) investigation, and supplied to me in raw form by Elizabeth Prather. The figure shows the percentage of all substitutions, at each of the seven sampling intervals, in which the intruding consonant was a member of the babbling repertoire of Irwin's subjects. Here there is no regular trend over time, but in each age group the intruder is considerably more likely to be a repertoire sound; overall, the average is 78% for repertoire segments compared to 22% for nonrepertoire segments.

It appears that a preliminary model of the child's early phonology is possible; some of the details and additional support will be introduced later in the chapter. According to the model, the infant—as he begins to speak—brings forth a set of sounds which are somewhat like those he is attempting to replicate. He will, in general, project the segments at his disposal onto the lexical terrain, as he perceives it, such that sounds fall both where they should and, overextensively, where they should not. According to this logic, which I will elaborate on later, the child does not substitute some sounds for other sounds. Rather, he projects

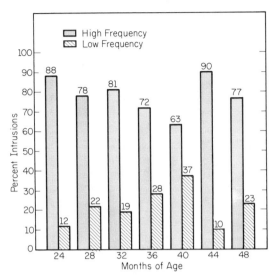

Figure 2.3. *Mean percentage of segmental substitutions by children of various ages in which the intruding consonant was in the infant babbling repertoire (high frequency) or outside the babbling repertoire (low frequency) (figure taken from Locke, 1980b).*

what he has into contexts where it seems to fit, and in some cases the fit—to the listener—is imperfect.

Phonological Development Cross-Linguistically

In the first chapter, I presented evidence that infant babbling is patterned at the segmental level, and showed that this regularity was similarly evident in the speech of children. As there appears to be little variation in the babbling of babies reared in different linguistic communities, one might suppose that in the face of functional links between babbling and early speech there also would be similar developmental patterns cross-linguistically. We would expect the acquisition data for English to look fairly similar to those of French, German, and Russian children.

Before we commence our cross-linguistic study of phonological development it is necessary to decide on the appropriate unit of linguistic analysis. One might think it best to select the phonetic segment, for it provided the basis for our earlier analysis of infant babbling. But with few exceptions, the segment will not do here, and for a number of disparate reasons. First, there is evidence that two or more languages may share *no* acoustically identical segments (cf. Ladefoged, 1980). Consequently, observing that French and English children do different things for /p/ may mean little more than that the French /p/ is not the same as the English one; the children might otherwise be doing much the same thing. In fact, one might regard children's differential treatment of two nominally identical segments as prima facie evidence that the segments are physically different—even if the adult perceptual system indicates otherwise—and in need of instrumental analysis. As we will see in Chapter 5, children's behavior, perhaps because we study it so attentively, sometimes tells us things about adult speech that had previously escaped our notice. Second, we would expect less than perfect agreement at the segmental level as we look across language groups, for the reason that the phonological systems will be different, even if the segments are not. The phonetic environments in which the sound occurs, the number of words in which the sound contrastively functions, its perceptual distance from other segments in the system, and a variety of other factors can affect the developmental fate of any particular phonetic unit.

Third, what plagued Leopold in 1947 in his review of the literature continues unfortunately to disturb cross-linguistic analyses today. I am referring to the nonuniform application of the International Phonetic Alphabet and the use of a variety of contrived and unexplained symbols and diacritics. Lacking a scientific language to describe phonetic behavior unambiguously, many of the published accounts have been tantalizing but difficult to reliably interpret.

There is a fourth factor that can defeat effective comparisons between two languages: I gathered several years ago (Locke & Ohala, 1980) and will report in Chapter 3 data showing that children's most commonly misproduced sounds are, in general, the most infrequent in adult languages. It is unfortunately the case that the sounds and sound patterns we would most like to compare we cannot, at least with a satisfying degree of rigor.

It follows from what I have said that to compare children's sound change patterns across a variety of languages, if using data reported in the existing literature, one needs to deal with a broader unit of analysis than the segment. Consequently, although I will examine specific sounds on occasion, more frequently I will deal in phonetic features.

Cross-Linguistic Developmental Patterns

I am clearly not the first to wonder about the kinds of phonological difficulties experienced by the children of the world, or the strategies they use to bail themselves out of their difficulties at the phonological level of language. In 1888, Edmund Noble wrote in his "Child Speech, and the Law of Mispronunciation" that

> studies of child-speech in such languages as English, French, German, Russian, Italian, Danish, Swedish, Magyar, Calmuck, New Greek, and Finnish, have

seemed to afford abundant justification [for the conclusion that there are] in the more prominent mistakes of child pronunciation, *tendencies to error in certain common directions* such as clearly implied some law as their inciting cause [p. 44; emphasis mine].

In 1916, Kroeber observed that a 2-year-old boy learning Zuni had difficulty with sounds which, "so far as they occur, . . . are precisely the sounds with which English speaking children have difficulty [p. 532]." Jespersen commented in 1922 that "children in all countries tend to substitute (t) for (k) [p. 107 in the 1964 edition]." Perhaps the strongest and most influential statement was made initially in 1941 by Roman Jakobson:

> Whether it is a question of French or Scandinavian children, of English or Slavic, of Indian or German, or of Estonian, Dutch or Japanese children, every description based on careful observation repeatedly confirms the striking fact that the relative chronological order of phonological acquisitions remains everywhere and at all times the same. . . . At a particular stage of development . . . the Swedish child says *tata* for "kaka", the German child *topf* for "kopf", the English child *tut* for "cut", and the Japanese child also changes *k* to *t* . . . in French children *ta* "carte", *tata* "kaka" . . . in Estonian children *taal* "kukal" [1941/1968, pp. 46–47].

Let us, then, examine some of the attested patterns that have occurred in the development of children learning a variety of languages. All the feature changes also occur in English, and have been thoroughly documented. I will identify a few segmental errors that occur in several languages but not, for some reason, in English.

Stopping

One has little difficulty locating examples of this pattern, which usually involves the production of a fricative (less commonly, the less common affricates) with a stoplike quality. Perhaps the most notorious of such "stoppings" is the expression of /s/ as [t] or [ts].

At 27 months, Piyush, the son of Srivastava (1974), produced [tuntar] for the standard Hindi /sundar/ 'beautiful'.

At 33 months, Maria, the subject of Drachman and Malikouti-Drachman (n.d.), expressed Greek /xalí/ 'carpet' as [kalí], and rendered /saɣapó/ 'I love you' as [tadapó].

In his Slovenian-learning grandchildren Maja and Tomaž, Kolarič (1959) observed that although /f/ was produced with a fricative quality, like [ɸ] or [h], the voiced labiodental /v/ was replaced by [b]. The affricate /ç/ also was expressed as a stop, [k].

Pačesova (1968) described the phonological development in Czech of a boy who expressed /ž/ as a palatal stop, [ɟ], and changed the voiceless cognate /č/

into alveolar [t] or palatal [t̡]. In a later work, Pačesova (1976) indicated that Czech children, like the American English children described by Ingram (1978), go through stages in the acquisition of the affricates. These stages, according to Pačesova, reveal an "ignorance of the feature of semiocclusivity and the substitution of the affricates by means of the stops in the first stage, by means of the fricatives in the more mature stages, thus illustrating the developmental order stop-articulation–fricative-articulation–semi-occlusive articulation [p. 194]."

In Eblen's (1982) data on Mexican Spanish children, there are several cases in which /s/ is expressed as [t], including [topa] for /sopa/ 'soup' and [tiya] for /siya/ 'chair'. Interestingly, Eblen observed that Spanish /s/ often is changed to [tʃ], which Ferguson (1964) observed in the baby talk of Spanish adults, but which has also been observed in the Pilaga Indian children of Argentina (Henry & Henry, 1940). For some reason, this sound change is extremely rare in English children. Olmsted (1971) observed just one occurrence of /s/ → [tʃ] among his 197 errors (his Table 13), and Snow (1963) tabulated only one [tʃ] in 146 substitutions for /s/. I note, however, that the 16 language-disordered children seen by Burton (1980) commonly replaced /s/ with [tʃ]. This seems logical, for /s/ frequently is expressed as [ʃ] and as [ts], both in Snow and in Burton, so one would think the palatal placement of [ʃ] and the affrication of [ts] would occasionally converge to yield a [tʃ].

A [ts] for /s/ change was observed by Lin (1971) in a 22-month-old Taiwanese girl. Chao (1951) reported that at 28 months his granddaughter Canta expressed Mandarin /tʃ/ and /ts/ as [t] and said [d] for /dʒ/ and /dz/.

Vanvik (1971) reported that his daughter Hilde said [hu:t] for Norwegian /hu:s/ 'house', [litə] for /lisə/ 'lace', and [dantə] for /dansə/ 'dance'. Thanks to Deville (1890, 1891), whose daughter's data are reproduced in Lewis (1936), we know something of the segmental errors occurring in his French-learning child. Though the environments are not specified, it is clear that the girl had a number of stoppings, including [t] for both /s/ and /ʃ/, [p] for /f/, and [b] for /v/. From 1:7 to 1:10, Vihman's (1971) Estonian subject, Linda, replaced /s/ by several voiceless stops. The most common was [t] followed, less frequently, by [k] and [p].

Fronting

We referred earlier to Jespersen's (1922/1964) observation that [t] is substituted for /k/ by "children in all countries." The examples supplied by Jakobson (1941/1968) supported Jespersen's simple statement, but dealt only with the fronting of /k/. In fact, the basis for the pattern is somewhat broader, and applies generally to velars and palatals. In its most general form, alveolars replace postalveolars.

Möhring (1938) observed that among the more common errors in his study of several thousand German school children were [d] for /g/ and [t] for /k/. The data of Hilde Stern from 1:7 to 1:9 (in Lewis, 1936) show no frontings of the stops, but do contain several examples of fricative fronting, including [s] for /ʃ/ in *ritsche* and [s] for /x/ in *horch*.

Srivastava (1974) lists among the sound changes of her son, at 23 months, a rendering of Hindi /pʰugga:/ 'balloon' as [budda:]; at 22 months he said [tui] for /cu:ri:/ 'bangle'.

Pačesova (1968) supplies several examples of fronting in Czech, one involving the voiceless stops (where [t] replaced /k/) and the other the voiceless fricatives (where [s] replaced /x/). Pačesova (1976) summarized the fronting tendency as "the substitution of the velars by means of alveolars, especially in the sphere of stop phonemes [p. 194]."

Omar (1973) noted that /k/ was somewhat late in children's development of Egyptian Arabic, probably because [t] replaced it. Two of her subjects said [taelb] for /kaelb/ 'dog' at 3:6.

Drachman and Malikouti-Drachman (n.d.) observed a 33-month-old girl to render Greek /k/ as [t], as in /kanapé/ → [tanaté], /ékino/ → [etíno], and /kumbíá/ → [tūdá].

There are many other examples of fronting, including [n] for /ŋ/ in Mandarin (Chao, 1951), [t] for /k/ in Slovenian (Kolarič, 1959), French (Lewis, 1936), and Estonian (Vihman, 1976), and [s] for /ʃ/ in French (Lewis, 1936). There does seem to be more fronting among the stops, especially the voiceless /k/, but this may reflect nothing more than the greater number of velar stops than velar fricatives in the languages of the world, and the greater number of /k/s than /g/s.

Initial Stop Voicing

The voicing (and deaspiration) of initial voiceless stops is exceedingly common, and has been observed perceptually as well as instrumentally. Initial voicing appears to be one of the first sound changes to dissipate in children's phonological development, an occurrence witnessed at close range by several investigators whose research will be considered in what follows.

Vanvik's (1971) daughter said [dætʰ] prelinguistically at 6 months of age. She was observed to say it again at 13 months upon receiving something; /tak/ is Norwegian for 'thank you'. At 15 months Hilde said (datʰ) in a context appropriate to 'thank you', and reached the form [dakʰ] by 20 months. Though the vowel and final consonant had finally come into conformity with the adult form, Hilde continued to voice the initial stop, and to Vanvik this was predictable from his analysis of her babbling. Hilde also said [dɔ:] for /tɔ:/ 'toe' at 19 months.

Celce-Murcia's (1978) daughter Caroline, at 2:4, was bilingual in French and English, and produced the French /papa/ and /pæ̃/ 'bread' as [baba] and [bæ̃]. Lin's (1971) 22-month-old girl was quite consistent in deaspirating word-initial stops, rendering /pʰ/, /tʰ/, /kʰ/, and /tsʰ/ as [p], [t], [k], and [ts]. In Lin's symbolization, Taiwanese /pʰah/ 'beat' was produced as [pah], /tʰo/ 'play' was expressed as [to] and /kʰi/ 'go' as [ki].

Some very interesting data on the acquisition of the word-initial aspiration contrast in Cantonese were reported by Clumeck, Barton, Macken, and Huntington (1981). They studied one little boy, Pak-Wa, from 1:7 to 2:6, determining voice onset times with spectrography and oscillography. At about 26–27 months, Pak-Wa first began to differentiate between aspirated and unaspirated /t/s, a contrast which by 30 months had spread to the bilabial and velar points of articulation. This paralleled the developmental sequence observed among English children for initial voiced and voiceless stops (Macken & Barton, 1980b).

Macken and Barton (1980a) found that Mexican Spanish children gradually acquire the voicing contrast between word-initial stops. Instrumental analyses showed that VOT distinctions were first evident at about 20–24 months, but only for the bilabials. Velar and dental voicing contrasts appeared soon after, though the childrens' VOT values were neither consistent nor adult-like even at 46 months.

Final Obstruent Devoicing

The devoicing of word-final obstruents is exceedingly common, and has been well documented in English (Naeser, 1970; Smith, 1979). Many languages have no word-final voiced obstruents, so this sound change cannot occur in those languages. Ironically, this may be the only reason that final devoicing does not occur in all languages. The tendency is so universal and strong that the candidates for it have been removed historically or never were created in the first place.

From Ohala's (1983) analysis of data in the Stanford Archive it is evident that many of the languages in the world have no voiced obstruents whatsoever, but none of the world's languages lacks voiceless obstruents. Ohala found that fricatives were more than twice as likely to be voiceless as were stops. There is agreement here with the child data: My analyses of the substitutions in Snow (1963) indicate that devoicings of fricatives—irrespective of word position— were 26 times more frequent than stop devoicings.

In Pačesova's (1968) account of a Czech child, we see in the data several instances of stop and fricative devoicing in word-final position. Standard /lod/ was expressed variously as [oť] [joť], and [loť] which—of relevance to generative theory—alternated with [lodička]. The child also said /had/ as [hat] and /garaz/ as [gala:s] (note the long vowel). In Kolarič (1959), the children reportedly produced /gospod/ as [pôt], /gozd/ as [gòst], /jaz/ as [jàs], and /riž/ as [riš]. Celce-Murcia (1978) observed her daughter at 2:4 to say *rouge* as [uš].

When English-learning children devoice a final obstruent, they typically produce a long preceding vowel as their language requires (Naeser, 1970). This has been interpreted by many phonologists to mean that the child has the appropriate internal representation, and that even in the absence of voicing (or a final segment at all), he faithfully generates by rule a vowel of the right length. I will examine this more carefully in Chapter 6.

Gliding

The gliding change is one in which sounds resembling /j/ and /w/—traditionally classified as glides—replace other sounds, frequently /l/ and /r/. In English one sees [j] replacing /l/ in *leaf* and *lamp*, [w] replacing /r/ in *rake* and *red* (Snow, 1963). The /l/ → [j] change is widely attested in the developmental literature, and has been recorded for Mandarin (Chao, 1951), Estonian (Vihman, 1971), French (Lewis, 1936), Taiwanese (Lin, 1971), and Czech (Pačesova, 1968).

The replacement of /r/ by a glide is comparatively inconspicuous cross-linguistically, but the reason has less to do with the generality of gliding than with the phonetic characteristics of non-English /r/s. Most of the languages of the world have an /r/ (Ruhlen, 1976), but fewer than 10%, by my calculations, have a sound corresponding closely to the American English /r/. In place of this retroflex approximant (/ɹ/), there are flaps and trills, dentals, alveolars, and uvulars. Among many /r/s one finds little that is glidelike, and it perhaps should come as no surprise that children substitute [d]s for the apicoalveolar trills and [ʒ] for the vibrant /ř/ (Pačesova, 1968).

The glides replace sounds other than those in the lateral and flap–trill–approximant family. The [w], at least, is commonly heard in place of standard /v/. This has been documented for Estonian (Vihman, 1971), Hindi (Srivastava, 1974), and German[1] (Leopold, 1947) as well as for English (Smith, 1973).

Consonant Harmony (Assimilation)

Though Smith (1973) suggested that consonant harmony was a universal characteristic of child phonology, from which the child needs to escape before he can progress very far, Marilyn Vihman's (1978) analysis indicates this may not be the case. Vihman compared the data from 13 children learning Chinese, English, Estonian, Czech, Slovenian, and Spanish. For the purposes of her study, she defined consonant harmony as "any child variant [that] shows agreement in place and/or manner of articulation between two non-contiguous consonants which differ in that respect in the adult model [p. 288]."

[1] According to Wolfgang Dressler, the German /v/ is more like an approximant, having less frication than the English /v/.

Vihman observed that harmony rates ranged from 1 to 32%, with much of the variation across subjects due to differences in the structure of the languages. That is, the opportunities for assimilative change are greater for some languages than for others. The majority of changes involved shifts of articulatory place. With liquids excluded from the data, place changes accounted for some 45% of the cases, with manner involved in about 20% and both place and manner involved in 35%.

In the typical case of consonant harmony, the source segment is in the final position of the adult model and the recipient is in the initial position. Vihman's data suggest that in about two-thirds of the cases the assimilation is "regressive." Of the regressive changes involving articulatory place, it would appear from Vihman's extended analysis of the Estonian child's data that harmony is particularly common when a velar is followed by a dental. For example, standard Estonian /kaesi/ 'hand' was produced by the child, at 1:9, as [tæsi]. In Chapter 4 I will point to the apparent unnaturalness of such velar–vowel–dental sequences in human language, which may account for the frequency of dental assimilation when the dental is word final.

Though Vihman observed, as had Lewis (1936), that in most cases of assimilation a developmentally late sound is influenced by an earlier one, she also observed that in many cases *both* sounds had already been mastered. This is why she tended to doubt Smith's (1973) supposition that harmony stands in the way of developmental progress. Rather, she viewed assimilation as an operation that, among other things, allowed the child to temporarily reduce the complexity of words so he could concentrate on those aspects that most urgently required his attention.

Cluster Reduction

Consonant clusters typically are reduced through the omission of one of the consonants (e.g., [mouk] for *smoke*), through their merger in a so-called conflation (e.g., [fid] for *speed*), or through vowel epenthesis (e.g., [nɛkəst] for *next*). This particular change, which results in a syllable restructuring, occurs in every language and undoubtedly is experienced by every child. I will identify the more common types of cluster reduction that occur in English-learning children and compare their patterns to those of children learning other languages, especially those with additional clusters not found in English. In doing so, I will concentrate mainly on two-member word-initial clusters.

Stop, Nasal, or Fricative + Liquid or Glide

English has five of the six possible combinations of stop, nasal, or fricative + liquid or glide, lacking only the combination of nasal + liquid. In English, as well as French and German (Lewis, 1936), Norwegian (Vanvik, 1971), Slovenian (Kolarič, 1959), and Czech (Pačesova, 1968), the changes I have examined all show the omission of the liquid or glide and the retention of the stop, nasal, or fricative.

STOP + LIQUID/GLIDE

In English, the six stops occur before /r/ and four of them precede /l/; except for /kj/ (as in *cute*) and /kw/ (as in *quick*), the stops are rare or nonexistent before the glides. Every reduction of these clusters by K, the American child described by Lewis (1936), involved the loss of the liquid or glide. This pattern is completely confirmed in other languages, where it applies also to the relevant non-English clusters. For example, in French, Deville's daughter omitted the /j/ in *pied* (/pje/) and *Dieu* (/djø/) and deleted the /w/ in *bois* (/bwa/). In Czech, Pačesova's subject reduced the non-English clusters /dl/ and /tl/ to [d] in *dlouhý* and [t] in *tlačit*.

FRICATIVE + LIQUID/GLIDE

Among British children (Anthony *et al.* 1971) *sleeping, three,* and *flower* have a high mortality rate; in each case the fricative is more commonly retained, the liquid lost. In French, Deville's daughter expressed *vrai* as [ve] and she omitted the /w/ in *voila* and *fois*. In German, Hilde Stern omitted the /r/ in /ʃr/ clusters but for some reason reduced *schlaft* to *laft*. Slovenian and Czech have a nice variety of fricative + liquid clusters that do not occur in English. In the Slovenian children, *vlasta, vrate, žlička,* and *hruška* all were observed to lose their liquid in child speech. In Czech, *vlásky, vrásky, hrob,* and *hlava* have been represented by children with their fricative portion only.

NASAL + LIQUID/GLIDE

At 1:11 the English-learning child K expressed *music* as [muŋi]. Nasal + liquid clusters have been expressed by Slovenian children without their liquid segment, for example, *mleko* → [méko].

Stop, Nasal, or Fricative + Stop, Nasal, or Fricative

FRICATIVE + STOP/NASAL

English-learning children readily reduce fricative + stop clusters to their aspirated or voiced/unaspirated stop portion. In Anthony *et al.* (1971), for example, the most frequent reduction of *spoon* was [pʰun] followed closely by [pun]. For *spot, stew,* and *ski*, I have found that 4-year-old cluster reducers are more likely to say [bat], [du], and [gi]—perceptibly—than they are to say the voiceless cognates. Moskowitz (1970) describes a 2-year-old girl, Erica, who reduced *study, store,* and *stack* to [déˌdi], [déˌɹ], and [t⁼akʰ]. Such cases are intriguing.

Some phonologists believe they suggest that children deaspirate by rule, implying their knowledge of the omitted fricative. A similar phenomenon is evident in the Anthony *et al.* study: Children's most frequent reduction of the /sm/ in *smoke* was [m̥mouk].

Eblen (1982) systematically elicited production of /sk/ and /st/ clusters in seven Mexican Spanish children from 3:4 to 3:11. In all 21 cases of reduction that I counted, the /s/ was the deleted element, hence standard /mos'ka/ 'fly' was ['moka] and /pɛskaðo/ 'fish' was [pe'kada] in several of the children.

A variety of non-English fricative + stop/nasal clusters exist. In Hilde Stern's German, /ʃp/ and /ʃt/ reduced to [p] and [t] in *Spiegel* and *Stall*. Hilde also stripped *schmutzig* and *Schnee* of their /ʃ/. In Slovenian, Tomaž expressed *škorenjček* as *kónćke* at 1:10. The Czech child at 1:8 expressed *školka* as *kolka;* at 1:5 he omitted the /s/ in *spivat*.

STOP + NASAL/FRICATIVE

Neither of these clusters occurs in English. The stop + nasal cluster occurs in German, Norwegian, Slovenian, and Czech. In all four languages, children have been heard to reduce the word-initial /kn/ cluster to [n], and in the Slovenian child at 1:6 *tma* was expressed as *ma*. In Hilde Stern's German [s] represented the initial /tsv/ cluster in *zwei* and the /ts/ in *Zähne*.

FRICATIVE + FRICATIVE AND NASAL + STOP

Except for the rare /sf/, English also lacks these clusters in word-initial position. There are child data on German, Slovenian, and Czech fricative + fricative clusters. Hilde Stern said [f] for the /ʃv/ in *Schwanz*. At 1:11 the Slovenian-learning Tomaž reduced the /sv/ in *svečka* to [v]. At 1:9 he produced *vzeti* as [zéla]. The Czech child at 1:7 said [šeski] for *švestka;* at 1:8 he produced *světlo* with an [f] but no /s/. Egyptian Arabic has nasal + stop clusters. In Omar's (1973) study a little girl at 12 months produced the baby talk word for 'water', *mbū*, as [pū].

Other Word-Initial Clusters

Other clusters that do not occur word initially in English are the stop + stop units. In Slovenian, Maja expressed *kdo* as [ko] and *ptiček* as [tícɔk]. The Czech child in Pačesova's study, on the other hand, reduced *kdo* to [do], *kde* to [de], and *kdepak* to [depak]. The general trend seems to be to reduce stop + stop clusters to the second stop.

In Slovenian, Tomaž at 1:9 reduced *mleko* to [meko]. I have found little additional data on nasal + liquid clusters. A nasal + nasal cluster in Czech, *mňau*, was expressed by Pačesova's subject as [ňau]. The same child reduced a

Czech liquid + fricative cluster, /lž/, to [ž] in the word *lžice* (/l/ is nonsyllabic in this word).

The patterning evident in children's two-member, word-initial cluster reductions, with few exceptions, may be summarized as follows. If there is a glide or a liquid present, it typically will be the *second* member, and children will omit it. In most other cases, the *first* member will be a stop or a fricative, and children will omit the stop or fricative. If both members are stops, fricatives, or nasals, the first stop, fricative, or nasal will be omitted. In general, this analysis agrees with the findings of Vihman (1979, Table 5).

Final Omission

Like cluster reduction (and reduplication), final omission affects the shape of syllables and words, though characteristics of the preceding vowel may continue to "mark" the original segment. Like final devoicing, perhaps the only reason this pattern does not occur in all languages is that many (e.g., Japanese, Italian) have no final consonants. In such languages, even the final obstruents in loan words tend to be rendered nonfinal by the addition of a vowel.

Lewis's (1936) data on the English-learning child K shows he frequently omitted final obstruents:

> *bath*   [ba]
> *garden* [ga]
> *plane* [pei]
> *sleep* [si:]
> *toast* [tou]

In French (Lewis, 1936), Deville's daughter expressed *place* as [fa]. In Slovenian (Kolarič, 1959), *bombon* was economized by the 17-month-old Tomaž to, simply, [bó]. At 1:7, the Czech subject of Pačesova's (1968) study produced *plavat* as [pave].

According to data reported in Taymans (1976, p. 81), 89% of the consonant segments produced by her English-learning subject between 16 and 18 months were in nonfinal position. In the 50-word vocabulary of the Czech child, 92.8% of the items had open syllables, only 7.2% had closed syllables. My analysis of Vihman's (1971) raw data from Linda, an Estonian-learning subject at 1:7–1:10, shows that 32% of all word-final errors involved segment omissions.

Cross-Linguistic Sequences of Phonological Mastery

We have seen that children learning different languages display many similar sound patterns. It follows from this that the sequence in which children master phonetic segments and features also would be similar across language groups. As the developmental sequence data are exceptionally scarce cross-linguistically, I will work from such empirical fragments as I have been able to locate and identify with the hope that the resulting reconstructions will be generally useful.

English

We may anticipate the non-English data with an examination of some cross-sectional findings on American English 2–4-year-olds. Figure 2.4 shows the Prather *et al.* (1975) data on which some of our earlier analyses were performed. In the figure, it is interesting to note that in some cases the sounds tested via elicitation were already "present"—that is, produced correctly by at least 70% of the subjects—at 24 months. These "early sounds" include /n, m, p, h, f, w, ŋ/. Six of these seven sounds are in the repertoire. The figure also shows that some sounds still were not said correctly by 90% of the children at 48 months. These "late" sounds include /l, r, ʃ, tʃ, ʤ, v, z, ʒ, ð, θ). None of these 10 sounds is in the basic sound repertoire.

German

Figure 2.5 shows some data gathered by Möhring (1938) from 2655 German schoolchildren, also through an elicitation technique. The figure gives an indication of the probability of error, though there is no ordinate. But from a table in Möhring it can be ascertained, for example, that /m/ was missed by 2% of the children, /g/ by 28%, and /z/ by 56%. The broad sequence of development looks a great deal like English, with nasals and stops occupying the most privileged status—being accurate at the outset—with liquids and glides a bit less accurate, and fricatives, affricates, and a variety of clusters further down the list.

For those sounds that could reasonably be called English equivalents (though obviously not phonetically identical), I calculated the mean percentage correct for repertoire sounds (/b, d, g, h, j, k, m, n, p, t/) and nonrepertoire sounds (/f, l, ŋ, z, s, v, ʃ/). The repertoire sounds produced were 89.3% correct, on the average, and the nonrepertoire sounds were 71.9% correct.

Japanese

Figure 2.6 shows a sampling of Japanese data from four children studied in spontaneous play situations by Nishimura (1980). In all four cases it can be seen

---

Figure 2.4. The developmental course of English phonology (data from Prather et al., 1975; figure from Shriberg, 1980). Average age estimates (50%) and upper age limits (90%) of customary consonant production are depicted. When the percentage correct at 24 months exceeded 70%, the bar extends to "less than 24." When the 90% level was not reached by 48 months, the bar extends to "greater than 48."

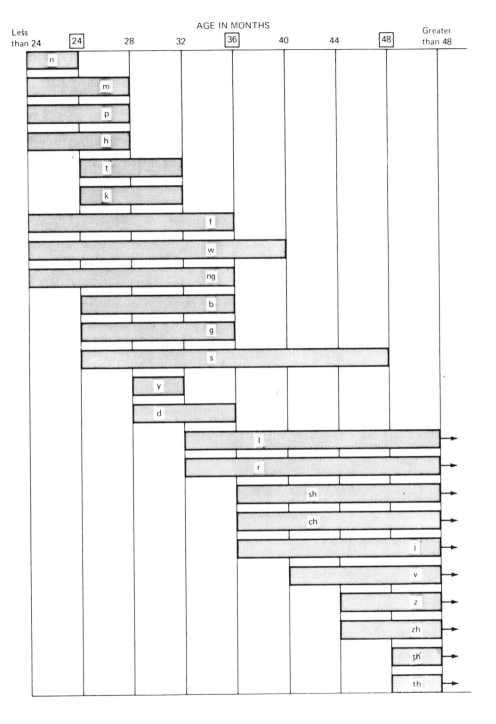

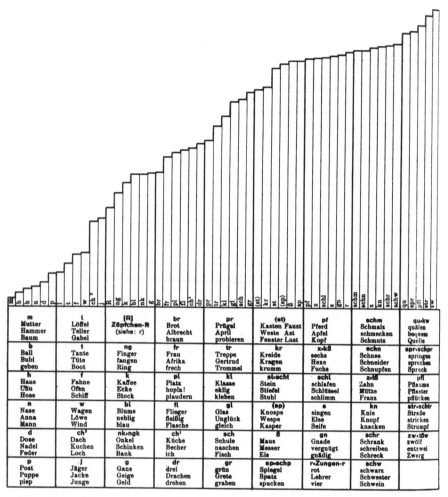

Figure 2.5. German children's error pattern in a large-scale articulation survey (from Möhring, 1938).

that /s/ was not produced correctly in words by age 6, whereas /p/ was said correctly at about 3 years. I will leave it to the reader to peruse these graphs, but in general it appears that stops and nasals were early, whereas fricatives and affricates were relatively late, especially /s/ and /dz/.

There are more extensive—though cross-sectional—data on Japanese. Yasuda (1970) observed 100 children ranging in age from 3:0 to 3:11 years. Their speech articulation was assessed in word-initial and medial positions with a picture-naming task. Table 2.2 shows the percentage of consistently correct production, with English equivalents or near equivalents separately designated. In general, stops, nasals, and glides were produced accurately, with /s/, /r/, and the apical affricates produced poorly. The palatal affricates were said with a surprisingly high level of accuracy.

The developmental sequence for Japanese is more lucidly depicted in Table 2.3, which comes from a table in Yasuda that summarizes two other studies, one of them his own. Again, the stops, nasals, glides, and palatal affricates were developmentally early, followed by some of the fricatives (including /s/), alveolar affricates, and /r/.

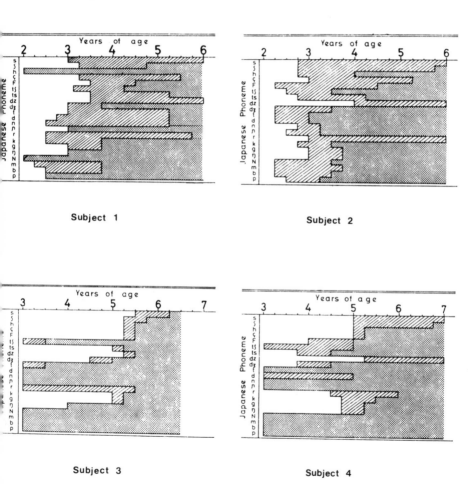

Figure 2.6. Developmental profiles on four Japanese children (from Nishimura, 1980). The shaded areas indicate correct production in words, the diagonally lined areas indicate correct production in syllables or in isolation but not in words, and unfilled areas indicate incorrect production.

Table 2.2
Articulation Scores of 100 3-Year-Old Japanese Children on a Picture-Naming Test

Yasuda's symbols	Closest English equivalent[a]	Mean percentage correct
m	m	100.0
n	n	100.0
t	t	100.0
ɲ	ŋ	100.0
N		100.0
p	p	99.2
j	j	99.2
bj		98.7
Pj		98.6
ʤ	ʤ	95.9
tʃ	tʃ	95.1
mj		94.0
g (n)	g	93.4
k	k	92.7
b	b	92.3
w	w	90.6
kj		88.9
gj (nj)		86.2
d	d	83.5
çj		81.3
h	h	75.7
rj		66.1
F		65.9
ç		63.2
ʃ	ʃ	60.3
ts		33.5
r		27.7
S	s	24.5
dz	z	14.7

Source: From Yasuda (1970).
[a]My English equivalents are based on an inspection of the Japanese consonant inventory and allophonic details described in the Stanford Phonology Archive, and a bit of inference as to what Yasuda had in mind.

Russian

Timm (1977) followed a Russian child from 1:7 to 2:9, transcribing nearly 12,000 spontaneous and elicited speech segments. Table 2.4 shows the percentage of incorrect productions for each of the Russian phonemes. Of the 16 sounds that also appear in English, half were repertoire and half were nonrepertoire sounds. The repertoire items had a mean inaccuracy of 23%, the nonrepertoire sounds had a 63% error rate.

Italian

A cross-sectional study of Italian was reported by Battacchi, Facchini, Manfredi, and Rubatta (1964). They used pictures to elicit word-initial and medial

Table 2.3
Developmental Schedule for Japanese Phonology According to Two Studies Cited in Yasuda (1970)

	Umebayashi and Takagi (1965); cited in Yasuda (1970)		Yasuda (1966)	
Age[a]	Initial or medial word position	Both word positions	Initial or medial word position[b]	Both word positions
Before 3:5	m p b tʃ ʤ h F ç n ɲ t d k g kj gj ʃ w N pj bj çj mj j	m p b w tʃ ʤ F ç n t d k g kj ɲ N bj pj çj mj j	m p b w j n N ɲ t d k g tʃ ʤ (mj) (bj) (Pj) h F ç (çj) kj gj	m p b w j n N ɲ t d k g tʃ ʤ kj gj
3:6–3:11	r rj	gj	ʃ r (rj)	h F
4:0–4:5		ʃ rj h	After 4:0, s ts dz	s ts dz ʃ r ç
4:6–4:11	dz ts			
5:0–5:5	s	dz ts		
5:6–5:11		s r		

[a]Age given is earliest age at which 75% of all subjects correctly articulated the sounds listed.
[b]Parentheses indicate that only the word-initial position was tested.

Table 2.4
The Error Scores of a Child, from 1:7 to 2:9, Learning Russian as His Native Language

Russian sound[a]	Error score	Russian sound	Error score
r	1.000	lʸ	.631
rʸ	1.000	v*	.602
xʸ	1.000	l*	.551
r	.994	bʸ	.541
x	.934	ʃ*	.534
sʸ	.920	k*	.486
f*	.875	g*	.410
mʸ	.837	gʸ	.389
tʃ*	.837	kʸ	.363
tʸ	.831	d*	.262
ʒ	.785	m*	.245
pʸ	.783	z*	.178
vʸ	.773	n*	.149
nʸ	.748	t*	.111
zʸ	.708	b*	.104
s*	.656	p*	.072
dʸ	.631		

Source: From Timm, L. A. (1977). A child's acquisition of Russian phonology. *Journal of Child Language 4*, 329–339, Table 5, with permission from Cambridge University Press.
[a]Asterisks indicate sounds having an English equivalent, as determined from an inspection of the Russian segment inventory and allophonic details presented in the Stanford Phonology Archive.

Table 2.5
Number and Percentage of 20 Italian 3- and 4-Year-Olds Producing Consonants Correctly on a Picture Articulation Test

Sound[a]	Position Word initial	Position Word medial[b]	Overall percentage
t	20	20	100.0
n	20	20	100.0
g	20	19	97.5
d	20	19	97.5
tʃ	19	19	95.0
b	19	—	95.0
l	19	—.	95.0
v	18	20	95.0
m	20	17	92.5
k	20	16	90.0
p	20	16	90.0
s	18	—	90.0
f	18	0	90.0
ʃ	16	—	90.0
dʒ	17	—	85.0
r	19	15	85.0
z	15	—	75.0

Source: From data reported in Battacchi, Facchini, Manfredi and Rubatta (1964).
[a] I have shown here mainly the sounds having reasonably close English equivalents.
[b] A dash indicates that a sound does not occur in or was not tested in medial position.

consonant production by children from 3:1 to 4:8. They reported the number who produced each sound correctly. Table 2.5 shows my analysis of their original data (which were analyzed differently in their Table 9), with consonants listed in descending order of overall accuracy. Though the accuracy variations were not large, they do indicate a hierarchy that favors anterior stops and nasals and disfavors fricatives. The liquids and affricates are not clearly patterned.

Arabic

Omar (1973) studied 37 children in the process of acquiring Egyptian Arabic. Her cross-sectional observations produced a developmental "schedule" for Arabic phonology, which appears here in Table 2.6. The "early" sounds in Arabic are anterior stops, the nasals, and the glides. The fricatives and more posterior sounds do not appear until later. As in Italian, the flap /r/ is one of the last to be mastered. Omar commented that "in Arabic, the order of acquisition of phonemes is about the same as in English. . . . The similarities in order of acquisition of Arabic phonemes far outweigh any differences with acquisition order in English, considering the dissimilarities of the two phonemic systems involved [pp. 58, 60]."

Table 2.6
Developmental "Schedule" for the Phonology of Egyptian Arabic

Age	Sounds with close English equivalents	Sounds without close English equivalents[a]
1:5	b m w j h	ʔ
2:0	t d s z n k	
2:3	f l g	
2:6		x
3:0		γ
3:6		ḥ
4:0	ǰ	ṣ z ḷ ṭ ḍ
4:6	š	
5:0		ʕ
6:6		ř
		q

Source: From data reported in Omar (1973).
[a]Sounds with a dot below them are the Arabic "emphatic" series, except for /ḥ/ which is a voiceless pharyngeal fricative. The voiced cognate to /ḥ/ is /ʕ/; /q/ is a voiceless uvular stop.

Slovenian

Kolarič (1959) observed that his Slovenian grandchildren acquired early the stops /b, d, g, p, t, k/, nasals /m, n/, and /l/. From his report it appears that the glide /j/, fricative /f/, and velar /ch/ were intermediate sounds. The most troublesome consonants for his grandchildren were the fricatives /s, š, z, ž/ and the affricates /tˢ, č/. The last sound to be acquired was /r/.

Swedish

Magnussen (1983) studied 32 Swedish children whose ages ranged from 3:9 to 6:6 years. Although the subjects had previously been diagnosed as language delayed, none had received treatment at the time the subjects' spontaneous speech was sampled. Table 2.7 shows the percentage of children whose consonants were phonemically correct. My analyses reveal that the highest accuracy was for nasals (77.1% correct), followed by stops (68.2%), glides (56.2%), and fricatives (51.3%), excluding /h/, with the lowest accuracy for the liquids (46.9%).

Norwegian

As mentioned earlier (p. 54), Vanvik (1971) observed that his daughter Hilde first acquired the stops /p, b, t, d, k, g/, nasals /m, n, ŋ/, fricatives /h, s, v/, and approximants /l, j/. It was not until some time later that the retroflexive /t, d, n, l/ the rolled /r/, and the fricatives /f, ʃ, ç/ developed, with /ç/ appearing latest.

Table 2.7
Percentage of 32 3–6-Year-Old Swedish Children Whose Consonants Were Phonemically Correct (from data reported in Table 10 in Magnusson, 1983)

Segment	Percentage	Segment	Percentage
m	93.8	d	59.4
p	90.6	ŋg	59.4
b	84.4	j	56.3
f	81.3	l	50.0
t	81.3	k	50.0
h	81.3	R	43.8
n	78.1	g	43.8
v	71.9	ç	25.0
s	68.8	ɧ[a]	9.4

[a]Classified by Magnusson as a voiceless dorsovelar fricative.

Czech

The emerging phonological system of Pačesova's (1968) Czech subject is shown in Table 2.8 as a function of vocabulary size at the time of analysis. This longitudinal study shows that stops and nasals comprise the 50-word system, with fricatives and affricates either unstable or nonexistent. It is interesting that /g/—a somewhat weak consonant in the languages of the world—is the only missing stop (even the palatal stops are present and stable). The main change at 100 words is the development of /g/ and the appearance, unstably, of /v/ and

Table 2.8
Status of the Consonants in a Czech Child's Developing Phonological System

	Stable	Unstable	Absent
50-word system			
Stops	p b t d t̆ d̆ k		g
Fricatives	j h	f s š x l ž	v z r ř
Affricates		c č	
Nasals	m n ň		
100-word system			
Stops	p b t d t̆ d̆ k g		
Fricatives	j	h v f s š x l z ž	r ř
Affricates		c č	
Nasals	m n ň		
500-word system			
Stops	p b t d t̆ d̆ k g		
Fricatives	j h x f s š l z v ž		r ř
Affricates	c č		
Nasals	m n ň		

Source: From data reported in Pačesova (1968).

/z/. At 500 words, the system is completely present and stable with the exception of the infamous /r/ and /ř/.

Error Prediction

It appears for developmental "schedules"—as it did for patterns of developmental "deviation"—that as we look across language groups and patterns of sound change we see commonalities. Just as there is a cross-linguistic tendency for children to express fricatives as stops, so is there a universal tendency for stops to be acquired prior to fricatives. And the same may be said for a number of other patterns, as we have seen. These tendencies are, I believe, the phonetic residue of a biologically driven system of vocal tract movements that become apparent as early as the later periods of premeaningful babbling. These sound patterns in the young child speaker suggest that the frequency of phonetic elements in babbling is linked to the availability of those same elements for lexical programming. If such is the case, it should be possible to *predict* the patterns of a particular child speaker from his articulatory patterns as a babbler.

Perhaps the "acid test" of a continuity hypothesis would be an investigation in which a fairly large number of infants are followed from late in their premeaningful babbling to the phonology of their first 50 or 100 words. Evidence favoring the continuity hypothesis would begin with the observation of separate patterns of consonantal preferences among many of the subjects, which continued observation would show were carried over—predictably—into correspondingly separate patterns of consonant substitution. As a separate but related component in the predictive formula, it would be helpful to know for individual subjects which segments were perceptually similar or indistinguishable.

As such data were unavailable, I undertook several years ago (Locke, 1980a) to see what the predictive possibilities might be using existing data on separate populations. Concerned about the still to-be-developed vocal physiology of the 1-year-old, I used Carr's (1953) data on 5-year-old deaf children as my basis for estimating phonetic preferences. Lacking appropriate data on children's speech perception, I turned to Wang and Bilger's (1973) adult confusion matrices for CV syllables of weak intensity. Having at the time no large sample of speech errors in the very young, I used the consonant substitutions of Snow's (1963) 7- and 8-year-olds as my "explicanda."

I then generated a set of "expected" substitutions based on the supposition that beginning talkers would *project* high-frequency-in-babbling segments upon perceptually similar low-frequency-in-babbling segments. For example, this model generated b/v on the basis that (*a*) [b] had a high frequency in babbling, (*b*) [v] had a low frequency in babbling, and (*c*) adult listeners replaced [v]—imperceptively—with [b] more often than with any other high-frequency-in-babbling segment. As Snow's subjects frequently expressed /v/ as [b], this prediction was successful. So, also, were f/θ, t/k, d/g, s/z, w/r, d/ð, f/v, and s/ʃ.

Not only did this initial attempt meet with general success, accurately predicting many of children's more "popular" substitutions, it also seemed to open up some potentially fertile new grounds of inquiry. For example, the model generated some errors that children do *not* make. In word-final position, the model produced m/ŋ. If children replace /ŋ/, the results of various studies suggest they will do so with /n/, not /m/. If the field of child phonology aspires to explain child phonologies, it seems one should be able to concretely rationalize such "nonerrors" along with the observed errors, showing why children *would not do* what they *do not do*.

Perceptual Similarities

At the time of my predictive study, there was little evidence on the perceptual similarity of various speech sounds to infants. Since then, however, an interesting study by Hillenbrand (1983) has shown that preverbal infants may be aware of consonantal feature categories such as those embodied in the distinction between the nasals and the voiced stops. In Hillenbrand's experiment, there were two groups of eight infants between 5½ months and 6½ months of age. The *phonetic* group was reinforced for head turns on trials involving a shift in the stimulus series from [m, n, ŋ] to [b, d, g] to [m, n, ŋ]. Performance on these change trials was compared to control trials in which there were no featural alternations. The *nonphonetic* group was reinforced for head turns to featurally arbitrary shifts in stimulus series, and could perform above chance only by remembering particular syllables that had been reinforced.

Hillenbrand's analysis showed that in both groups head turns during change trials occurred significantly more often than during control trials. However, the difference between change trials and control trials was significantly larger for the phonetic group than for the nonphonetic group. This finding indicates that the 6-month-olds in Hillenbrand's study were aware of the distinction between nasals and voiced stops. As other research has shown that even younger infants typically can discriminate place contrasts within the [b, d, g] set, that Hillenbrand's infants treated the voiced stops as equivalent implies they perceived a similarity between them.

We can return now to our prototypical infant who has been babbling many more [d]s than [g]s, and wishes for the first time—at *12* months—to say [go]. With Hillenbrand's data, it is a small step to assume the infant, perceiving the similarity among the voiced stops, will deploy his highly available [d] to represent /g/ as well as /d/.

A Working Model of Early Phonology

At this point, I believe something can be said of the child's phonological debut; how he breaks into a phonological system, and why his system initially is different from his parents'. It appears that as the child reaches that point in his social and cognitive life in which it is both desirable and possible to designate things with strings of sound, the child reaches—as it were—into his collection of readily available articulations. The available articulations, at this point, are the segments of his babbling repertoire. It is a foregone conclusion that these artic-ulations will be projected, much as they are in the case of "invented words" in which there is no identifiable adult model (cf. Leopold, 1949; Ferguson, 1978b). Since the infant at 12–18 months has a fairly well developed perceptual system (Eilers & Oller, 1981), in projecting his available articulations the infant will produce a number of "hits." Many of his [d]s and [b]s will land on lexically standard /d/s and /b/s. A number also will land elsewhere, on /ð/s and /v/s, because the child (*a*) may not notice that those sounds differ from [d] and [b]; (*b*) may not know that the difference matters, in some sense; or (*c*) could not make the necessary articulatory adjustments even if he did notice or respect the dif-ference between the adult form and his own.

Figure 2.7 schematizes the model I have just described, which I believe applies initially in the *cognitive stage* of phonological acquisition, as I will detail later (p. 97). In that stage, the child becomes aware that some phonetic strings make reference to something (e.g., [fɪʃ]). If the child wishes to refer to the same thing, or to toy with the same sound pattern, what will he shoot for? What is the child's underlying representation for *fish*? Indeed, even if we assume the child "has the adult surface form as his underlying representation," as many so glibly do, we should still be compelled to ask, as Peters (1974) did,

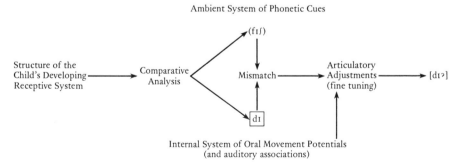

Figure 2.7. A model of low-level operations involved in the cognitive stage of phonological development.

what is this? The last instance he heard? An average of the last five instances he heard? (Whether slow, fast, kidding, angry, sloppy). What if the mother and the father have different "averages". . . . If a child is aiming at a constant target then why do we observe that her pronunciation of a specific word may improve right after an adult has pronounced the word—and then revert to her current level of accuracy [p. 97].

It may be a while before answers are available to such questions. Proof of the child's perceptual capabilities is insufficient, for it will not reveal the nature of the internalized phonetic shapes which guide his articulatory maneuvers, nor will it tell us what the child perceives when he hears his own sounds (cf. Locke, 1979b). But we must assume the child in Figure 2.7 has *some sort* of internal representation for [fɪʃ], and we assume he asks, in essence, "What do I have (and what can I do) that sounds like (fɪʃ)?," where parentheses imply the child's correct or approximate perception of [fɪʃ]. He finds [dɪ]. It may or may not be considered a match. If it does not match, he may or may not care; if he does care, he may or may not be able to do much about it. But in Figure 2.7 I have assumed that he notices the mismatch, cares, and can do a little "fine tuning." He comes out with an accommodation of sorts, [dɪ²].

What is systemic about this? What involves learning, compromise? Very little, possibly just the glottal stop in the child's [dɪ²], and perhaps not even that. Later in this chapter, I will suggest that no genuine accommodations to the adult system will be evident until the child reaches the *systemic stage* of phonological acquisition, which probably occurs at some time after the first 50 words are in use. In the meanwhile, the young speaker will take maximum advantage of his incumbent oral movements, deploying them as he can, enjoying the benefits of a linguistic system that is tailored to the constraints of a vocal tract very much like his.

This model contains physiological, perceptual, and cognitive components. The physiological components are responsible for the segmental repertoire and the child's limited ability to make articulatory adjustments. The perceptual components refer to the child's recognition of the appropriate contexts to project his repertorial segments, and to his failure to recognize limitations on the assignment of those segments. The cognitive component, which is linked to the perceptual one, refers to the child's systemic innocence, his ignorance of the complex system of cues and contrasts and their functional status in language and communication. Indeed, why should he fret over the indeterminate noises of adults when not even with his most practiced motor programs can he hope to truly replicate any of the forms, whether phonemic or allophonic?

The continuity model implicates several different mechanisms of phonological development, whose operations are distributed through several different stages of phonological acquisition.

Mechanisms of Phonological Development

As far as the *system* is concerned—the phonotactic rules, the composition of consonant clusters, the pattern of syllabic stress, and so forth—it seems reasonable to assume that the child has to "get" some knowledge of what his native language requires of its speakers. The child has to "discover" certain facts about English, for example, that vowel nasalization is not one of the "-emic" properties of the system, or that final /z/ can function morphologically. It seems probable that children must—through their own powers of perceptual analysis and deduction—"gain" the impression that /m/ is a unit in the sound system, that /ʒ/ is rare, or that /ŋ/ cannot occur initially.

Much of the efficiency of a sound system is determined by the nature of its internal structure, the rules of relationship among the constituent parts. One has little difficulty in accepting that the bulk of this internal structure is arbitrary, that is, need not on purely physiological or perceptual grounds be precisely as it is. And if it is arbitrary, is it less likely that one will master it quickly? Might one even need special strategies, specialized mechanisms?

But what of the constituent parts? Are they as arbitrary as the rules of their interrelationship? Are there languages with no /m/s and /d/s and /h/s; are there more that have no /tʃ/, no /v/, and no /θ/? If /m/ and /dʒ/ function contrastively, occur without restriction as to word position, and so forth, they are "emic" units of a certain, more or less equal linguistic status. But how do they get into the child's system? To what physiological, cognitive, and perceptual processes do we owe their appearance? Can the "environment" take equal credit for both?

I have developed the view, expressed elsewhere in brief (Locke, 1980b), that the child's increasing use of all and only the units of a phonological system is the result of no fewer than three mechanisms, which I have called *maintenance, learning,* and *loss.* I believe the operation of these mechanisms is supported by the Stoel-Gammon and Cooper (1981) data in Table 2.1, and by a variety of other sources of evidence.

Maintenance

In Figure 2.1 we saw that children of 16–22 months had a speaking repertoire that looked very much like a babbling repertoire. In Figure 2.2 we saw continuations of this at 24 months and beyond. If Jakobson (1941/1968) had been correct in his assertion that the child "loses nearly all of his ability to produce sounds [p. 21]" in the transition from babbling to speech, we would not find that certain sounds have a developmental "head-start," as do those that figure prominently into babbling. Consequently, it seems compatible with the data to suggest that at the time of the child's first words certain sounds are already present. One might suppose that the child's primary task is to maintain them—to learn where they go and when not to use them but in any case to hang on to them.

An analogy in second language acquisition comes to mind. Though it may be true that no two languages have *exactly* the same placement for /s/ or *identical* VOTs for /d/, one frequently "bursts into" a new system by using "old" segments that are perceptually similar to new ones. The learner does this automatically. And based on the results of contrastive analysis, it frequently is possible to predict the errors in L_2.[2] Likewise, knowing something of the rule system of a language, it is possible to predict the damage a loan word can expect to sustain.

What I am asserting about the development of phonology in children differs from the analogy mainly in the origin of the interference. In second language acquisition the interference is from an acquired system whereas in first language acquisition the interference is from an unacquired system. And I would be perfectly happy to call the infant's consonants "protoconsonants" or "prephonemes," or practically anything else that removes unfortunate connotations. For the fact is that adult listeners *recognize* the sounds of their language in the vocalizations of babies. And if phonemicization accompanies the adult perceptual event, then it hardly matters what we call the audible product of an infant articulation or what the absolute truth is about its acoustic structure, or the ways in which it might differ from a prototypical rendering in standard adult speech. For when phonetic entities see lexical service, even in [mama], they potentially do phonemic work, and in the long developmental run it is less important how linguists view the activity than how parents view it.

Learning

We also saw in Figure 2.2 a pattern of change that started low—the 35% mean accuracy of nonrepertoire segments—and climbed considerably over the succeeding months to finish at a respectable 83%. Templin's (1957) data showed a 99% performance level at age 8 for these same nonrepertoire segments. If many of the repertoire sounds creep into early phonology via a mechanism such as maintenance, how are we to account for such monotonic improvements in the remaining sounds? We might suppose that every sound makes its appearance ultimately through the maturation of relevant musculature, each sound—like its unique articulation—dependent upon its own schedule of neuromuscular "unfolding." However, we saw in the babbling of deaf children that certain classes of sound never do appear, convincingly, at least by the age of 5 or 6. By that time most of the fricatives and liquids and glides have been mastered by the typical

---

[2]Or to predict the general structure of an intermediate system analogous to Selinker's (1972) "interlanguage."

child speaker (Templin, 1957). So it seems reasonable to ascribe the child's articulatory progress for nonrepertoire segments to an environmentally interactive process we might inelegantly term *learning*. Under the social compulsion to say *cheek* and *matches* and *witch*, the child struggles to gain control over /#tʃ/, /VtʃV/, and /tʃ#/.

I am not aware of a phonetic or phonological learning model that appropriately incorporates biological and social factors, and that evenly values the contributions of perceptual, articulatory, and organizational learning. I am assuming, obviously, that such factors and forms of learning must be present for a model to have adequate explanatory power. In the meanwhile, I will use the term *learning* to designate levels and types of whatever cognition is responsible for the getting of what would otherwise not be provided by the mechanisms of "emergence."

Loss

Several years ago I (Locke, 1978) wrote that "much of his phonological acquisition is described not by what the child gains but—perversely—by what he is forced to give up [p. 3]." I went on to look at the infant's "relinquishment" of consonant-like sounds with no functional equivalent in his (future) native language. In Locke (1980b), I plotted Figure 2.8, which depicts the gradual reduc-

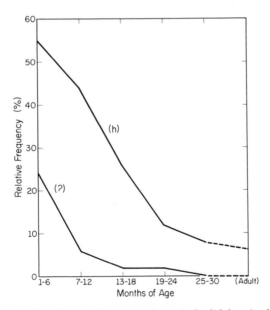

Figure 2.8. *Gradual decline of glottal fricatives and stops in English-learning babies, eventuating in the systemic loss of word–initial glottal stop (from Locke, 1980b).*

tion of glottal fricatives and stops over the different sampling intervals in Irwin's (1947) data. Where the glottal fricative remains as English /h/, with a word-initial frequency of 5.8%, the glottal stop essentially becomes extinct, with a word-initial frequency of .4% (from data in Mines et al., 1978). Unfortunately, so few data were available on this process that it was difficult to do more than to suggest loss as an important area for future research. And important it is, for one can think of few kinds of evidence on the child's phonological acquisition that "tell" so unambiguously. As the young child's articulatory ability is doubtful, his utterances convey little reliable information about his knowledge of phonological categories, and one frequently is unsure of how much weight to attach to phonetic transcriptions. There is the suspicion that the child literally knows more than he tells. But the same child ought—as the better part of a more cognitive process—to be free to *abandon* that which he can say but which no longer fits.

There is a real theoretical need for the loss mechanism. Vihman et al. (1981) observed in the babbling of their subjects what they, after Jakobson, called "wild sounds." Frequently these wild sounds—in this case, labioalveolar trills——were carried over into speaking. Two of the children blended their trills in with conventional English sounds in word production.

Several linguist-parents have observed their child to lose some first-language knowledge in the process of acquiring a second language. Burling (1959) observed that his 16-month-old son was just beginning to express English /f/- and /v/-like sounds when he was exposed to Garo, which contains neither sound. Burling commented that "the disappearance of *f* and *v* can be taken as marking his real transition to the Garo language. Everything earlier might be considered to be just as much English as Garo, but only Garo influence can explain *the loss of these phonemes* [p. 47, emphasis mine]."

Berman (1979) moved from Israel to the United States at a time when her 3-year-old daughter understood Hebrew and English and spoke Hebrew. Subsequently, the daughter switched from Hebrew to accented, and then unaccented, English. According to Berman, after 6 months in the United States her daughter "was no longer bilingual," which the author termed "a special instance of the phenomenon of language loss [p. 157]."

There are studies of children's speech discrimination—or what I prefer to call differential identification—that particularly implicate the loss mechanism as it relates to language reception. Bond and Adamescu (1979) tested 4-year-olds, adolescents, and adults on an identification task in which the voiced English stops were contrasted with voiced ingressive stops as are found in Hausa. Each CV syllable has proffered as the name of a cartoon figure, and following practice trials subjects were to identify the named figure in a series of cartoon pairs. In all, there were 20 trials each on [ba–ɓa], [da–ɗa], [bi–ɓi], and [di–ɗi]. Adult and adolescent subjects performed in the 50–60% range, whereas the 4-year-olds identified the syllables at a significantly greater (72%) level of accuracy. Bond and Adamescu suggested that those with "more stable and mature phonological systems . . . have a correspondingly lessened ability to discern and employ phonetic information that is completely novel [p. 185]."

Allen (in press) studied 4- and 5-year-old French-, German-, and Swedish-speaking children with respect to their performance on the TAKI test, which was designed by Allen to assess children's acquisition of lexical stress rules. Children in all three languages and at both age levels were presented with three pairs of toylike forms, which were assigned stress-contrastive nonce labels (e.g., *táki* and *takí*. As expected, the older children generally did better than the younger ones in all three languages. However, the 5-year-old French children made more perceptual errors than did the 4-year-old French children on the one stress contrast not relevant to French. Moreover, in a special retest administered 6 months later only to the younger French group, three of the six 4-year-olds worsened on the non-French contrast while improving on the two contrasts relevant to French. Allen concluded that his findings were consistent with the notion that innate perceptual abilities "may become attenuated or completely lost if they are inappropriate or irrelevant for the child's language [p. 1]."

In a second cross-linguistic study, Oller and Eilers (1983) presented seven English and seven Miami Cuban Spanish 2-year-olds with the "shell game task" they had invented and used earlier for the purpose of studying children's differential perceptual identifications. Unlike the TAKI task, in the shell game technique one of the forms is an identifiable object and the other is a nonsense object which is named for the purpose of the experiment. Each child is trained in the nonce label, and his identification of the appropriate name (and, therefore, segment) is tested by instructing the child to find a raisin, for example, under one or the other of the two objects. In this experiment, Oller and Eilers used a native and a nonnative contrast for each language group. For the English subjects, a native liquid–glide contrast was created by pairing the word *rabbit* ([ɹæbɪt] in the authors' notation) with the nonce word [wæbɪt]. A non-English tap–trill contrast was formed by pairing the word *ladder* [læɾər] with the nonce word [læɾər]. For the Spanish subjects, a native tap–trill contrast was created by pairing the Miami Spanish word for 'car' [káro] with the nonword [káro]. A non-Spanish liquid–glide contrast was achieved by pairing the word for 'egg' [wéβo] with the nonce word [ɹéβo]. The "phonetics" of the contrasts, then, were well controlled, with the primary distinction being the functional status of the contrasts in the respective languages.

Oller and Eilers found that the two groups performed equivalently in their identification of the nonnative contrast, with a mean of 5.29 correct trials out of 10 possible, and nearly alike in their identification of the native contrasts, with the Spanish children scoring 8.29 on the tap–trill contrast and the English children scoring 8.43 on the liquid–glide contrast. As the authors had observed good discrimination of the liquid–glide contrast in 6–8-month-old English and Spanish babies in an earlier study (Eilers & Oller, 1978), they could only conclude that the Spanish children in the present study had experienced *loss* of the contrast:

> We suspect . . . that by age 2, children have acquired a conception of their native phonology that specifies certain contrasts as relevant and others (*even if they are easily discriminable*) as irrelevant to the language's meaning system. Thus, the child may ignore contrasts that do not pertain to the system, at least in tasks involving identification of meanings. It is possible, of course, that *systematically ignoring certain contrast types at the level of linguistic meaning may ultimately result in changes in the child's lower level perceptual abilities* [p. 53; emphasis mine].

I find it particularly interesting that Oller and Eilers implicated meaning in their discussion of perceptual performance, especially as I collected some data several years ago with a procedure that has been viewed as more psychoacoustic than psycholinguistic (Locke, 1980d, 1980e). As I have not reported these data elsewhere, I will present them here in detail.

SUBSEMANTIC PERCEPTUAL LOSS

In 1978, I conducted an experiment in which 30 native American children were tested on their ability to discriminate [ta] from three other syllables. In an English phonemic contrast, the opposing syllable was [ka]. In two non-English (or allophonic) contrasts, the opposing syllables were the dental [t̪a] or the retroflex [ṭa]. These contrasts were presented in an ABX format (which is considered allophonically sensitive; Locke, 1980d, 1980e), modified for children by using puppets. Where an adult would be asked which of two different syllables a third one was more like, the first or the second, the children were asked which of two puppets had said a particular syllable, the hippopotamus or the tiger. The child had merely to point to the correct puppet.

Children first were trained in this procedure using an [a–i] contrast; they then proceeded with the experimental items. There were eight blocks of six contrasts in the experiment proper. Each block contained two of the three different contrasts, for 16 each of the [ta–ka], [ta–t̪a], and [ta–ṭa] contrasts or 48 items overall. The stimuli were presented live-voice in a sound-attenuated room near the day care center from which the children were selected.

The children ranged in age from 2:11 to 5:11. In the analysis, data were examined separately for six groups of five children whose mean ages increase regularly in 6-month intervals: 3:3, 3:9, 4:3, 4:9, 5:3, and 5:9.

My initial expectation was that discrimination of the [t–k] contrast would improve or remain the same across the different groups, and that discrimination of the other two contrasts would decline with age, that is, with development in English phonology. The results are shown in Table 2.9. The mean performance of each age group was above chance on the [t–k] contrast, ranging from 71.3 to 93.8%, with an overall mean of 81.7%. There was no upward (or downward) trend discernible with increasing age. On both nonphonemic contrasts, the mean performance of each age group was at chance. The mean [t–ṭ] accuracy for groups ranged from 50.0 to 65.6%, with an overall mean of 56.1%. The mean [t–ṭ] accuracy for groups ranged from 46.9 to 58.8%, with an overall mean of 52.5%. The expected decline in children's discrimination of these nonphonemic contrasts did not occur, and there was no apparent trend of any kind.

Though it was not observed in this experiment, I assume young English children are able to discriminate [t–ṭ] and [t–ṭ], and that they lose this ability—even in subsemantic performance—before the age of 3. My youngest subject, 2:11, scored 87.5% on [t–k] and exactly 50% on the nonphonemic contrasts. The mean age of Oller and Eilers's (1983) English subjects was 2:6, and they could not discriminate the nonphonemic tap–trill contrast. The greater age at which loss was inferred in Allen (in press) may mean only that different phonetic features are lost at differential rates just as they are acquired at differential rates.

Werker, Gilbert, Humphrey, and Tees (1981) have reported data which support these assumptions. They presented two Hindi contrasts to 6- and 7-month-old English infants, to adult Hindi speakers, and to adult English speakers. The VRISD head-turning paradigm was used with infant subjects. Adult listeners were exposed to the same tapes as the infants, but pressed a button when they detected a shift from one syllable to another. Of particular interest, in light of my own study, is the fact that one of the contrasts was [ṭa–ta]. The other Hindi contrast was between [tʰa] and [dʰa], which were very different in voice onset time. All test syllables were produced by a native Hindi speaker.

Table 2.9
Performance of Native English Children on [ta–ka], [ta–ṭa], and [ta–ṭa] Discriminations as a Function of Age

Age	Percentage correct		
	[ta–ka]	[ta–ṭa]	[ta–ṭa]
3:3	83.1	56.9	46.9
3:9	93.8	56.3	49.4
4:3	71.3	52.5	54.4
4:9	80.0	55.6	50.0
5:3	85.6	65.6	58.8
5:9	76.3	50.0	55.6
Grand Mean	81.7	56.1	52.5

Note: My research assistant, Richard Cureton, tested the subjects and analyzed the data.

Analysis of the results revealed that both Hindi contrasts were discriminated by the infants and the Hindi-speaking adults, but that neither contrast was discriminable to the group of adult English speakers. It also was evident that the dental–retroflex contrast was less discriminable to all these groups than the voicing contrast. Werker *et al.* concluded that infants "possess the ability to discriminate natural linguistic contrasts without prior specific language experience," but with reference to the more difficult [ṭa]–[ta] contrast, "there may be a decrease in speech perceptual abilities with either age or linguistic experience [p. 354]."

In Locke, the stop in contrast with retroflex [ṭ] was alveolar, not dental. But since my subjects failed to discriminate alveolar and dental phones, and alveolar and retroflex phones, they may also have been unable to discriminate [ṭ] from [t]. If so, the best conjecture is that Werker *et al.*'s English-speaking adults lost their ability to discriminate [ṭ]–[t] as young children, probably before the age of 3 years.

Concluding Remarks on Loss

Where phonetic output is concerned, it is apparent that extrasystemic sounds are present in babbling, and that they eventually disappear. On the input side, a number of experiments have now shown that infants can discriminate a variety of contrasts that are nonphonemic in the ambient phonology (cf. Eilers & Oller, 1981). It seems likely that in my study, and in Oller and Eilers (1983), Bond and Adamescu (1979), Allen (in press), and Werker *et al.* (1981), nonphonemic discrimination—through a lack of environmental stimulation and systemic function—was lost.[3]

A Unified Model for Production and Perception

In an attempt to put in perspective the diverse studies on infant speech perception, Aslin and Pisoni (1980) created the model shown here in Figure 2.9. The model was inspired by certain of the papers of Gottlieb (1976a, 1976b), a behavioral embryologist, and it shows that at birth perceptual abilities may be fully or partially developed or may be undeveloped. The fully developed perceptual abilities are either maintained by the environment or allowed to slip away. The partially developed perceptual abilities are facilitated by environmental interaction, are maintained in their partially developed state, or are permitted to

---

[3]Incidentally, perceptual loss need not be permanent. Even without training, Japanese adults typically can discriminate changes in the third formant, which distinguishes /r/ and /l/, when the third formant is heard by itself (Miyawaki, Strange, Verbrugge, Liberman, Jenkins, & Fujimura, 1975). With training, Japanese adults tend to discriminate /r/–/l/ categorically, as do native English speakers (MacKain, Best, & Strange, 1981).

EFFECTS OF EARLY EXPERIENCE ON PHONOLOGICAL DEVELOPMENT

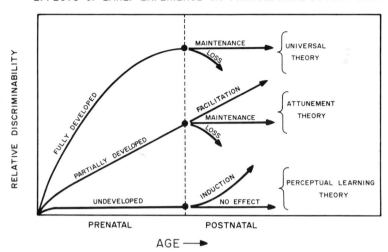

AGE ──▶

Figure 2.9. *A model of the child's perceptual development, applicable to productive development as well (from Aslin & Pisoni, 1980).*

decline. Perceptual abilities that are undeveloped at birth may be induced to develop or may be left in their undeveloped state.[4]

One can also imagine Figure 2.9 as a sound *production* model for phonological development. Among the fully developed sounds that are maintained would be repertoire sounds such as [m] and [d]. Lost would be syllable-initial glottal stop. Partially developed sounds that are facilitated would include [l] and [n]; maintained would be [ɵ] and [j]. Partially developed sounds that are lost might include, for English, [ç] and [x]. Candidates for undeveloped sounds that are induced would be the affricates [tʃ] and [ʤ], which show up on none of the infant charts, but which obviously appear eventually in child speech. We might put [β] and [ɸ] in the final category for English, sounds whose neonatally undeveloped status is undisturbed by the environment or subsequent development.

Stages of Phonological Development

It should be clear by now that I consider phonological development to be a continuous process whose beginnings predate the child's first words. This view

---

[4]There also are some related arguments in Rozin's (1976) excellent article on the evolution of intelligence. Rozin argues that aspects of learning may involve increases in the level of accessibility of innate dispositions. Rozin considers that environmental stimulation "often has the function of calibrating a prewired system [p. 252]."

is consistent with contemporary models of child development which assume that biological and psychological maturation are continuous (Kagan, Kearsley, & Zelazo, 1978). It may also be evident to some readers that I have been using the words *development* and *acquisition* differently. Perhaps some clarification is in order before I examine discernible stages in the child's development of expressive phonology, only some of which involve acquisition.

If asked *when the child's phonological system begins,* my inclination would be to say "when an elaborate pattern of phonetic preferences and capabilities is first evident," as in variegated babbling. I would say this even though the child, at that time, may not have actively targeted for a phonetic structure and may not have intended to "mean anything" with a segmental or prosodic pattern. It is clear that the infant's variegated babbling is intimately related to his early speech patterns, and if we afford linguistic status to the latter, we must similarly recognize the behavior from which it arose.

If asked *when the child's acquisition of phonology begins,* my inclination would be to say "when he moves away from what would continue to be *his* pattern and closer to an ambient one." According to this, *mama* is not a *phonological* acquisition—even when used in the appropriate situations—if the probability is that he would have uttered [mama] without knowledge of the ambient system. An implication of this assertion, which I accept, is that lexical acquisition may precede phonological acquisition. If phonology is a *system,* to be credited for an acquisition the child will have to do something *systemic* which could validly be traced to his linguistic environment (e.g., introduce clusters or final stops).

As phonological development merely includes and is not equivalent to acquisition, it follows that the larger developmental process must be realized in *stages.* The mere existence of stages is not antithetical to continuity in children's phonetic development (Kent & Murray, 1982), though as I use the term here, stages do represent inferable changes in the child's intentions, knowledge and proactivity.

The Pragmatic Stage

In what I have chosen to call the pragmatic stage of phonological development, the child discovers that his vocal tract activity (probably through its audibility) conveys information to others, and the child begins consciously to favor certain movements (or to try to achieve certain auditory patterns). This discovery marks the beginning of the *function* of phonology for the child, even though others may previously have used his vocal sounds to impute attitudes and states to the child. The pragmatic stage occurs well before babbling ceases, anticipating the child's "first (standard) word" by as much as 6 months.

We might be suspicious that something like a pragmatic stage occurs from the testimony of such observers as Werner Leopold. Leopold (1947) noted that in the second half of her 9th month, his daughter Hildegard began to produce "a short, sharp scream" in an apparent effort to engage his attention.

This utterance was in form farther removed from standard speech than many of her babbling combinations. But it was distinguished from them by an important addition: the intention of communication, which must be considered the chief criterion of language. Encouraged by the result, she used this sound very often during the following week, and it assumed the more articulate form [ʔa!], very short and vigorous. The intention of communication was beyond doubt . . . [p. 21].

In order to ascertain the existence and nature of several different pragmatic categories of vocalization, D'Odorico (1982) videotaped an Italian infant, Mattia, in a variety of situations. Mattia was seated in a high chair, alone or with his mother and/or the experimenter. D'Odorico specifically analyzed for three categories of vocalization. *Discomfort sounds* were all cries that occurred when the mother did anything that might irritate Mattia (e.g., dressing him), when he was "fed up," as D'Odorico put it, or when he had lost interest in a toy with which he had been playing. *Call sounds* were all cries that occurred when Mattia, having lost interest in a toy, and having been left alone, began to look around for his mother. *Request sounds* were all noncrying vocalizations that occurred in the same situations as calls, but without the facial expressions that typically accompanied Mattia's crying (e.g., frowning, squinting). Both call and request sounds typically ceased when the mother entered the room.

From 3 to 6 months, 93% of Mattia's cries were discomfort sounds, with calls accounting for the rest. In other words, there was not much pragmatic differentiation in Mattia's vocalizations. At 7 months, however, D'Odorico observed that Mattia began "to use his utterances to induce a change in the situation [p. 7]." Discomfort sounds account for about 37% of the total, with calls and requests amounting to 13 and 50%, respectively. Table 2.10 shows an analysis of Mattia's intonation contours as a function of pragmatic category. The majority of all three categories involve level contours, though the magnitude varies by category. There is a low percentage of rising patterns in the discomfort category,

Table 2.10
Distribution of Intonational Contours in an Italian Infant as a Function of Communicative Category

	Level	Rising	Falling	Convex	F_o variation[a]
Discomfort	66.7	2.7	19.4	11.1	105.16
Call	84.6	7.7	7.7	0	131.80
Request	71.4	20.4	2.0	6.1	151.14

Source: From data in D'Odorico (1982).
[a]This column shows within-utterance variations in fundamental frequency.

with more in the call category, and with request sounds clearly dominating in this regard.

Falling contours have much the opposite trend. They were involved in many of the discomfort cries, but relatively few of the calls and requests. Convex intonation contours were those that smoothly rose and fell, as in an inverted U-shape. They also claimed a greater share of the discomfort sounds than did the requests and calls.

In the last column of Table 2.10 I have shown D'Odorico's analyses of fundamental frequency shift for all but the level patterns. These analyses show that the greatest shift occurred among the requests, with less extreme frequency shifts among the calls and discomfort sounds. D'Odorico (1982) concluded that "even in the prelinguistic period, the infant is able to change systematically the melodic pattern of his vocalization. . . . [even if idiosyncratic] the existence of this melodic differentiation is nevertheless indicative of an early sound–meaning correspondence, that is to be considered in the process of language acquisition [p. 9]."[5]

Tuaycharoen (1977) observed a Thai infant longitudinally, recording that between 5 and 7 months "the baby's desire for communication had increased [p. 77]." Though Tuaycharoen did not identify the function or the meaning of the infant's utterances, she indicated that "regular patterns of pitch occurred more frequently and were used to convey 'meaning' in interaction [p. 189]."

Something similar was observed by Vihman et al. (1981) in their longitudinal study of 10 American infants. Rejecting Jakobson's discontinuous view of phonological development, Vihman et al. remarked that "certainly for all of our children the productive pairing of sound and meaning for communicative purposes antedates the emergence of the first adult-based words [p. 17]."[6]

The pragmatic period begins with the demonstrated desire to vocally communicate, as I have indicated, and may be said to end with the demonstrated ability to speak. The time lag between these two events may reflect the infant's insufficient phonetic perception and speech-motor production. Of interest in this regard is the work of Bonvillian, Orlansky, and Novack (in press). Noting that the visual cortex typically develops in advance of the auditory cortex, and that hand control generally precedes voice control in the developing infant, Bonvillian et al. followed the sign language acquisition of 11 infants born of deaf (signing) parents. As the authors expected, subjects were linguistically advanced relative to infants learning to speak. On the average, the infants produced their first

[5]It perhaps should be noted that D'Odorico's functional analysis of the vocalizations of a human infant is not different in any formal way from Green's (1975) analysis of the "coo" sounds of Japanese macaque monkeys. Green observed seven acoustically and perceptually distinct sounds which could be associated with 10 different situations. To the extent that the coo of the Japanese macaque is nonlinguistic, so must the intonations studied by D'Odorico be considered prelinguistic.

[6]Cruttenden (1982) has a helpful review of the literature on infants' use of different intonation patterns for different illocutionary purposes.

recognizable sign at just 8.5 months; at 13.2 months they produced their tenth sign. Both events antedate the corresponding lexical developments of children raised in speaking environments by 2–3 months. In light of this, I suppose one might argue that some cases of delayed lexical development may be viewed as articulatory problems.

The Cognitive Stage

At about 12 months, the child's awareness of the linguistic environment is for the first time conspicuously reflected in his vocal output. This marks the beginning of a cognitive stage during which the child produces his nonadult form of standard language words through the operation of cognitive processes such as attention, storage, retrieval, and pattern matching. The child's first words, however, provide scant evidence that a phonological system is being acquired. Rather, the child's productions of *dada* and *bye-bye* have surface characteristics quite similar to his premeaningful (babbling) patterns.

Some things, relative to the pragmatic stage, will not, then, be different. The organization and substance of the child's system will not discernibly vary. The child's use of "invented words" will persist. But the majority of his words will be those that he has heard. As such, the operations governing their use must necessarily be different from those that produce invented words and communicative patterns of pitch and voice quality. Patterns originating with the child need not have an auditory reality for the infant, who might merely make certain movements of his vocal muscles when he wants attention, food, and so forth. However, lexical forms derived from the child's linguistic environment must begin as auditory phenomena, and one assumes they therefore must be attended to, stored, analyzed, and mimicked. Do these operations include error detection and error correction? Such operations, if formed, are not particularly evident in the child's phonetic output. Rather, the phonology of the early lexicon is quite like the phonetics of his babbling, as we saw earlier in Figure 2.1 and in the testimony of Cruttenden, Leopold, the Labovs, and others.

Though during the cognitive stage children may accommodate little to the ambient system, they evidently are aware of their own system. For even before the age of 18 months, children are more likely to attempt new words if compatible with their established inventory of sounds (Leonard, Schwartz, Morris, & Chapman, 1981). There are, then, "permissibilities."

It is in the cognitive stage that the first and most passive of the three mechanisms of phonological development—maintenance—begins to operate.

The Systemic Stage

The onset of the systemic stage of phonological development is marked by changes, not of intentionality or in the nature of the lexicon, but rather in the phonetic characteristics of the child's phonological system. The child's system moves in the direction of the adult system in ways it would not be expected to without environmental stimulation. For example, consonant clusters, rarely observed in Sykes' (1940) 3–6-year-old deaf children, make a timid appearance. Voiced fricatives and final consonants also creep in here and there.

At the same time that these gains occur, the child abandons certain of his excess phonetic baggage. Glottal stops are on the decline. "Wild sounds" are diminishing, labial trills are on their way out. The child begins to experiment with sound patterns. As Ferguson and Macken (in press) point out, "as children acquire new vocal skills they have new resources to play with; as children play with speech sounds they consolidate and extend their control over the phonological system [p. 27]." Consider here the serial efforts of Scollon's (1976) Brenda, 1:7, who while trying to say *sick* produced first [š], then [šz̧kɛ], and finally [šik]. Scollon observed that "a target word is repeated until a reasonably acceptable form is achieved. . . . In some cases, the 'best' form was not reached until a week or more later [p. 29]."

Jakobson Revisited

I began the previous chapter by asking "when is the beginning?" and by quoting Jakobson's answer, "the first acquisition of words." In light of the material that has been reviewed here, it appears that Jakobson, ironically, may have been *generous* in his assessment. Where phonology is concerned, it appears that the first genuine stage may well await the first 50 words, and may not be discerned until 18 months or more.

3

The Phonetic Tendencies of Adults

In the two previous chapters it was demonstrated that many of the speech behaviors of very young children were traceable not so much to the linguistic environment as to "child internal" factors. This was first observed in infant populations, whose patterns of babbling were essentially uniform in spite of variations in their phonetic environment and their sensory access to that environment. Certain of the phonetic elements in the repertoire were rationalized on anatomical and physiological grounds, and all characteristics of their phonetic output were assumed to be susceptible to such rationalization. With the beginnings of lexical production and the formation of a phonological system, the persistence of these internal factors was apparent, but now with an additional mechanism evident, perception. That is, the phonetic repertoire still was constrained largely by physiological factors, but how that repertoire was manifest in lexical production was seen to be a function of an emerging sense of the perceptual similarity between repertoire segments and adult forms.

If very young children's speech is initially patterned by physiological constraints, does maturation free the individual of such constraints and, therefore, of such patterning? Or, is maturation continuous, with control increasingly but never completely acquired even in adulthood? If so, one ought to see certain parallels between child and adult (cf. Stampe, 1969, 1973). Indeed, it has recurrently been attractive to consider the child's sound change patterns to be similar to those of the adult and—it has been implicitly assumed—for similar reasons. Kiparsky allowed that "rules are susceptible to loss if they are hard to learn

[1971, p. 627]." Slobin stated, as a general principle of language contact, that "forms which are late to be acquired by children are presumably also relatively difficult for adults to process, and should be especially vulnerable to change [1977, p. 194]."

Such statements seem to ascribe sound change to limitations on the *human* produceability of the system undergoing that change. If so, one might expect certain parallel speaking behaviors in children and adults, though obviously different in measurable degree. Since, as we saw earlier, the weakening of word-final obstruents is exceedingly common in children, we will begin a comparison of the two populations by examining whatever evidence exists on weakening in adult speakers.

Laboratory Studies versus Naturalistic Studies

Before we examine laboratory studies of weakening and other sound changes it is appropriate that the nature of this empirical setting itself be examined briefly. In the laboratory it is necessary for the subject to fully cooperate, and he immediately becomes aware that his speech is being monitored. His speech is in a different register; it is laboratory speech. Test material is carefully preselected, often repeated after the experimenter, or read. Frequently the materials consist of isolated mono- or disyllabic words or nonsense syllables. In real-life conversations, the rate typically is fast, the articulation slurred, and very little speech is in the utterance-final position. In the laboratory, the rate typically is slower, the articulation more precise, and the target sounds frequently are preceded or followed by silence.[1]

Nowhere is the difference in precision more clearly documented than in the social dialect studies of Labov (1966). Figure 3.1 depicts Labov's data on the production of /r/-words by native New Yorkers. As the figure indicates, /r/ was said rarely in conversational speech, with a slight increase during a formal interview. There is a second increase when reading a prose passage, and there are sharp increments—to about 50 and 70%—in reading single words and minimal pairs (e.g., *sauce–source*). Of course the reading of words and word pairs is more typical of laboratory studies of speech than is speaking in a conversational situation and formal interview. Figure 3.2, taken from Labov (1964), shows the production of [ɵ] words by New Yorkers of various socioeconomic classes. The prestige form is /ɵ/, the stigmatized forms /t/ and /tɵ/. As the figure indicates,

---

[1]An acoustic consequence of these differences, according to Best and MacKain (in press), is that "finding phonemes and syllables in everyday speech is like an especially complex Embedded Figures Test [whereas] in the laboratory, syllables are disembedded and often acoustically simplified."

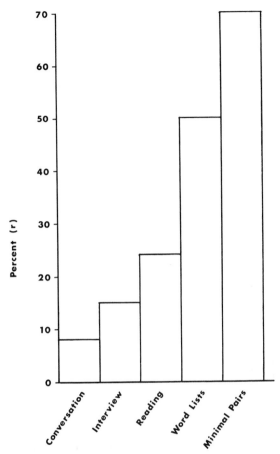

Figure 3.1. *Situational variations in the production of /r/ words by New Yorkers (from data in Labov, 1966).*

all groups are closest to the prestigious /θ/ in word lists, less close in reading, careful speech, and casual speech. The reading of isolated words so conceals speakers' natural tendencies that it nearly erases their dialectal differences!

Baran, Laufer, and Daniloff (1977) measured the VOTs of voiced and voiceless stops in three adults while speaking conversationally, reading a passage, and reading single-word citation forms. They found VOT values to be most discrete for citation forms, where there was no overlap between voicing categories (essentially confirming Lisker & Abramson, 1967). In speaking and reading, there was less difference between voiced and voiceless stops; in conversational speaking there was a "noted trend for increased rate of utterance and less precise articulation [p. 348]."

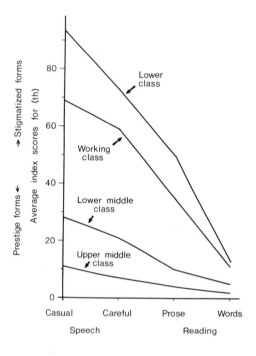

Figure 3.2. *Situational and social class variations in the production of /ɵ/ words by New Yorkers (from Labov, 1964).*

The greater care and precision of laboratory speech is to a degree offset by the greater precision of instrumental analysis. That is, although speakers may be phonetically on their best behavior, even the slightest articulatory nuances are likely to be detected. As a consequence, many of the instrumentally detected cases of, for example, devoicing, may be imperceptible to listeners. This is not necessarily bad, for in many cases the question may not be what speakers do under certain conditions, but why they do it. If they shave a few milliseconds off this and add a little aspiration to that, and the magnitude of such modifications is *subperceptual,* one may regard the motivation for such changes as internal to the speaker. That the phonetic cues are, or might be, perceivable makes them potentially linguistically significant, but not ipso facto less physiological in their motivation (though perhaps greater in their degree of stability).

In the perceptual analysis of natural speech, there must be a different set of concerns. For example, it is clear that certain sympathetic relationships exist between the production and perception mechanisms of speakers. To a degree, speakers perceive as they do because they produce as they do, and vice versa. There is some correspondence between speakers' VOT values for the labial–alveolar–velar stop series and listeners' VOT boundaries for voiced and voiceless categories in the same series. This kind of effect, to the extent that it operates in perception-based studies of natural speech, ought to cause listeners to miss, in speakers of the same dialect, those phonetic variations that fall within their own normal ranges of speech variation.

An additional problem is that most phonological contrasts are multiply cued at the phonetic level. A speaker may devoice a final stop but produce an appropriately long vowel before it. As vowel duration is an important cue to final "voicing," the listener may not detect the devoicing. The listener can know that he heard a /b/, but what he cannot know, even with training, is exactly *why* he heard a /b/.

One's perceptions may be constrained additionally by situational and grammatical context. For example, listeners' ability to detect a particular phonetic target may be greatly enhanced or reduced merely by changes in contextual redundancy (cf. Locke & Yakov, 1982).

In naturalistic studies, then, a variety of perceptual illusions or restorations will occur, mostly charitable to the speaker. The errors and changes are those sufficiently bold to survive the processes of "corrective perception."

Laboratory Studies

Adult Checking of Word-Final Stops

Word-final stop consonants may be fully released, with a resultant puff of air in the case of voiceless stops or faint schwalike vowel in the case of their voiced cognates. They may also be imploded or checked, with no audible release. Evidence on the checking of final stops is available in Rositzke's (1943) report on the final stop production of five male college students or recent graduates who spoke a General American dialect of English. In a phonetics laboratory, the subjects read 372 monosyllabic words ending in a voiced or voiceless stop consonant. Each word was preceded by an unaccented particle (e.g., *to keep, a beet, the gate*). Rositzke made kymograph recordings of each speaker, and on the basis of these recordings he determined whether each word-final stop was released or checked. Both for voiced and voiceless stops, alveolars were the most likely to be checked, followed by bilabials and by velars. Averaging across the five speakers, some 61% of the final /t/s were checked, followed by mean implosion rates of 42 and 7% for /p/ and /k/. The corresponding voiced stops were less likely to be checked; about 37% of the final /d/s were checked, compared to a 33% rate for /b/ and an 18% rate for /g/.

One might think that a speaker's tendency to check final /t/ is somewhat inconsequential as the /t/ still would be present, more or less, in its unreleased form. Its presence is decidedly less rather than more. Malécot (1958) removed the final release cues from VC syllables ending in voiced and voiceless stops. For /t/, listeners' identifications went from 88% correct for the fully released forms to 12% for the forms without release cues. For the entire stop series, the figures were 94 and 69% for the stops with and without releases.

Adult Devoicing of Word-Final Obstruents

Smith (1979) analyzed the medial and final voicing of /b/ and /d/ in 2-year-olds, 4-year-olds, and adults in a nonsense syllable repetition task. From oscillograms, Smith measured the duration of each stop closure period and the duration of the period in which voicing was present; from these figures he calculated the percentage of the closure period in which voicing was evident. In both child groups more than 90% of the final /b/s and /d/s were less than fully voiced. Typically, there was voicing in just the first third of the stop closure period. Some readers might have expected such results, in light of the impressionistic data on children's devoicing of final stops. However, Smith found a parallel behavior in his adult speakers, who devoiced 50% of *their* final /b/s and /d/s. On devoiced trials, voicing was evident over the first two-thirds of the stop closure periods. Children and adults differed, but mainly in the frequency and the magnitude of their devoicing.

Smith noted the existence of other research showing that children typically generate greater intraoral air pressures in stop production than do adults. He observed that based on this fact, aerodynamic theory would predict more devoicing in children than in adults. Smith concluded that "one need not attempt to account for devoicing in terms of phonological rules or processes [p. 27]."

Smith also studied the voicing characteristics of final /t/. He obtained the following measurements for /d/ and /t/:

	/d/	/t/
Adults	64	20
4-year-olds	34	4
2-year-olds	36	5

Perhaps unexpectedly, the adults *voiced* the first 20% of the closure periods for final /t/s, and children voiced the first 4 or 5%. In other words, the difference between "voiced" and "voiceless" final stops was one of *degree*, as both were partially voiced in both populations. It was apparent that the 2- and 4-year-old children had the voicing contrast, inasmuch as they voiced about the first third of the closure period for /d/. Relative to the adults, the children devoiced both voiced and voiceless alveolar stops. As this study was limited to oscillographic measurement, it is not known whether any of it was perceptible.

One may add to Smith's evidence on devoicing a curious bit of additional information: Smith (personal communication, 1981) *instructed* his subjects to release their final stops to ensure that the termination of closure periods would be discernible. Left to their own devices, even in careful, laboratory speech subjects seem to use final stops mainly to check the preceding vowel, granting the consonant little physical identity apart from its postvocalic transitions.

Parrucci (1983) analyzed oscillosocopically the utterance-final stops of eight adult speakers of American English. Each stop was preceded by a variety of different vowels. The results showed that a significantly lower percentage of the closure period was voiced for /g/ than for the other phonemically voiced stops:

/b/	/d/	/g/	/p/	/t/	/k/
79.9	79.00	69.1	11.5	11.6	9.8

The tendency for velars to be the least voiced was evident also in the phonemically voiceless series, with /k/ following (nonsignificantly) behind /p/ and /t/.

Plevyak (1982) performed a similar study of the voicing values of eight 3-year-old children. As expected, the children gave less voicing to /b, d, g/ than did the adults, though /p, t, k/ were similar for the two groups. Plevyak found that /g/ *and* /b/ were significantly less voiced (again, according to percentage of closure period that contained periodic pulsing) than was /d/:

/b/	/d/	/g/	/p/	/t/	/k/
45.3	54.7	44.7	9.8	6.9	9.1

Flege (1982) studied medial and final /b/ production in 4-, 7-, and 10-year-old children and in adult speakers. Oscillographic analysis revealed that final /b/s were fully voiced by only about 20% of the 4- and 7-year-olds, and about 58% of the 10-year-olds. Adults did no better; in fact, just 40% of their final /b/s were fully voiced. All groups supplied more voicing to medial /b/s.

Haggard (1978) looked at adults' devoicing of fricatives oscillographically. He defined devoicing as the cessation of the periodic component prior to the cessation of the friction component. The words read by Haggard's British English subjects were embedded in sentences. He found that more than 90% of the fricatives were devoiced when in word-final position and also when prior to voiceless stops. Haggard attributed fricative devoicing to physiological and aerodynamic constraints, noting somewhat less devoicing of /v/ than of /z/. As oral pressure has been observed to be less for /v/ than for /z/ (Subtelny, Worth, & Sakunda, 1966), the reduced devoicing for /v/ was predictable by the aerodynamic model.

Adult Voicing of Word-Initial Stops

In Olmsted (1971), we observed earlier that children's productions of phonemically voiceless stops frequently are transcribed as voiced. This was especially true of bilabial stops, less true of alveolars, and the least true of velar stops. A similar trend was apparent for Spanish children in Ferguson (1975). Though there are no directly comparable data available on adults, measurements have been made of adults' *prevoicing* of word-initial voiced stops. Smith (1978a) asked 20 adults to read a list of four /b/, four /d/, and four /g/ words five times each. Analyzing oscillographically the onset of voicing relative to the consonantal burst, he found a consistent pattern of prevoicing:

	Lead		Lag	
	Percentage	msec	Percentage	msec
Labial	56	74	44	11
Alveolar	50	71	50	18
Velar	39	65	61	26

Labial prevoicing exceeded alveolar and velar prevoicing both in frequency and in magnitude. In the cases of voicing lag, a sympathetic trend was apparent: There was less lag among labials than among alveolars and velars. This was confirmed a year later in a study by Westbury (1979).

Smith explained his results as follows. The point of maximum articulatory constriction for labials is at the periphery of the vocal tube, creating a large volume between the vocal folds and that constriction. In producing /b/, it would take some time, following the onset of voicing, for the air pressure in the mouth to become so high that it had to be released. In the case of /d/, where the point of maximum constriction is farther back in the vocal tract, that time would be less, and it would be the least for /g/.[2] If children were subject to these same constraints, they would be more likely to voice bilabials than alveolars and velars, and this is exactly what the child transcriptions show. It also is what spectrographic analysis reveals. In the following chart, I have shown the VOT (in msec) of repeated productions of *bear, dime,* and *goat* by 2-year-old, 6-year-old, and adult speakers (from Zlatin & Koenigsknecht, 1976).

	Bear	Dime	Goat
2-year-olds	6.43	11.47	21.28
6-year-olds	−3.03	12.10	19.10
Adults	−12.02	−5.20	−.08

Negative values indicate prevoicing. The data indicate that all three groups consistently gave more voicing to labials than to alveolars and velars. As seen earlier (p. 18), this pattern also describes the voicing of syllable-initial stops of Swiss German infants at 9–12 months of age (Enstrom, 1982).

Perceptually, a similar pattern was revealed by a little Czech boy between 15 and 17 months of age, who had a vocabulary of 100 words. From data reported in Pačesova (1968, p. 95), I calculated the number of voiceless and voiced stops that occurred in word-initial and medial position. The following shows the occurrence of voiceless and voiced stops by place, and the ratio of voiceless to voiced:

	Bilabial		Alveolar		Velar	
Voiceless	[p]	73	[t]	84	[k]	90
Voiced	[b]	94	[d]	28	[g]	2
−V/+V		.78		3.00		45.00

At the bilabial place, voiced stops predominate. At the alveolar site, voiceless stops predominate by a ratio of three to one; in the velar region, the ratio of voiceless to voiced stops increases dramatically to 45 to 1. From data reported in Kučera and Monroe (1968), I calculated the word-initial ratios of voiceless to

---

[2]Ohala and Riordan (1979) found that passive enlargement of the supraglottal cavities associated with /b/, /d/, and /g/—which evidently accounts for much of the VOT variation among the stops— also is greater for bilabials than for alveolars and velars.

voiced stops in the speech of Czech adults. The ratios were 1.35 for bilabials, 1.61 for alveolars, and 37.07 for velars. The place trend is similar to that evinced by Pačesova's little boy, but the boy's voicing pattern is even more exaggerated.

Field Research

When people are interviewed on the street or in their homes they give us a more natural picture of their speech than we get in laboratory testing. Conversational forms frequently bear little relationship to the entries in standard dictionaries. Even linguists tend to forget that oral language has a phonetic level, a mode that can be related to speakers' internal representations with only the greatest difficulty. Consider Malécot's (1975) finding that conversational French abounds with glottal stops. My calculations (re Malécot, 1974) indicate that 7.2% of the French stops are glottals, an incidence that exceeds even the phonemic /b/ and /g/. Yet Malécot was surprised to find, upon checking the literature, that there is

> a great deal of confusion among phoneticians about the matter. Of 20 well-known books on French pronunciation, in which we have searched for references, only 7 mention it at all, and 3 of these deal only with cases where its absence in French offers a contrast with English. The other 4 are either wrong in their observations or indicate only a small part of what is in reality an interesting and complex system [p. 51].

In the next few pages I will examine some characteristics of ordinary adult speech. One purpose in doing so is to show the degree to which adult speakers are constrained by phonetic factors. A second purpose is to provide a glimpse of the kind of speech the child may be exposed to, a matter to which we will return in Chapter 5.

Adult Omission of Final Consonants

It has been observed for some time that there is a strong tendency for American English speakers to omit the /t/s and /d/s from word-final clusters. In fact, the tendency is so strong that Zwicky (1972) has named it: Dentdel. According to Zwicky's formulation of Dentdel, alveolar stops are omitted in final position when preceded by continuant consonants. The application of this rule was studied by Neu (1980), who obtained 10 min of natural continuous speech from each of 15 adults of various ages and geographic backgrounds. She found that stop omissions were affected both by phonetic and grammatical factors. Specifically, when the following sound was a consonant there was a 36% rate of stop omission, compared to a 16% rate when the next sound was a vowel. There was a

32% rate of omission when the stop was part of a monomorphemic cluster (e.g., *fast*) compared to a 9% omission rate when the cluster was bimorphemic (e.g., *passed*). A generally confirming and phonetically more detailed account of the same phenomenon is available in Guy (1980).

Wolfram and Fasold (1974), in their analysis of Detroit Black English, found that among working classes the incidence of /t, d/ omission in stem-final clusters approached 100% in certain phonetic environments (before a consonant).

It is interesting to note one other point in Neu's study. Of the 2379 final /t, d/ clusters in her sample, Neu had transcribed 55 glottal stops. It is significant that 54 of these glottal stops replaced /t/, with only 1 replacing /d/. Zwicky (1972) also has commented on speakers' preference for replacing /t/ rather than /d/ with [ʔ].

Shockey and Bond (1980) calculated the frequency with which eight middle-class British women expressed word-final /t/ as glottal stop. When speaking to another British woman, the rate of /t/-to-glottal conversion ranged from 8 to 68%, with an average of 32%. When speaking to their own child, the mean glottalization rate increased to 44%.

In Mines *et al.* (1978), an analysis was done not for final consonant omission but for the usage frequency of various consonantal and vocalic elements in the conversational speech of 26 American adults of different ages and geographic backgrounds. Fortunately for our purposes, Mines *et al.* transcribed and tabulated their data in detailed phonetic form. Their results show a high incidence of glottal stop and flap. The percentage of occurrence of these sounds is shown here, as well as the number of less frequent (NLF) English *phonemes:*

	Initial		Medial		Final	
	Percentage	NLF	Percentage	NLF	Percentage	NLF
Flap	.35	2	3.06	13	2.04	10
Glottal stop	.38	1	.55	2	1.66	10

With an occurrence of 3.06%, medial flap was more frequent than [ð, w, z, f, h, g, j, ŋ, ɵ, ʤ, ʃ, tʃ, ʒ]; at 1.66%, glottal stop was more frequent than [ð, b, p, f, g, ɵ, ʤ, ʃ, tʃ, ʒ].

I tape recorded a young adult native of Baltimore and examined the phonetic expression of all word-final /t/s over several minutes of her spontaneous conversation. Five phonetically sophisticated listeners categorized each final phonemic /t/ as released or unreleased, replaced by a glottal, a flap, or another phone (i.e.,

Table 3.1
Incidence of Various Surface Manifestations of Final /t/ When Followed by a Pause, a Vowel, or Another Consonant

	Pause	Vowel	Consonant	Total	Percentage
Released	1	2	4	7	11.5
Checked	2	5	19	26	42.6
Glottalized	1	0	3	4	6.6
Omitted	1	1	10	12	19.7
Merged	0	1	0	1	1.6
Flapped	0	11	0	11	18.0
Total	5	20	36	61	100.0

Note: Linda Morris was helpful in obtaining the original recording.

a merger with the following consonant), and tabulated all omissions. Though this notation system was briefly practiced, it was surprising that sophisticated listeners agreed so rarely: In 89 of the 150 final /t/s, only three or fewer of the listeners agreed on any particular notation. This perceptual variation occurred in the face of perfect lexical intelligibility. Often, judges complained that the rate of speech simply was too fast for them to make a confident decision of any kind. In 61 cases, four or five of the listeners agreed. Their data, shown in Table 3.1, indicate that final /t/ was expressed as an identifiable form of /t/ in just 54% of the cases and the majority of these were unreleased. Some 20% were omitted, mainly when a consonant followed.[3]

Other raw data available on adult speech permit a similar analysis. With the assistance of Debra Yakov, I examined the conversational speech data in Carterette and Jones (1974), which appear both in conventional text and in phonetic transcription. Omissions and glottal stops are shown in the transcriptions, and flaps (one assumes) are represented as /d/s. Based on my examination of 578 final /t/s, 89 (15.4%) were replaced by glottal stops, 115 (19.9%) were omitted, 48 (8.3%) were [d]s, 8 (1.4%) were merged with a following consonant, and 318 (55%) were heard as a form of /t/. The grammatical and contextual variations noted by Neu (1980) and Guy (1980) were basically confirmed.

There is some generality to final consonant omission; it does not involve just /t/ and /d/. Poplack (1980a, 1980b) studied the final omissions of /s/ and /n/ in the Spanish of native speakers of Puerto Rican Spanish now residing in the United States. She documented an extremely high omission rate for plural /s/ and /n/, regardless of whether this caused the loss of grammatical information, though there were grammatical as well as phonetic constraints.[4] Poplack com-

---

[3]It is clear from Henderson and Repp (1982) that many of the preconsonantal /t/s that were not released *perceptibly* probably were released *articulatorally*, but were too faint to be heard.

[4]Uber (1982) observed in comprehension testing that ''native speakers of Puerto Rican Spanish are now relying heavily on . . . contextual factors for disambiguation, thus laying the foundation for categorical deletion of -*s* and -*n*.''

mented that "final (s) deletion in Puerto Rican Spanish is a sound change which has advanced so far that, rather than being treated as a morphological marker, Puerto Rican (s) is now mainly a phonological entity, undergoing well-defined rules of weakening and elision in certain environments and being retained in others . . . . [This quote is reprinted from Poplack, G. (1980a). Deletion and disambiguation in Puerto Rican Spanish. *Language, 56,* p. 383; with permission from Linguistic Society of America.]" She also observed that /s/ omission was common in other dialects of Spanish and paralleled in some ways the loss of /s/ in the Old French plurals *les* and *las* to Modern French /le/.

Data of Sankoff (reported in Table 10 of Bailey, 1973) indicate that speakers of Montreal French are strongly inclined to drop the /l/ in *il* (personal and impersonal), *ils,* and *elle.* The omission rate among professional people was about 69.1%, among the working class it was about 96.3%. There also was a fairly high omission rate for /l/ in *les* and *la* (pronoun and article): 13.4% among the professional class, 45.2% among the working class.

Bonnin (1964) studied the perceived voicing and intensity of word-final stops in the conversational speech of Germans. From an earlier field survey, Bonnin selected tapes of speakers of major dialects who were "of unquestionably high educational attainment and/or socio-economic background living in metropolitan areas . . . representing an elevated standard [p. 72]." The sample contained over 7 hours of continuous speech, or about 50,000 words. Bonnin classified all final stop allophones as tenuis aspirata (e.g., [p^h]), tenuis fortis (e.g., [p]), tenuis lenis (e.g., [b̥], or media [e.g., [b]).

The first column of Table 3.2 shows the percentage in each allophone class of all the final stops occurring without pause prior to a continuant ($N = 986$). It is apparent that very few stops were aspirated or fortis, with the great majority produced weakly or in lenis fashion. As German phonology calls for no voiced stops in word-final position, there were expected to be few cases allophonically, and there were few (.2%) in spite of the fact that there always was a voiced consonant immediately following.

Table 3.2

German Speakers' Conversational Treatment of Final Stops in Particular Phonetic Environments and by Place of Articulation

	All environments	When followed by				Before nasals/liquids		
		[m]	[n]	[l]	[r]	Bilabial	Dental	Velar
Tenuis aspirata	4.6	10.2	5.1	2.4	24.5	5.6	5.3	12.3
Tenuis fortis	8.4	8.2	5.6	9.2	11.3	8.5	5.4	21.0
Tenuis lenis	86.8	81.6	88.8	88.2	64.2	85.9	89.1	66.0
Media	.2	.0	.5	.2	.0	.0	.1	.6

Source: Calculated from data reported in Tables II–X of Bonnin (1964).

Columns 2–5 show variations in final stops as a function of the initial consonant in the following word. The variations seem relatively slight, though there were more aspirated and fewer lenis allophones when the following consonant was a "palato-alveolar or uvular trill or flap," shown in column 5 as [r]. The articulatory place analysis in the final three columns shows that velars are more likely to be aspirate and fortis, and less likely to be lenis, than are bilabials and dentals.

All of Bonnin's speakers were linguistically "elevated," to repeat his words, people of unusually great educational or socioeconomic background. For them to produce weakly almost 90% of their final stops (in the contexts specified) seems to suggest that such a final "weakening process" has considerable generality among human speakers, and one may suppose—as Smith (1979)—that the basis is phonetic.

Loss of Initial /ð/

Shockey (1977) observed from previous research, including her own (1974), that word-initial /ð/ frequently assimilates completely to a preceding nasal, lateral or fricative, causing their lengthening. Examples are *effects the* [ifɛks:ə] and *seen the* [sin:ə]. To test listeners' use of these length effects in processing ongoing speech, Shockey made a tape of the phrases *miss a guy* and *warn a guy*. Using digital splicing techniques, she varied the duration of the [s] in the first utterance from 80 to 200 msec in 20-msec steps, and the duration of [n] in the second utterance from 0 to 120 msec in 10-msec steps. Listeners were asked to judge whether they heard *a* or *the* in the phrases. At the shorter durations, listeners reported hearing the indefinite article. But at about 130 msec for [s] and 120 msec for [n], listeners began to "hear" the word *the*. I find this result interesting, for if casual speech is the usual register of oral communication, it follows that systems of ancillary cues would evolve so listeners could deal with phonetic reduction and distortion. According to Shockey's research, they have.

In a more recent report, Shockey and Bond (1980) calculated the frequency with which British women omit word-initial /ð/ when preceded by a word-final continuant-coronal sound. The percentage of rule application ranged from 36%, when the women were speaking to another adult, to 56% when talking to their own child.

Devoicing of Final Obstruents

The tendency of adults to devoice final obstruents is common but somewhat difficult to detect, and so there are few studies reporting precise incidence figures. According to Labov (1981), "in English, the progressive devoicing of final consonants seems to be a regular, Neogrammarian shift [p. 302]" (i.e., it is phonetically gradual, affecting all relevant words simultaneously). Hyman (1975) commented—even more generally—that "English is in the process of losing its voice contrast in consonants (note the loss of the /t/–/d/ contrast in most intervocalic positions): the final voice contrast is being replaced with a length contrast and the initial contrast is being replaced with an aspiration contrast [p. 173]."

By "length contrast" Hyman meant the length of vowels preceding final voiced and voiceless obstruents. Since this contrast effectively signals the voicing category of final obstruents in English, the impressions of listeners as to the incidence of final devoicing may no longer be completely reliable. This topic will be explored further in Chapter 6.

Baby Talk

Though I discuss baby talk later (p. 189), it should be noted here that adults perform a number of changes in standard forms, and create altogether new lexical items, when talking to children. The changes imply some knowledge of child speech tendencies, and include cluster reduction, gliding, velar fronting, and reduplication.

Historical Sound Change

Under "Field Research" I described some phonological habits of contemporary adult speakers, including a variety of unintended phonetic effects and the variations of several dialects and several languages. Such variations are the raw material from which "permanent," that is, historical, change is derived. Historical change is not, then, a change *by a language* but a change *of a language by its speakers.*

It was evident, earlier, that children and adults tend to produce similar phonetic changes synchronically, including stopping, final devoicing, segment omission, and initial stop voicing. Indeed, nearly a century ago Sully (1896) commented that "in reproducing the sounds which he hears a child often illustrates a law of adult phonetic change [p. 152]." More recently, Wang (1978) suggested that microhistory (measured in years and decades) and mesohistory (spanning centuries or millenia) were but "different time windows through which we are viewing the same phenomenon [p. 73]."

If synchronic changes are, in fact, the seeds of phonological restructuring, then we should expect that historical change would resemble the developmental "errors" of children. And here we have the testimony of Grammont (1902): "all the phonetic, morphological, or syntactical modifications that characterize the life of languages appear in the speech of children [p. 61]."

Let us, then, take a look at some of the parallels between child patterns and historical change, beginning with one of the more frequently attested cases of both, final devoicing.

Final Devoicing

The devoicing of word-final obstruents—if frequency of occurrence means anything at all—must surely be one of the more "natural" of phonological changes. It has happened in Polish, Northern Belorussian, Silesian, Southwestern Ukranian (cf. King, 1976); it apparently affected certain Old English fricatives, and just as apparently is happening to Modern English (Labov, 1981). Perhaps the clearest case is German. According to Russ (1978), Old High German had word-final voiced stops in words such as *wib, tag,* and *sid.* In Middle High German these words were spelled *wîp, tac,* and *sît* (with letters appropriate to voiceless stops). In New High German there is alternation between medial voiced and final voiceless stops, now masked through spelling change, as *Tage* (/tagə/) and *Tag* (/tak/). This devoicing of final stops in Middle High German even has a name—*Auslautverhärtung*.

Stopping

German has also undergone a variety of other changes, including certain cases of stopping. For example, Modern High German /d/ is traceable to /ð/, derived from /θ/, spelled þ (Russ, 1978, p. 49). Ferguson (1978a) has described two other cases of /ð/ → /d/—one in Middle English in a post-/r/ environment (e.g., *burden*), the other involving most dialects of Arabic. It is understood, however, that in general, stopping is diachronically rare (Dressler, 1974).

Final Deletion

Hock (1975) has documented a number of cases in which final consonants were omitted, often going first through one or more intermediate stages. For example, Chinese oral stops became glottal stops, which were later eliminated. In Spanish, /s/ was replaced by /h/, which was eventually omitted altogether. Italian and Old French lost final /s/ and /θ/, respectively. In French, loss of final nasal consonants occurred with such generality that it represents a stage in the creation of nasal vowels (cf. Ruhlen, 1978).

Final Fricativization

Hock (1975) has provided a nice catalog of cases in which fricativization has applied, whether to syllable-final forms (Western Romance, Spanish, Greek,

Celtic, Iranian) or word-final forms (Old French, Old Irish, Cornish). Grimm's Law described—for German—the replacement of noninitial voiceless stops by fricatives. Dressler (1974) has indicated that /p/ is particularly vulnerable to this change, possibly because it requires—and in some phonetic environments is denied—high levels of oral air pressure. However, it will be noted shortly that in the context-sensitive (synchronic) rules of languages there is a decided tendency toward the fricativization of *voiced* stops.

Cluster Simplification

Greenlee and Ohala (1980) have listed several languages in which fricative–nasal clusters have been reduced through loss of the fricative. This has left behind, interestingly, a voiceless nasal. For example, the written Tibetan *sna* was expressed, in Burmese, as /na/. Indo-European *sm, sn, sr,* and *sl* in Primitive Greek were expressed as /m̥/, /n̥/, /r̥/, and /l̥/.

Other Changes

Greenlee and Ohala (1980) have identified a number of sound changes that are frequent in both acquisition and language history. It is assumed by them, and by others, that such changes probably have a common motivation. Specifically, the motivation is considered to be phonetic, arising from vocal tract constraints. In their paper, Greenlee and Ohala list the following historical–developmental commonalities:[5]

1. The resistance of initial nasals to change
2. The nasalization of vowels before velar nasals
3. The alternation of /n/ and /l/
4. The replacement of initial /sn/ by /n̥/
5. The tendency for final /nt/ to be expressed as /t/, but for /nd/ to be expressed as /n/
6. The tendency for friction + /w/ clusters to be expressed as a labial fricative (e.g., /f/ or /ɸ/)
7. The tendency for palatalized labials to be expressed as apicals

Clumeck (1979) also has documented (6) in a Mandarin-speaking child who expressed /hw/ as /f/ or /ɸ/, as occurred historically in a number of Chinese dialects.

---

[5]Dinnsen (1980, and in a personal communication) has pointed out that some of these changes are particular to a language. For example, in Catalan a homorganic stop deletion process is characterized by /nt#/ → /n#/.

Who Starts Sound Change?

It is clear that sound change ultimately involves both child and adult, and that many of the historically confirmed cases of phonological change are remarkably like the transient developmental changes of childhood. But, in point of fact, little is known about the relative contributions to sound change of children and adults. Classically, the child was regarded as a perpetrator of change (Sweet, 1888; Sully, 1896), an idea that has subsequently been regarded both favorably (King, 1969; Kiparsky, 1968) and skeptically (Drachman, 1976; Vihman, 1979).

After reviewing some of the parallels between historical and child sound change, Greenlee and Ohala (1980) placed the issue in a sharper focus, and perhaps in a slightly more tractable form:

> What we do not know, and what is crucial to this issue is: once a speaker makes a sound substitution (or 'mispronunciation'), whose speech, child or adult, is more likely to serve as a model for others' pronunciation? . . . We would claim that all speakers, children and adults, by virtue of shared articulatory and perceptual constraints, are eligible to be the initiators of ''mini'' sound changes. . . . But whose sound changes, once initiated, spread to other speakers to become ''maxi'' sound changes, i.e., sound changes proper, characteristics not only of an isolated speaker, but of whole speech communities [p. 14]?

My own view is that the child is both an *agent* of sound change and a *victim* of sound change, a contention I will elaborate in Chapters 5 and 6.

Context-Sensitive Phonological Rules

As we noted in the previous section, the value of historical records is attenuated somewhat by the fact that they frequently are incomplete or ambiguous. Fortunately, the raw material of diachronic change is readily observable in living languages in the form of their context-sensitive rules. From reference sources such as Stanford's *Handbook of Phonological Data from a Sample of the World's Languages* (1979)—hereafter referred to as the Stanford Archive or the *Handbook*[6]—one can determine the phonetic environments in which contemporary languages (i.e., adult speakers) devoice final voiced stops, nasalize vowels, and perform a variety of other transformations from internal representation to surface form. It also is possible to determine the frequency with which similar changes occur over the course of children's phonological development, and, therefore, to

---

[6]The Stanford collection was obtained between 1971 and 1979 under the direction of Charles Ferguson and is based entirely on published materials. The *Handbook's* 197 languages represent a geographically and genetically balanced sample. This reference speaks invaluably to the phonetic constraints and preferences of adults, although one needs to remember that many of the available language descriptions contain precious little phonetic detail and ''do not give a valid indication of the capabilities of the speech production mechanism [Ladefoged, 1983, p. 187].''

observe similarities between the two populations. Adults, by definition, have an established phonemic production and perception capability, so to observe adult–child similarities is to identify developmental errors whose motivation may be explainable in phonetic terms.

For the most part, the allophonic or implementation rules of a particular language simply are those tendencies of its speakers that are sufficiently strong and consistent that they are identified with the formal properties of that language. In context-sensitive rules, the phonetic environment in which the rule applies is explicitly stated. Those phonetic contexts which favor the application of a rule may also be correlated with the acquisition and loss of phonological contrasts in a variety of cases. For example, the phonetic conditions favoring the change $X \rightarrow Y$ allophonically may also be the optimal ones for the earliest expression of Y in children, and the most difficult contexts for the production of X. In cases of loss, whether in an aphasic adult or a dying language, the same phonetic conditions may be associated with the extinction of a phonological segment or feature. There may also be some teaching and clinical implications, with the conditions favoring the application of a rule also constituting the optimal environment for training in sound production.

From an inspection of Stanford's *Handbook,* I have identified some contextual changes that have parallels, under approximately the same conditions, in children's developmental changes. I will present these rules, identify a sample of the attesting languages, and list such environmental details as appeared in the *Handbook* documentation.

Final Devoicing of Obstruents

Table 3.3 shows a listing of 17 languages in which the analysis conducted by field workers contained a reference to frequent or regular devoicing of stops, fricatives, and affricates in the final position of syllables or words. It is difficult to determine whether final devoicing applies more to stops than fricatives, or more to a particular stop, because in many cases there are more stops than fricatives in a particular language, or the stop series is incomplete. For example, Icelandic has a rule that devoices final fricatives, but has no (voiced) stop candidates. In Ket, /b/ and /d/ appear voiceless in final position, but Ket has no /g/ which could undergo this process.

Though some languages have voiced obstruents that devoice *initially,* my impression is that these cases are less common than are the attested examples of final devoicing.

Glottalization of Final Stops

Table 3.4 lists the languages in the *Handbook* that express lingual stops as glottal stops in word-final position. In all cases, the replaced stop is voiceless,

Table 3.3
Devoicing of Final Obstruents

Language	Segments	Notes
Somali	b d g	Expressed without release
Iraqw	ɓ	
Tigre	b d g ǰ z ž	
Wolof	b d g	Expressed without release
Luo	b d g ð j	
Icelandic	v ɣ	Has no voiced stops
English	Voiced obstruents	"Partly or wholly devoiced"
Ostyak	ɣ	
Yakut	b	Expressed without release
Even	ß	
Chukchi	ɣ	
Ket	b d	Has no /g/
Vietnamese	ɓ	
Chontal	b	
Hopi	v	
Wapishana	ʔb ʔd	
Amuesha	ʐ	

and in three of the four it is /k/. This differs from the child data in that glottals are most commonly heard in place of /t/, but agrees with the tendency in children to substitute glottals for voiceless more than for voiced stops.

Voicing of Voiceless Stops

A number of languages produce voiceless stops with apparent voicing in two specific environments. Table 3.5 shows that in most cases the word position is medial, and the candidate either occurs intervocalically or postnasally. In many cases, the nasal is homorganic, but it is difficult to determine whether homorganicity is crucial to the process because heterorganic clusters are not permissible.

That a voiceless stop would appear voiced between vowels is explainable, as

Table 3.4
Glottalization of Lingual Stops

Language	Segments	Environments
English	"Before consonants it is not uncommon in RP to find [ʔ] alone for /tʰ/, particularly if the following consonant is a stop."	
Cambodian	k	Finally
Cantonese	k	Finally
Malay	k	Finally

Table 3.5
Voicing

Language	Segments	Environments
Maasai	p t k	After nasals
Icelandic	p t k	After homorganic nasals
Armenian	p t k ts č	After nasals
Cheremis	p t k č	After nasals
Ainu	p t	Intervocalically, in two dialects
Korean	p t k č	Intervocalically, and after nasals or liquids
Georgian	pʰ tʰ kʰ čʰ tsʰ	Partly voiced in medial position after vowels, liquids, or nasals
	p t č ts	Intervocalically and in clusters when directly preceding a vowel or voiced consonants
		Initial clusters are voiced before or after liquids or nasals.
Western Desert La	p t-laminal t ṭ k	When preceded by a nasal consonant medially
Nyangumata	p t k	After voiced consonants and intervocalically
Kunjen	p t-laminal t	Before a nasal, sometimes following /l, r/
Maung	p t-laminal t ṭ	In prestop position and after nasals
	k	After nasals
Nunggubuyu	p t k	Intervocalic and in postconsonantal position
Alawa	p t ṭ ç k	Most word-initial and -medial positions, and after nasals
Wik-Munkan	p t ç k	After nasals
Ojibwa	p t k č s š	Between vowels, especially after a nasal
Delaware	p t k č .	After homorganic nasals
	s š	After initial /n/
Oneida	t k	Intervocalically; following a vowel, silence, glottal stop; and before /j, l, n/
	č	After a vowel; before /j/ or /i/
		Word initially or after a glottal stop; before /j/ or /y/
	s	Intervocalically; sometimes word initially or after glottal stop; before a vowel
Totonac	p t k ts č q	Between a nasal and a voiced vowel in the same word
Tarascan	p- t- k-lax ts- č-lax	After a nasal (which is always homorganic in practice)
Mixtec	p k kʷ	After a homorganic nasal consonant (t and č excepted)
Campa	p t ç k	After nasals (affricates excepted)
Jivaro	p t k č	Medially, after nasal consonants /p/ may voice before r-flap; /k/ may voice before /m/ and /n-palatoalveolar/
Amahuaca	p t k	Morpheme initially after a nasalized vowel; /k/ is voiced between glottal stop and a vowel and as the first segment of a bound morpheme before a voiced segment.

is the postnasal case, on the grounds of aspiration differences. That is, it may be that voiceless aspirated stops deaspirate and, especially for English-speaking analysts, seem devoiced mainly because nonaspiration is a potent cue to "voicing" in English (Winitz, LaRiviere, & Herriman, 1975). The intervocalic deaspiration of voiceless stops in English is well known (Houlihan, 1982); in fact, in Carterette and Jones's (1974) analysis of conversational speech, /t/ frequently was transcribed as /d/ intervocalically. Following a nasal it is likely that some of a stop's aspiration is lost to the nasal cavity (Ohala, 1983) and, therefore, is imperceptible, or as Malécot (1960) has indicated, the nasal "consonant" may actually be a nasalized vowel and the candidate for "voicing" is intervocalic.

In children, the tendency to *devoice* voiced stops characteristically applies less to intervocalic position, and there is some additional evidence that voiceless stops may appear voiced in that position or after nasals (where the oral air pressure would be reduced, favoring voicing). For example, several children in the Edinburgh study (Anthony, Bogle, Ingram, & McIsaac, 1971) produced *monkey* with a voiced stop [ŋg]. As children's consonant productions typically are not tested in medial position or in phrases (e.g., Prather *et al.,* 1975), or the environment is unspecified (Olmsted, 1971), there are not many other data on this question.

Labialization of /l/

Numerous studies document the tendency of children to replace /l/ with [w]. In Olmsted (1971), 56% of the substitutions for /l/ were [w]. In Snow (1963), 64% of the /l/ substitutions were [w]. According to the *Handbook,* /l/ is expressed as a labialized glide in Kashmiri before /w, u, ū/ and in Hakka before /ɔ/.

Stopping of Continuants

One of the more common types of sound change in children involves the substitution of (usually) homorganic stops for fricatives and, to a lesser extent, nasals. The following is an indication of the percentage incidence of a more stopped substitute (i.e., stop for a fricative or affricate; affricate for a fricative) in the speech of 24–48-month-old children (from data supplied by E. Prather):

	Word initial	Word final
f θ s ʃ tʃ	7.89	2.56
v ð z ʒ ʤ	30.71	8.19

It is apparent from these data that stopping applies differentially to word-initial and word-final positions as well as to voiced and voiceless continuants. The overall ratio of initial to final stopping exceeds three to one (17.8 to 5.1%), as does the ratio of voiced to voiceless (18.9 to 5.2%).

The relevant data in Olmsted are not broken down by word position, but they show 19.9% of the substitutions for voiceless fricatives to be stops, compared to 78.5% for the voiced fricatives. When /ð/ is subtracted, the voiced fricative stopping is reduced to 26.9%. But when /ð/ is subtracted from the voiced fricatives in Prather, the incidence stays roughly the same (32.3%). So it is clear that stopping applies mainly to voiced fricatives in the initial position, less to voiced fricatives in word-final position, with very little stopping of voiceless fricatives in either position.

An examination of the *Handbook* shows stopping to be fairly common in standard languages. Table 3.6 lists the languages that treat stopping as a context-sensitive rule and describes the segments affected and, in some cases, their environments. It appears from the table that across languages—as with children—stopping applies more to voiced than to voiceless fricatives. In fact, this preference is even stronger than the tabled data suggest; voiceless fricatives and affricates are more numerous in the first place, and consequently there are more voiceless than voiced candidates for stopping. Thus, /f, θ, ɸ, x/ are stopped in 1.19% of the languages where they could be stopped, /v, ð, β, ɣ/ are stopped in 7.51% of the languages having those sounds in their segment inventory. The ratio of voiced to voiceless stopping is over 6 to 1, which is roughly the ratio in children according to data reported in Olmsted (1971).

It is not clear from these rules what the precise effect of word position is. Children are more inclined to replace fricatives with stops in word-initial position. If the same is true of adults, it might follow that fricativization should apply more to voiceless stops in word-final position. According to Grimm's Law it does, and in Liverpool English voiceless stops in postvocalic positions often are expressed as affricates and fricatives (Labov, 1981).

Spirantization

Adults are known to replace stops, in certain environments, with fricatives. This so-called spirantization is something children rarely do. But even here one finds a compatibility of sorts—for adults are most likely to spirantize voiced stops in final position, and children are the least likely to replace final voiced fricatives with stops. So even if children tend not to *create* spirants (finally), they at least *respect* them!

I have included in Table 3.7 a list of *Handbook* languages that incorporate spirantization rules for /d/. "Intervocalic" is the environment most associated with spirantization.

Table 3.6
Stopping of Fricatives and Affricates

Segment	Environment	Language
	Voiceless cases	
f	p-labiodental, word finally and before consonants	Albanian
ɸ	p "occasionally"	Hausa
θ	t̪ word finally and before consonants	Albanian
s	ts	Mixtec
č	t^h	Irish Gaelic
	t̪	Ostyak
	t̪ʲ	Even
	t̪ʲ word finally	Asmat
	t̪ intervocalically	Araucanian
	c preceding homorganic affricates, laterals, and nasals	Irish Gaelic
	c⁻ syllable finally	Cambodian
	c	Apinaye
v	b-labiodental, word finally and before consonants	Albanian
ß	b except prevocalically	Atayal
	b following a bilabial nasal	Gadsup
	b after /m/	Digueno
	b after voiced bilabial stop and bilabial nasal	Paez
	b word initially and after nasals	Quechua
ð	d̪ word-finally and preconsonantally	Albanian
	d initially after pause and following nasals and /l/	Spanish
	d following nasal consonants	Mixtec
	d initially and after vowels	Quechua
ɣ	g initially after pause and following nasals and /l/	Spanish
	g except prevocalically	Atayal
	g	Kaliai
	g before a consonant	Dakota
	g initially and after nasals	Quechua
ž	j	Mixtec
ǰ	d	Irish Gaelic
	d̪ʲ	Even
	d̪ʲ	Ticuna
	c⁻ in final position	Khasi

Ferguson (1978a) analyzed these tendencies in six languages and in child acquisition. He also determined that /d/ spirantization is mainly a post- or intervocalic phenomenon. If children are subject to the same constraints, one would predict that children's tendencies toward stopping might first abate in post- or intervocalic positions, that children's [d] for /ð/ may become fricative-like in *mother* before *this*, even if insufficiently so to be heard as a fricative. There seem to be no data on this at present.

As spirantization is patterned so obviously, applying mainly to *voiced* stops in inter- and *postvocalic* position, one might suppose that spirantization can be explained phonetically. In this regard, it is interesting that bilabial stops may be produced with somewhat less labial pressure when they are *voiced* and in inter-

Table 3.7
Spirantization of /d/

Language	Environments
Somali	Intervocalically, especially after a stressed syllable
Maasai	Intervocalically
Sinhalese	Intervocalically
Basque	/d/ occurs initially and after /n, l, r-flap/; ð occurs elsewhere
Yurak	Intervocalically
Azerbaijani	Intervocalically
Telugu	Intervocalically
Maranungku	Intervocalically and after /n/
Tzeltal	Intervocalically, preconsonantally, and postvocalically
Tarascan	Intervocalically
Otomi	/d/ is a stop following nasals, varies freely with fricative allophone elsewhere

and *postvocalic* position (though see Malécot, 1970). In Lubker and Parris (1970; Table 1), the mean pressure values (in cm aq) for three speakers were:

	Prevocalic	Inter- and postvocalic
Voiceless	16.42	15.23
Voiced	16.74	13.30

As fricatives are produced with less articulatory pressure than stops, even small across-the-board reductions in force should spirantize inter- and postvocalic voiced stops while leaving unaffected the naturally higher pressure voiceless stops and initial voiced stops. And as indicated earlier, the allophones of /v/ sound very much like the tokens of /b/, so the spirantized product is likely to be acceptable both to speaker and listener.

Palatalization

There are several context-sensitive changes that occur commonly in adult language but are relatively rare as *error patterns* in child speech. One of them is palatalization (cf. Bhat, 1978). Although there is some frequency of /s/ palatalization in Snow's data (*saw:* [ʃɔ]), children are more likely to depalatalize /ʃ/. Table 3.8 shows the languages and environments in which /s/ is expressed as [ʃ]. In general, it appears that /s/ is palatalized before and after high front vowels, with some exceptions. It would be interesting to determine whether children's tendencies in the opposite direction (i.e., to depalatalize /ʃ/) would be inhibited by this phonetic environment in which adults so commonly palatalize.

Table 3.8
Palatalization of /s/

Language	Environment
Kashmiri	Before /j/ and front vowels
Kirghiz	Initially, immediately preceding /ɛ, ø/
Yakut	Under the influence of front vowels
Gilyak	Before /I, j, e-mid/
Ainu	/s/ has palatalized free variants
Kota	Following /i/ or /ī/ or vowel-plus-/j/
Tagalog	Before /j/
Kunimaipa	Before low vowels

Fronting

Children also exhibit in their error patterns several changes that adults are not known to make allophonically. One such change is "fronting," in which children express a consonant with an atypically anterior occlusion of the vocal tract. For example, children unidirectionally replace the voiced and voiceless linguadental fricatives with labiodental ones. The following chart shows the unidirectional fronting errors for fricatives in 24–36-month-old children (E. Prather's data). Errors of the reverse direction are indicated in parentheses:

	Word-initial	Word-final
/ʃ/ → [s]	.19 (.01)	.34 (.01)
/θ/ → [f]	.35 (.00)	.21 (.00)
/ð/ → [v]	.00 (.00)	.38 (.00)

Note that /θ/ → [f] occurs in word-initial and in word-final position, whereas /ð/ → [v] occurs only in word-final position. The incidence of [d] for [ð/ word initially was .54, and in word-final position it was .14. So in some sense children prefer to stop this particular fricative in word-initial position, and to substitute a more anterior continuant for it in final position.

Children's tendency to front the stops is less clear, partly because the stimulus words in elicitation procedures often include readily depicted objects such as *kite* and *dog*, which allow for assimilation. In Prather's data on 24–36-month-olds, [t] for /k/ and [k] for /t/ substitutions were less than 5% in both word positions, as were substitutions of [d] for /g/. In initial position [g] for /d/ was 14%, but this probably was due to the use of the item *dog*. Olmsted's data are not presented by word position, but they show that [t] for /k/ (.25) exceeds [k] for /t/ (.12), and that [g] for /d/ (.31) exceeds [d] for /g/ (.19). Ingram (1974) suggested that children's fronting of stops may be more likely in word-initial than in word-final position, which I have confirmed in analyses presented in the next chapter.

Other tendencies perhaps more identifiable with children than with adults are the lateralization of /s/ and the labialization of /r/.

Special Populations and Conditions:
Systems Stressed and Speakers Liberated

It is understood that many of the behaviors identified with childhood are not necessarily lost to maturity, but instead become less overt. Consider, for example, the beginning reader's conspicuous subvocalizations during silent reading. As reading facility is increased, the whisperings and lip movements typically become less observable, seem to subside. Since electromyographic recordings show that subvocal articulatory activity occurs in the reading of adults (Locke & Fehr, 1971), it is apparent that the reader's inclination to subvocally pronounce persists, but occurs less noticeably. Subvocal speech may be brought to the surface, however, when the clarity of print is degraded (Edfeldt, 1960), when there is interfering noise in the environment (McGuigan & Rodier, 1968), or when the difficulty of the material is increased (Edfeldt, 1960).

Analogously, the experimental conditions that heighten subvocal speech may be simulated by nature, with attendant exaggerations of vocal speech tendencies. The subject's level of internal noise, the quality of his oral–motor programs, and the difficulty level of to-be-spoken material may be adversely affected by insult to the brain. As a consequence, diminution of cerebral capacity may exaggerate the usually subtle behaviors observable mainly under laboratory conditions in normal speakers.

In this section, I will consider the sound change patterns of adult speakers whose systems have been stressed by alcohol or brain damage. I also will examine some conditions under which normal speakers may be liberated (to a degree) from the motor programs and rules of their language, whether due to slips of the tongue or episodes of protracted glossolalia.

Inebriate Speech

Lester and Skousen (1974) administered alcohol to a small group of adult volunteers who read prepared word lists and spoke spontaneously at several points during the gradual loss of sobriety. From their report, it is clear that many of the alcohol-induced changes were not unlike the allophonic rules of languages and the errors of children still in the process of acquiring proficiency in their native system. One inebriated speaker had numerous devoicings of final obstruents in words such as *tease, bed, dog, judge,* and *hand.* In *tease* he very consistently preserved the voicing–vowel length rule, evoking voiceless percepts by prolonging the devoiced portion of the final fricative. There were several other kinds of change, including the deaffrication of /tʃ/ and /dʒ/. But the most prominent changes, in addition to devoicing, were modifications of articulatory place. All place changes occurred in the production of /s/, which was retracted to [ʃ], with no changes in the opposite direction. This tendency toward palatalization is less common in children, though it conforms to a general tendency of adults to palatalize in slips of the tongue, as we will see later.

Cerebral Palsied Adults

Platt, Andrews, and Howie (1980) and Platt, Andrews, Young, and Quinn (1980) analyzed the speech errors of 32 spastic and 18 athetoid adult males. All had been diagnosed as having congenital cerebral palsy, but with adequate intelligence and hearing. Subjects were asked to repeat 29 CVC words which contained 40 selected consonant phonemes. Confusion matrices of segmental replacements provided for some interesting additional analyses for our purposes. For example, there was considerable omission of final consonants. According to Table 3.9, final consonants were omitted more frequently than initial consonants by a ratio of more than 4 to 1. Of the omitted finals, voiceless stops were omitted more commonly than voiced stops and fricatives of either voicing. It is interesting, in light of earlier remarks about the special vulnerability of /g/ to various weakening processes, that the omission frequency for the voiced stop series was /g/ = 5, /d/ = 2, and /b/ = 0. For the voiceless stop series, the omission frequencies were very nearly reversed: /k/ = 2, /t/ = 6, and /p/ = 5.

One thing is particularly striking about the sound changes of these dysarthric adults. As their intelligence and hearing were within a range adequate for the acquisition of a phonological system, one assumes that nearly all of their errors were primarily the result of neuromotor constraints. Yet their substitutions are

Table 3.9
Obstruent Omissions of Cerebral Palsied Adult Speakers

	Segment omissions	
	Initial	Final
p t k	1	13
b d g	2	7
f θ s	3	8
v ð z	2	7
Total	8	35

Source: From data reported in Platt *et al.* (1980a, 1980b).

Table 3.10
Percentage of 50 Dysarthric Cerebral Palsied Adults Committing Substitution Errors

Word initial			Word final		
w/r	26	P, S[a]	tʃ/ʤ	48	P, S
s/z	22	P, S	ө/ð	42	P, S
f/v	20		f/v	34	P, S
ө/ð	16		f/ө	28	P, S
f/ө	16	P, S	s/z	20	P, S
ө/s	14	P, S	ʃ/s	10	
d/ʤ	12	P	ʃ/tʃ	10	
b/v	10	P, S	s/ʃ	8	P, S
s/ʃ	10	P, S	f/ð	8	
tʃ/ʤ	10	P	v/ð	8	P, S
w/v	8		t/s	6	
ө/z	8		ө/s	6	S
d/ð	8	P, S	tʃ/ʃ	6	P
t/tʃ	6	P	t/tʃ	6	
k/g	6				
g/k	6				
g/d	6	P			
n/d	6				
w/l	6	P, S			
ʃ/s	6	S			

Source: From data reported in Platt, Andrews, Young, and Quinn (1980).
[a]P, also committed by the 24–32-month-olds in Prather *et al.* (1975; raw data supplied by E. Prather); S, also committed by Snow's (1963) 7–8-year-olds.

quite like those of normally developing young children, whose errors have been "explained" as the output of abstract rules and phonological processes (cf. Ingram, 1976; Shriberg, 1980; Weiner, 1982). Table 3.10 lists in descending order the most frequent word-initial and word-final errors, which range from a 48% incidence of [tʃ] for /ʤ/ in word-final position to a 6% incidence of a number of initial and final errors. The greater range of initial substitutions is mainly a reflection of the fact that more initial consonants were tested. In the table, the substitutions also produced by young normal children in two different developmental studies are indicated. Twelve of the 20 initial and 8 of the 14 final substitutions were committed by Prather's 24–32-month-olds (her raw data); 9 of the 20 initial and 8 of the 14 final substitutions were committed by Snow's (1963) 7–8-year-olds.

Table 3.11 shows in descending order the percentage accuracy of production of the consonants tested by Platt, Andrews, and Howie (1980) and Platt, Andrews, Young, and Quinn (1980) across both word positions. The corresponding percentage accuracy also is shown for 2–7-year-old cerebral palsied children (Byrne, 1959) and the normal 36-month-olds in Prather *et al.* (1975). It is obvious that the sounds *spared* by various error processes in the dysarthric adults

Table 3.11
Consonant Production of Cerebral Palsied Adults and Children and Normal Children

Consonant[a]	CP adults	CP children	Normal children
w	94	87	88
m	90	69	100
h	80	72	100
p	87	66	100
k	86	57	100
n	86	70	100
$\bar{X}$	(87.2)	(70.2)	(98.0)
f	86	55	92
j	86	80	100
l	86	32	75
b	84	70	94
ŋ	84	70	94
d	83	66	94
$\bar{X}$	(84.8)	(62.2)	(91.5)
t	80	60	91
tʃ	78	35	69
g	78	59	95
ʃ	75	27	65
s	67	32	85
r	66	27	64
$\bar{X}$	(74.0)	(40.0)	(78.2)
θ	56	16	35
v	52	44	39
z	50	36	38
ʤ	48	33	43
ð	43	36	39
$\bar{X}$	(49.8)	(33.0)	(38.8)

Source: Data for cerebral palsied adults from Platt, Andrews, Young, and Quinn (1980), for cerebral palsied children from Byrne (1959), and for normal children from Prather *et al.* (1975).
[a]Data concerning /ʒ/ were not available on either cerebral palsied population.

also were said more correctly by the normal young children, and that both populations tended to be troubled by the fricatives, affricates, and /r/.

Aphasic Adults

Depending on the nature of the insult, aphasic adults may experience one or more disorders expressed at the phonological level of language. Some patients display either of two types of jargon, "neologistic" or "phonemic." Other aphasic patients may experience mainly one of two types of motor disorders, apraxia or dysarthria. It is not in all cases clear the extent to which any particular patient's pattern reflects aspects of his previous linguistic experience or characteristics of his vocal system.

NEOLOGISTIC JARGON

Some aphasics' spontaneous speech includes a number of neologisms, or nonsensical patterns of sound. Buckingham has written extensively on the nature of neologisms (Buckingham & Kertesz, 1976; Buckingham, 1981), and has attributed their occurrence to lexical (or supraphonological) dysfunction rather than to failures of motor output. Buckingham has pointed out, for example, that lingual apraxia often persists long after neologizing has stopped, and that the phonotactic and segmental characteristics of neologisms typically conform to the rules of the patient's preinsult language. Neologisms also are selective; contentives, especially nouns, are affected more than functors.

Neologisms are relevant to the matter of adult phonetic dispositions because their phonetic form is neither lexically determined nor necessarily tied to motor constraints. Therefore, though Buckingham has shown neologisms to be broadly consistent with phonological rules, a phonetically "elective" flavor is present in neologisms. And the question of what adults say when their phonology is not obviously driven by their lexicon is an intriguing one.

Using the phonetic transcriptions for an American English patient, B.F. (in Buckingham & Kertesz, 1976), and a British patient, K.C. (in Butterworth, 1979), I was able to analyze a total of 373 neologisms containing 1251 consonant sounds. The results are interesting in view of universal phonetic tendencies I have discussed previously and will treat later in this chapter. Table 3.12 shows the combined phonetic inventories of B.F. and K.C. according to a conventional schema and without respect to "word" position.

In Table 3.12 one sees certain trends immediately. In each of the eight voiced–voiceless cognates the voiceless member is of greater frequency, the overall ratio being 2.4 to 1. The dominance of /k/ over /g/ is particularly large (6.4 to 1), as we might expect. It is also apparent that on the average there are

Table 3.12
Combined Phonetic Inventory for Patients B.F. and K.C.

	Bilabial	Labiodental	Linguadental	Alveolar	Palatal	Velar	Glottal
Stops	p (50)			t (98)		k (128)	
	b (24)			d (78)		g (20)	
Affricates					tʃ (17)		
					ʤ (4)		
Fricatives		f (49)	θ (10)	s (132)	ʃ (27)		h (12)
		v (18)	ð (5)	z (62)	ʒ (0)		
Approximants	w (28)			r (130)	j (7)		
Nasals	m (87)			n (120)		ŋ (19)	
Laterals				l (101)			

Source: From data reported in Buckingham and Kertesz (1976) and Butterworth (1979).

many more stops ($\bar{X}$ = 66.3) than fricatives ($\bar{X}$ = 35.0). There is a general trend for alveolar sounds to exceed bilabial sounds, which in turn exceed velar (or palatal) sounds (with the exception of /k/). As in normal language, the nasals and liquids are prominently represented. Generally, one will notice that frequencies conform to child substitution patterns, such as /b/ exceeding /v/, /t/ exceeding /tʃ/ and /θ/, /d/ exceeding /ʤ/ and /ð/, etc. Children's "gliding" of liquids would be an exception.

When neologistic frequencies are analyzed separately for initial and final "word" positions, some interesting patterns become apparent. For example, in initial position /b/ (19) exceeds /d/ (17) which exceeds /g/ (8). In final position /k/ (26) exceeds /t/ (25) which exceeds /p/ (6). Thus the relative "strength" of /b/ and /k/—referred to earlier (pp. 106–107)—seems to prevail in these non-lexical utterances as well. There is a slight advantage of stops over fricatives initially (116 versus 111), and a slight advantage of fricatives over stops finally (99 versus 95). These differences surely are not significant in a statistical sense, but they are interesting in light of the fact that allophonic stopping is more nearly an initial position phenomenon, spirantization a word-final effect. Initial consonants exceeded final consonants (227 versus 194).

Table 3.13 shows in descending order the combined segment frequencies of B.F. and K.C. as a function of the frequency of English consonants in stressed and unstressed syllables (after Denes, 1963). The stress differences are of theoretical interest in that Buckingham and others have observed that neologisms very neatly replace contentives in the spontaneous speech of aphasics, with considerably greater frequency than they replace functors. As contentives are more likely to be stressed, one would expect B.F.'s and K.C.'s segment frequencies to agree more closely with stressed syllable counts, and they do. I obtained a correlation of r = .79 between B.F.–K.C. and stressed English syllables, and a correlation of r = .59 between the neologistic frequencies and the unstressed syllable tabulations. This finding has some intresting implications for the cognitive level at which neologisms originate, as, of course, does the general result that neologistic frequencies agree so closely with lexical frequencies in the native language of the patients.[7]

PHONEMIC JARGON

Perecman and Brown (1981) distinguish phonemic jargon from neologistic jargon: Whereas the latter typically affects nouns and other contentives disproportionately, the former cuts across grammatical categories equally. Perecman and Brown report on an aphasic patient who had phonemic jargon, K.S. The

---

[7]This general result is violated in the case of device-generated neologisms (see Butterworth, 1979, Table 7).

Table 3.13
Frequency of Phonemes in Neologisms of B.F. and K.C. and in Stressed and Unstressed Syllables of English (after Denes, 1963)[a]

		Neologisms		English (%)	
Rank	Phoneme	Frequency	%	Stressed	Unstressed
1	s	132	10.74	9.67	7.39
2	r	130	10.60	4.61	4.63
3	k	128	10.44	7.08	2.76
4	n	120	9.79	11.28	12.29
5	l	101	8.24	6.41	5.92
6	t	98	7.99	13.47	14.51
7	m	87	7.10	5.78	5.21
8	d	78	6.36	7.48	6.49
9	z	62	5.06	3.12	5.12
10	p	50	4.08	4.15	1.84
11	f	49	4.00	3.27	2.52
12	w	28	2.28	4.15	4.40
13	ʃ	27	2.20	.91	1.41
14	b	24	1.96	2.72	1.84
15	g	20	1.63	2.72	1.21
16	ŋ	19	1.55	1.14	2.92
17	v	18	1.47	2.42	3.71
18	tʃ	17	1.39	.79	.45
19	h	12	.98	2.72	2.85
20	θ	10	.82	1.32	.68
21	j	7	.57	1.87	3.17
22	ð	5	.41	1.55	8.15
23	ʤ	4	.33	1.34	.41
24	ʒ	0	0.00	.05	.13
		1226	99.99	100.02	100.01

[a]Denes reported consonants in percentage of *total* sounds (including vowels). I have adjusted his figures to sum at 100%.

speech of K.S. was "clearly articulated, consisting of fluent, voluble jargon produced with an apparent logorrhea [p. 180]." K.S. was tape recorded in monologue and dialogue, and in oral readings of English and German, both of which he had spoken prior to onset. Though K.S. rarely produced a recognizable word, even in naming, his utterances were highly patterned at the phonological (or phonetic) level. Analysis of the K.S. system (from data in Perecman and Brown's Appendix 5) showed a number of agreements with certain characteristics of the neologistic patients, K.C. and B.F. For example, consonant singletons exceeded consonant clusters by a ratio I calculate to be 3.9 to 1. In unit-initial position, stops in one corpus outnumbered fricatives, 171 to 111. However, in noninitial position, fricatives exceeded stops, 129 to 104. This pattern is consistent with the allophonic tendency toward "spirantization" of medial and final stops that describes so many standard languages.

In the largest dialogue sample (their Appendix 1), the incidence of /b/ exceeded that of /p/ by 1.9 to 1, whereas /k/ exceeded /g/ by 1.3 to 1. This conforms to the "strength" scale for voiced and voiceless stops described by Ferguson (1975) and observed in K.C. and B.F.

It is interesting that K.S. also had some segmental preferences that are not easy to explain. For example, among his most frequent consonants was /r/, a preference also observed in French and other English patients (cf. Table 4.5). These sounds typically develop late in children's acquisition schedule, but they tend to be very frequent in conversational speech. This makes it appear that the jargon patients are revealing an effect of "learning" as opposed to an internal phonetic disposition. On the other hand, K.S. also produced /m/ and /b/ with high frequency. These sounds are more rare in English and German conversational speech, though relatively early in children's acquisition. Perecman and Brown (1981) said that "although one might prefer to find a single explanation for why jargon is what it is, it may in fact be the case that some form of the 'nature–nurture' question is as relevant to the study of aphasic jargon as it is to the study of language development [p. 213]."

Before one can understand the segmental contents of jargon it may be necessary to learn why /r/ and /s/ are (*a*) developmentally late and (*b*) conversationally frequent. This—in itself—seems to involve a certain irrationality. But perhaps /r/ and /s/ are not late phonemically, just phonetically, their *articulation* requiring the retroflection and central grooving that are (*a*) *motorically* late but (*b*) motorically inevitable, nonetheless.

APRAXIA AND DYSARTHRIA

In the jargon of aphasic adults we can do no substitution analyses, for the speaker's target is completely unknown.[8] However, there are other brain-damaged patients with severe phonological disorders, whose lexical intentions are known or inferable with some confidence. Johns and Darley (1970) tested the production of 20 word-initial consonants by dysarthric and apractic adults, reporting segmental substitutions in matrix form. Apractic patients made considerably more errors than the dysarthrics, and the two groups differed as to the types of errors committed. Table 3.14 shows the more common singleton errors of the two groups (each making a number of errors in which consonant clusters were created or destroyed). The most common error among the apractics (s/θ) was never committed by the dysarthrics. Though t/θ was fairly common in the dysarthrics, the only error involving these sounds in the apractic group was its reverse, θ/t, which was about equally frequent. The errors shared by the two

---

[8]An exception is Butterworth's (1979) Category 2 neologisms, which are related to a prior or following word, or to an unrealized but highly predictable word.

Table 3.14
The Most Frequent Segmental Substitution Errors of 10 Apractic and 9 Dysarthric Patients[a]

Apractics			Dysarthrics		
Error	N	%	Error	N	%
s/ɵ	17	11.3	w/r	16	11.9
b/v	14	9.3	b/v	13	9.6
tʃ/ʤ	8	5.3	n/m	12	8.9
n/m	6	4.0	tʃ/ʤ	10	7.4
f/v	6	4.0	t/ɵ	8	5.9
f/ɵ	6	4.0	ʃ/tʃ	7	5.2
ɵ/t	6	4.0	ɵ/f	7	5.2
ɵ/z	6	4.0	m/b	6	4.4
tʃ/ʃ	5	3.3	n/d	5	3.7
d/ʤ	5	3.3	v/b	4	3.0
k/n	5	3.3	f/s	3	2.2
w/r	5	3.3	v/f	2	1.5
d/n	4	2.7	p/b	2	1.5
k/g	4	2.7	ʃ/s	2	1.5
s/ʃ	4	2.7	b/m	2	1.5
z/v	4	2.7	d/b	2	1.5
n/l	4	2.7	m/v	2	1.5
s/z	4	2.7	m/n	2	1.5
w/l	4	2.7	n/l	2	1.5

Source: Adapted from Johns and Darley (1970).
[a]Each patient made 15 attempts.

populations (b/v, tʃ/ʤ, w/r) tended, as well, to resemble developmental errors. But there also were a number of featural oddities and reversals of the typical child pattern. Both groups produced n/m errors frequently, and errors such as b/st and st/ɵ. The dysarthrics said [v] for /b/ and [ɵ] for /f/; the apractic patients frequently replaced /t/ with [ɵ]. The dysarthrics in particular seemed to lack velar control, producing a number of /b/−/m/ and /d/−/n/ commutations.

An examination of the most and least frequently erred consonant singletons proved to be interesting. With the exception of /k/ distortions by the dysarthrics, the 10 most frequently misproduced sounds (regardless of the type of error) were identical for the two groups, including /ɵ, v, l, tʃ, z, ʃ, ʤ, s, r, g/. They occur in a mean of 91.1 or 46.2% of the languages in the Stanford *Handbook*. The 10 least misproduced phonemes occurred in a mean of 136.9 or 69.5% of the languages in the *Handbook*. It is clear that there is, as Jakobson (1941/1968) suggested, *some* relationship between the phonological errors of aphasia and the patterns evident in children's development and linguistic universals. What is not evident is the basis for many of the similarities observed here. If English is to some degree "natural," then perhaps even aphasia, as a linguistic disorder, ought not disrupt the "English-like" phonetic patterns of an aphasic patient. Ultimately, the best question is not whether the neologisms of a patient are

English, but whether they are more like English than French and German. This is because it is possible to produce patterns that are permissible (or impermissible) in all three languages. Were a patient set free of the constraints of his language, presumably he would drift in his phonetic output no further than would be allowed by vocal tract constraints. To the extent that his preinsult language conformed to such constraints, analyses would make it appear that the patient was conforming to linguistic rules when he really was just constrained by his articulatory hardware.

But let us examine once again the phonetic patterns of B.F. and K.C. shown in Table 3.12. We saw, among other things, that voiceless obstruents predominated over their voiced cognates by a ratio of 2.4 to 1. What is the ratio of voiceless to voiced obstruents in English, the native and only language of K.C. and B.F.? An analysis of the English frequency data for stressed syllables in Table 3.13 shows that the ratio of voiceless to voiced obstruents is 1.97 to 1. The difference in ratios could be due to sampling error or to an "elective" property of neologisms. Unfortunately, frequency data on stressed syllables seems to be unavailable for other languages.

By combining the Johns and Darley (1970) data with those of Trost and Canter (1974), MacNeilage was able to achieve a single group of 20 nonfluent aphasics with a corpus of 1055 substitution errors. MacNeilage's (1982) analyses turned up some phonetic regularities, especially in the voicing and devoicing patterns for stops. All 32 of the word-final voicing errors involved *de*voicings, with the more interesting cases distributed as follows:

p/b:	3
t/d:	9
k/g:	13

In word-initial position, there were voicing and devoicing errors, but together they show some place agreements with the final errors:

p/b:	5	b/p:	9
t/d:	2	d/t:	2
k/g:	8	g/k:	1

In summary, the nonfluent aphasics were more likely to devoice a stop if it was velar, more likely to voice a stop if it was bilabial.

Slips of the Tongue

We have seen that child *errors* and adult *behaviors* are not always different in kind. They must at least be different in degree, for we tend to notice the errors of children much more than the variations of normal adults. A somewhat analogous situation exists with respect to the so-called slips of the tongue. In spontaneous speech or in reading, we hear others and ourselves commit unintended speaking behaviors. These slips frequently are detected and immediately repaired by the perpetrator. Again, this is not to say that these slips differ in kind from other behaviors on the part of speakers. Rather, in many cases the slip may merely be more noticeable.

In the visual patterns of spectrographic and oscillographic records we see tendencies to deaspirate and devoice that we do not perceive in listening. One of the reasons for these imperceptions is that phonetic categories allow for variation. Perceptual boundaries are drawn—by nature or by language conditioning—with a tolerance sufficient to render most variations undetectable. Any production that strays beyond these perceptual boundaries may be noticed by the listener because of this difference in degree.

The context-sensitive rules of a language are a slightly different case. There, the deviations are conditioned by phonetic environment. As long as they occur only in the recognized environments, they may be detected, but not as errors or slips. One may allophonically devoice the first /v/ in *I have to have it* ([aɪhæftəhævɪt]) but a devoicing of the second /v/ ([aɪhævtəhæfɪt]) will be regarded as a slip, probably a transposition. Hence one may achieve a slip by means of a production that violates either the perceptual boundaries of one's listeners or the phonetic environments in which they expect such productions to occur. Since slips are detected only by ear, it is not known to what extent their analysis tells us about disturbances in the motor programming of speech movements by the speaker as opposed to the perceptual processing of acoustic patterns by the listener (see, e.g., Garnes & Bond, 1980; Tent & Clark, 1980; Cutler, 1981). Here we will consider slips as context-independent deviations that violate the listener's perceptual boundaries for the expected segments.

Due to the vigilance of Fromkin (1973) and Shattuck-Hufnagel (1975), several massive corpora of phonemic slips of the tongue are available for English; some German, Dutch, and Norwegian slips also have been tabulated (Nooteboom, 1969; van den Broecke & Goldstein, 1980; Foldvik, 1979). The dissertation of Shattuck-Hufnagel (1975) is based on 1000 consonant confusions; her later article with Klatt (Shattuck-Hufnagel & Klatt, 1979) is based on 1620 consonant confusions. As these MIT corpora have been rather extensively analyzed at the segmental level, they are useful in examining the relationship between adult slips and child errors.

Though consonants comprise about 60% of the phonemes in spontaneous speech (Mines *et al.*, 1978), they are involved in about 85% of the segmental intrusions. The proportion of children's errors that involves consonants probably runs closer to 95% (or more) in many of the populations that have been studied.

A further similarity between child errors and adult slips is their source. Of the slips involving either anticipation (e.g., *some s paint spent*) or perseveration (e.g., *practical cr– classes*), the majority according to most studies are of the anticipatory type. Though it is true that anticipatory slips also are more detectable (Tent & Clark, 1980), in the London–Lund corpus all slips were *tape recorded*—hence verifiable—and the analysis showed that about 87% were anticipatory (Garnham, Shillcock, Brown, Mill, & Cutler, 1981). From Vihman's (1978) analysis of the assimilation errors of children across six languages, the "corresponding" cases of so-called regressive harmony (e.g., *trolly* → [lɔli], constitute about 67% of the errors.

A major similarity between child and adult speakers can be found in the featural analysis of their errors. Table 3.15 shows the most common intrusions for 23 of the 24 English consonants, in adult slips and in children's substitutions. Of the most common intrusions in the adult slips, 25 share the voicing of the target phoneme. Interestingly, the only exception is /g/ → [k]. In the children's substitutions, 23 of the 27 most common intrusions share voicing. Furthermore, in 15 of the 26 adult slips a place change occurred, as was also the case in 18 of the 27 children's errors.

Table 3.15
The Most Common Consonantal Intrusions in Adult Slips (from Shattuck-Hufnagel, 1975) and Children's Substitutions (from Snow, 1960)

	Most common intrusion	
Target phoneme	Adult slips	Child errors
p	f	t, k
t	k	k
k	t	t
b	v, m	v, p
d	b, z	g, t
g	k	d
f	p	v
v	ð	b
s	š	θ
z	d	s
š	s	s
ž	g	ǰ
č	ts	ts
ǰ	d	dz
θ	s	f
ð	v, z	v
r	l	w
l	r	w
w	r	m, n, r
j	l	l
m	n	n
n	m	—
ŋ	—	n
h	k	—

Table 3.16
Adult Slips Involving Alveolar and Palatal Consonants[a]

Target consonant	Intruding consonant				
	s	t	ʃ	tʃ	ΣX
s		25	68	17	195
t	21		1	14	123
ʃ	33	2		6	50
tʃ	1	4	3		22
ΣX	130	101	81	54	

Source: From data reported in Shattuck-Hufnagel and Klatt (1979).
[a]Totals given include all errors in the original corpus.

There is an important difference in the directionality of errors in adult slips and child errors. Children's errors are highly unidirectional, with many cases of /θ/ → [f], /ʤ/ → [d], and /v/ → [b]. In adult slips, the errors are mostly bidirectional when targets and intrusions are adjusted for their relative frequency of occurrence in conversational speech. That is, even though there are more cases of /θ/ → [f] than of /f/ → [θ] in adult slips, there are more /f/s in English speech. There appear to be two exceptions to this bidirectionality. One was observed by Shattuck-Hufnagel and Klatt (1979), the frequent intrusion of palatal consonants for alveolar consonants. Their raw data appear in Table 3.16.

Using the data of Table 3.16, I calculated the probability of a palatalizing slip using the formula

$$p_{X/Y} = \frac{A + B}{A + B + C + D}$$

where

A = probability of X/Y given that Y was replaced
B = probability of X/Y given that X was intruded
C = probability of Y/X given that X was replaced
D = probability of Y/X given that Y was intruded

Calculated in this way, the probability of ʃ/s was .563. As perfect bidirectionality would yield a probability of .500, the tendency to palatalize /s/ seems slight. However, the tendency to palatalize /s/ by replacing it with [tʃ] was greater (p = .885), and replacement of /t/ with [tʃ] had a probability of .628. These calculations confirm Shattuck-Hufnagel and Klatt's own chi-square analyses which originally suggested a palatalization rule.

Similar calculations revealed asymmetry in the stop series as well. Table 3.17 shows the relevant raw data from Shattuck-Hufnagel and Klatt (1979). Again using the formula, I calculated the probability of a voiced stop replacing its

Table 3.17
The Voicing Substitutions for English Stops in Adult Slips of the Tongue[a]

Target consonant	Intruding consonant						
	p	t	k	b	d	g	ΣX
p		16	31	10	0	1	112
t	22		23	0	9	1	123
k	16	28		0	1	6	90
b	4	1	3		10	11	78
d	0	3	1	14		10	77
g	0	1	10	9	7		41
ΣX	96	101	103	70	75	35	

Source: From data reported in Shattuck-Hufnagel and Klatt (1979).
[a]Totals include all errors in the original corpus.

voiceless cognate. I found that [b] and [d] were more likely to replace /p/ and /t/ than [g] was to replace /k/. The probabilities were:

b/p:	.712
d/t:	.735
g/k:	.410

This finding is exactly what one would expect from evidence, reported earlier, that velars are the hardest to fully voice.

It is interesting that both cases of unidirectionality in the data of Shattuck-Hufnagel and Klatt correspond to sound change patterns attested in adults and/or children. In fact, the correspondences present us with a sort of theoretical puzzle. On the one hand, they argue that unidirectional slips betray a certain phonetic naturalness which is revealed in allophonic and historical change. According to this view, slips represent the inexorable pressures of the articulatory system upon the phonological system. On the other hand, if correspondences between slips and sound change patterns speak to the "naturalness" of certain deviations, why are these deviations so noticeable to the listener—and so extreme—that they are regarded as slips? Speakers commonly delete stops in word-final clusters (pp. 108–112) but listeners just as commonly do not regard them as slips. In fact, I have had difficulty getting listeners to notice them. Wondering why she had so little vowel omission in her dissertation corpus, Shattuck-Hufnagel (1975) commented that vowel omission "is so common in conversational speech that [it] may easily escape notice [p. 31]."

Does this mean that palatalization and stop voicing patterns are unnatural, or that the phonetic environments in which they "naturally" occur were violated in the cases reported as slips? I am inclined to suspect the latter, though it is apparent that such matters cannot be resolved until slips corpora are constructed to include environmental details.

Glossolalia

Glossolalia, often referred to as "speaking in tongues," is a linguistic or pseudolinguistic activity engaged in by members of various religious groups, notably the Pentecostals. Under divine inspiration, glossolalians fluently generate—without previous training, or even, perhaps, example—extended monologue which sounds to others like a foreign language. Although many of the sounds may be familiar, not all are, and the intonation pattern and vocal affect may also seem to be that of a foreign language. Except by occasional accident, not even multilingual listeners hear recognizable words, though all syllables are wordlike.

It is odd that relatively little is known about glossolalia, especially given the large number of people who have produced it (in 1964, Sherrill estimated that there were 8.5 million producers of glossolalia). But as an important aspect of religious ritual, glossolalia, like other practices, is performed privately. It is only because a few speakers have consented to be tape recorded that we know anything about it at all. The following is a sample of glossolalia, from Motley (1967):

travioxóta xiá exítamakapasán denisisiantiáda// ainimóta iamemóte exitakantrao exitakantraviande// livísta lavasiándo/ ↓ nemórta meporpampırándara sontinisisian tiáda/ ↓ kepáltala patrabas tinisisiantiadádeviox\ó:ta// tómoxiada kepáltala patrávo patra patándenisisiantelió// dibóŕnitas ımpiádadevisisiıntadór// patravas timisiantáda dináda

The 60-year-old man who produced that "paragraph" was a monolingual speaker of English, who had never been trained in, or particularly exposed to, any other language. He spoke several "dialects" of glossolalia, each of them fluently, with no obvious pauses or hesitations. This is no small feat, as most of us can do little more than repetitively and gropingly mumble a few phonetically simple syllables.

Glossolalia is potentially of interest in any discussion of universal phonetics as, of all the known kinds of evidence, it probably comes the closest to the case of a healthy adult speaking without a demonstrated need to obey the constraints of a conventionally learned language. Consequently, one can ask unique questions of the glossolalian. We have seen that adults—in their contextual variations (allophonic rules) and their slips of the tongue and their dialect differences—have certain phonetic proclivities. They tend, for example, to devoice final obstruents, to discard or weaken final stops. Ordinarily, there are real-life pressures which block these tendencies from significantly eroding functional contrasts. But in glossolalia, no such pressures apparently exist. What will we find, then, in glossolalia—will we encounter more stops than fricatives, more voiceless than voiced obstruents, more singletons than clusters?

Motley (1967) has fortunately provided us with an extensive and careful analysis of the two dialects of glossolalia produced by the individual mentioned earlier. One of the dialects sounds like Spanish, the other like Russian, at least to those who know those languages. But they are neither, and the speaker knew nothing of either language.

Table 3.18 shows in a conventional schema the actual number of times the speaker produced each of the consonants in the sample, collapsing across the two dialects (whose individual inventories were correlated at .67 for rank-order frequency). It is apparent from the table, as Motley (1975) also observed, that there was a fairly complete inventory of sounds, and that glossolalia may be highly patterned in that some sounds occur frequently and others occur rarely.

Motley compared the frequency rankings for glossolalic consonants to the conversational frequencies in English, Spanish, and Russian. He found, first, that the highest frequency sounds were frequent in all three languages. He found, second, that the overall frequency rankings of glossolalic consonants were not more highly correlated with English values than with Spanish or Russian. Whatever the constraints on this glosslalian, they apparently were not, or were not limited to, the constraints of English phonology.

What, then, of this speaker's phonetic patterning? Motley (1975) reported extensive lists of "morphemes," or frequently recurring phonetic strings. I did a syllable shape and cluster analysis on these 784 morphemes, finding that in only 9 cases (1.1%) did a morpheme end in a consonant cluster, and these were all /rt#/. I calculated from Table 21 of Roberts (1965) that the conversational English frequency of final clusters is about 13%. So Motley's glossolalian took advantage of his freedom to speak as he wished, and did what Guy's (1980) and Neu's (1980) informants did, he "dropped" the stops in final consonant + stop clusters.

In English conversation, about 24% of the words begin with a vowel and

Table 3.18
Consonantal Repertoire of a Sample of Glossolalia

	Bilabial	Labiodental	Dental	Alveolar	Palatal	Velar	Glottal
Stops	p (231)			t (679)		k (242)	ʔ (1)
	b (125)			d (433)		g (5)	
Affricates					tʃ (2)		
					ʤ (0)		
Fricatives	ɸ (0)	f (32)	θ (0)	s (454)	ʃ (229)	x (64)	h (0)
	β (6)	v (295)	ð (1)	z (4)	ʒ (3)	ɣ (0)	
Approximants	ʍ (11)			r (600)	j (7)		
	w (8)			r̄ (34)			
Nasals	m (213)			n (587)	ñ (30)	ŋ (0)	
Laterals				l (180)			

Source: From data reported in Motley (1975).

about 13% end with a vowel (Roberts, 1965, Table 5). In the glossolalia sample, however, about 5% of the "words" begin with a vowel and 46% end with one. Even more than the architects of English, the glossolalian seems to like to begin words with consonants and end them with vowels.

From Table 3.18 one gets a further impression of the glossolalian's segmental and featural preferences. His most frequent class of sounds was the stops (38.6%), followed by the nasals (18.7%), sibilants (15.3%), vibrants (14.2%), fricatives (9.1%), laterals (4.0%), and affricates (0%). This ordering is not greatly different from the universal feature hierarchy which appears in Table 3.19.

The glossolalian's preference for stops over fricatives is evident, the ratio being 4.2 to 1. The ratio in conversational English is 1.14 to 1 (from data reported in Mines *et al.*, 1978). In the glossolalian, the ratio of voiceless to voiced obstruents is 2.5 to 1 for fricatives, 2 to 1 for stops. Note the large velar difference relative to alveolar and bilabial stops.

I compared the glossolalian's segmental frequencies to those of English, and to those of the brain-injured neologizers (B.F. and K.C.). I found that *both* the glossolalian and the neologizers had a lower frequency of /ð/, and a higher frequency of /ʃ/. The former fits with the fact that /ð/ appears mainly in functors; the latter is predictable if, as the slips of the tongue data suggest, palatals are preferred over alveolars.

Phonological Universals

Roman Jakobson (1941/1968) was among the first to take seriously the parallels between children's phonological development and the collective structure of adult languages. Jakobson noted that all of the world's languages apparently possessed stop consonants, though many lacked fricatives, and that children generally acquired stops prior to fricatives. Although Jakobson did not speculate on the basis of such parallels, it is now generally accepted that a sound or a class of sounds would not be strongly represented in the languages of the world if its mode of production were not compatible with the structural and functional characteristics of the human vocal tract (and auditory system).

It may be instructive, at the outset, to ask what a "natural" phonology is like, using adult language characteristics as the metric. From the languages in the UCLA Archive, Maddieson (1980) constructed a sort of modal consonant inventory, as shown here.

p	b	t	d	tʃ	k	g	ʔ		plus
f		s		ʃ					/z/ or /ts/
		m	n		ɲ	ŋ			or
		w	l	r	j		h		/x/ or /v/ or /ʤ/

Table 3.19
Phonological Universals and Children's Production Accuracy

	Percentage of languages having[a]	Percentage of correct production[b]
Stops	100.0	98.5
Nasals	99.6	96.0
Sibilants	90.6	80.2
Laterals	81.7	93.4
Vibrants	77.3	88.4
Fricatives	73.0	73.2
Affricates	69.8	86.6

[a]Based on 693 languages listed in Ruhlen (1976).
[b]Based on 438 children tested by Snow (1963).

There are seven stops, four fricatives, and one affricate, with voicelessness predominating over voicing. The nasals are well represented and so are the glides and liquids. Eighteen of the 20 consonants occur in English as phonemes, the other 2 as allophones. The English sounds not in this modal system—/θ, ð, dʒ, ʒ, v, z/—are exceptionally difficult for children to produce at early ages, and hence would not typically appear in their systems either.

Table 3.19 shows the percentage of 693 languages reported in Ruhlen (1976) having stops, nasals, etc., and the percentage of correct production for members of those feature categories by 7- and 8-year-old normally developing children (from data in Snow, 1963). It is apparent that stops and nasals (i.e., "nasal stops") are more prevalent both for adults and children. Except for the low articulation score for sibilants, and the relatively high one for affricates, the two sets of data agree rather closely overall.

The first column of Table 3.20 lists, in descending order of frequency, the number of languages (of 197) in the Stanford *Handbook* having each of the consonants that also function in American English. The nasals and glides are high in frequency, followed by voiced and voiceless stops, with the fricatives generally (except for /s/) low in frequency. The second column shows the frequency of these same sounds among the 317 languages of the UCLA Phonological Segment Inventory Database (1981). My rank-order correlational analyses indicate a moderate agreement between the two archives ($r = .809$) for the segments of Table 3.20. The third column shows the accuracy of Prather *et al.*'s (1975) 2-year-olds in producing the same sounds. In general, as frequency in the Stanford *Handbook* becomes less, children's accuracy is diminished, though the relationship is clearly imperfect. The Stanford data correlate with child performance at $r = .725$, the UCLA data correlate with children's speech scores at $r = .699$.

If sounds unusually vulnerable to error are less frequent in the languages of the world, it follows that their replacing segments would be somewhat more

Table 3.20
Segment Universals and Children's Production Accuracy at 2 Years

	Universals				Universals				Universals		
	Stanford	UCLA	Children		Stanford	UCLA	Children		Stanford	UCLA	Children
/m/	194	299	89	/h/	147	202	86	/pʰ/	87	82	75
/n/	191	106	91	/g/	142	175	86	/ǰ/	80	80	40
/j/	187	271	75	/d/	141	65	58	/z/	77	36	25
/s/	172	102	50	/š/	123	146	50	/v/	61	67	25
/w/	167	238	100	/č/	116	141	36	/ž/	53	51	0
/l/	155	93	38	/f/	106	135	67	/ð/	33	21	20
/ŋ/	155	167	100	/kʰ/	94	79	89	/ɵ/	22	18	13
/b/	154	199	100	/tʰ/	88	19	82	/r/	12	15	9
%	87	58	80	%	61	38	69	%	24	15	26

Source: Child data after Prather et al. (1975).

Table 3.21
Stanford Archive Frequencies for Intruding and Replaced Phonemes in Children's Substitutions

X/Y	p	X frequency	Y frequency
w/r	.61	167	12
b/v	.60	154	61
d/ð	.53	141	33
d/ʤ	.37	141	80
f/θ	.34	106	22
s/θ	.23	172	22
s/ʃ	.23	172	123
w/l	.22	167	155
j/l	.22	187	155
t/tʃ	.20	88	116
g/d	.18	142	141
s/z	.18	172	172
t/s	.17	88	172
d/z	.14	141	77
s/tʃ	.12	172	116
$\bar{X}$ =		147	91
% =		75	46

phonologically universal. Table 3.21 shows the 15 most common word-initial substitutions in Prather's 24–32-month-old children. In 12 of the 15 cases, the X or intruding segment was more frequent in the Archive, the overall average frequency being 75%. In contrast, the Y or replaced segment occurred in an average of 46% of the Archive languages.

In the two cases in which the intruding segment was actually less frequent in the *Handbook* than the replaced segment, the intruder was /t/. As the American English /t/ is aspirated initially, I took the Archive value of /tʰ/.[9] I am not sure how important the difference is to the present analysis, but if the *unaspirated* cognate is used (/t/ = 177 languages) there are *no exceptions* to the rule, that is, the intruding segment is uniformly more frequent.

The parallels between phonological universals and child phonology have some generality, as one might expect, and apply broadly across children's acquisition of a number of languages. Table 3.22 shows the percentage of languages having sounds which are high in child accuracy (roughly the top third), of intermediate accuracy (the middle third), or low in accuracy for children acquiring English (Prather *et al.*, 1975), Egyptian Arabic (Omar, 1973), Japanese (Yasuda, 1970), German (Möhring, 1938), and Russian (Timm, 1977). It is apparent that the sounds children say the most accurately occur in the most languages.

[9] I have placed the aspirated form in slashes because it is *phonemically* inventoried in the *Handbook*.

Table 3.22
Percentage of Sampled Languages Having Sounds Produced with High, Intermediate, and Low Accuracy by Children Learning English, Arabic, Japanese, German, and Russian

Acquisition language	High accuracy segments (e.g., /m/)	Intermediate segments (e.g., /f/)	Low accuracy segments (e.g., /r/)
English	76	59	27
Arabic	81	43	19
Japanese	64	39	31
German	78	50	46
Russian	68	15	16

Source: Data for English from Prather, Hedrick, and Kern (1975), for Arabic from Omar (1973), for Japanese from Yasuda (1970), for German from Möhring (1938), and for Russian from Timm (1977).

Stopping

Children are notorious for their frequent and persistent production of fricatives as stops, though this occurs more commonly with voiced than voiceless fricatives (at least for the bilabials). The following shows the frequency of b/v in Prather's data on children from 24 to 48 months of age, and in Olmsted's data on children from 15 to 54 months of age:

	Prather		Olmsted	
	N	%	N	%
/v/ → [b]	71/127	56	37/54	69
/f/ → [p]	6/132	5	2/26	8

It is clear that the incidence of b/v is some 8–10 times greater than p/f. As we look in the Stanford Archives at the ratio of /b/ to /v/ in the world's languages (154/61 = 2.52), we see that it exceeds that of /p/ to /f/ (87/106 = .82). That is, on the basis of archive frequencies alone one would predict greater "stopping" of /v/ than /f/. The reason for this disparity is not clear, however. Both sounds are very rare in the babbling of infants, with [v] at about 1% and [f] at less than .5% of the consonantal repertoire at 11–12 months. At the same age, [b] had a frequency of just under 10%, with [p] just under 2%. According to the logic of substitutions described in earlier chapters, [b] would be more available to serve as a substitute than [p]. But additionally, perceptual confusion studies show that /b/ sounds more like /v/ than /p/ sounds like /f/. In Wang and Bilger

(1973, Tables 5 and 7), the confusions in CV position caused by low signal intensity were:

	Set 1	Set 2
p/f	43	28
f/p	16	21
b/v	128	129
v/b	133	143

The sum of /b/–/v/ confusions (533) was five times greater than the sum of /p/–/f/ confusions (108).

Voicing and Devoicing

Ferguson (1975) identified 65 languages that have a stop series, and a voicing contrast within that series, but one stop "missing." The missing element typically was /p/ (27) *or* /g/ (23), less commonly /b/ (4) or /k/ (1). Among languages missing two stops, typically both /p/ and /g/ were absent from the stop series. This suggests, as Gamkrelidze (1978) also observed, that "voicing is best combined with labiality, and voicelessness with velarity [p. 17]."

Ferguson (1975) also observed that Spanish children tend to mirror these universal statistics in their acquisition patterns. From his data, I have calculated that the incidence of b/p substitutions (33%) exceeds p/b (10%), and the incidence of k/g substitutions (75%) exceeds g/k (11%). Macken and Barton (1980a) report that of the 2–4-year-old Spanish children in their study, the initial voicing contrast was first established for bilabial stops; according to their Table 3 it appears that alveolars, as one might expect, were slated to be second, velars third. The same trend is apparent in English-learning children. The following are my calculations, from data reported in Olmsted (1971), of the percentage of substitution of voiced for voiceless stops and vice versa.

b/p	56/89	63%		p/b	10/59	17%
d/t	135/297	45%		t/d	33/112	29%
g/k	45/140	32%		k/g	30/62	48%

There is a regular decrease in the frequency of substitution of voiced for voiceless stops as the place of articulation is progressively retracted from bilabial to alveolar to velar. There also is an increase in devoicing as place is progressively retracted. It is apparent that children's tendency to voice (word-initial forms, presumably) and to devoice (word-final forms, presumably) is closely tied to articulatory place. These data confirm predictions one would make on the basis of phonological universals, namely, that if *children* have an incomplete stop series with voicing contrasts, the missing elements are most likely to be /p/ and /g/.

The rationale for such place-selective behaviors undoubtedly lies in the phonetic domain, with the principal factors being cavity size, air pressure, and passive enlargement of the vocal tract (Ohala & Riordan, 1979). With /b/ we assume that there is relatively little danger of devoicing because the larger supraglottal area—and capability for expansion—can accommodate glottal flow for some time before oral pressure would exceed subglottal pressure (causing the vocal folds to cease vibrating). The relatively smaller supraglottal area for velar stops would make /g/ more vulnerable to this effect. As we saw earlier, this selective vulnerability also is evident in adult slips of the tongue.

Contrasts

Maddieson (1980) has pointed out that languages are very unlikely to contain both /φ/ and /f/, and both /β/ and /v/, because they are insufficiently distinct phonetically to function contrastively. The lack of cooccurrence of phonetically similar segments should make us suspicious that their contrast would be difficult for children to acquire, and conceivably for adults to sustain over the history of the language. Adult perceptual evidence is admissible here, and when we turn to such evidence it becomes apparent that English has some contrasts that are exceptionally difficult to appreciate in the presence of interfering noise or low signal levels. After /w/–/hw/, the two most confusable pairs in Wang and Bilger (1973) are /v/–/ð/ and /f/–/θ/. With slightly unfavorable listening conditions (6 and 12 dB S/N ratios), /f/–/θ/ and /v/–/ð/ were the first and third most common interconfusions. Children also have difficulty discriminating these contrasts (Graham & House, 1971; Rudegeair, 1970; Locke, 1980d), and it is generally understood that even the finest audio equipment may be of insufficient quality to preserve them.

It is interesting to examine the languages that have *both* /f/ and /φ/ relative to the languages that have *either* of the two, and to look as well at languages containing both /f/ and /θ/, /v/ and /β/, or /v/ and /ð/. There are 106 languages in the Stanford Archive that have /f/ in their segment inventory. Of these, 21% also have /φ/. Of the 91 /f/-less systems, 24% have /φ/. It appears that the reason for the scarcity of /φ/ is not the presence of /f/. The same can be said of /f/ and /θ/; 15% of the languages with /f/ also have /θ/, whereas only 7% of the /f/-less systems have /θ/. Similarly, 20% of the languages with /v/ also have /ð/, as do 13% of the /v/-less languages. On the other hand, Maddieson probably was right in suggesting that the phonetic similarity of /v/ and /β/ may discourage their use in phonological contrasts: /β/ occurs in 52% of the languages without /v/, but in only 26% of the languages with /v/.

Some sounds may be essentially uncontrastable. On the basis of frequency alone, the probability of a language having an /s/ is about .87. There are at least five languages in the *Handbook* that have dental /s/. According to the probability figure above, four of the five dental-/s/ languages should also have alveolar /s/. In actuality, only one does, Digueno, and according to the allophonic entry in the *Handbook,* the /s/ is "pronounced with great tenseness, with the apex almost touching the upper edge of the alveolar ridge, which gives it for some speakers a very distinctive 'whistling' quality [p. 429]." It is not known whether this apparently remarkable /s/ was driven to such uniqueness through its coexistence with·dental-/s/, or whether its unique properties allow dental-/s/ to coexist with it.

Syllable Shapes and Word Positions

It has been claimed that all languages have words that begin with consonants, whereas many languages have no words that end with consonants. The degree of preference for initial over final consonants is hard to establish precisely. In a study of consonant *clusters,* Greenberg (1978) reported data on 104 languages. According to my own calculations, 39% had initial clusters only, compared to 13% that had final clusters only.

In the 32 languages in the Stanford *Handbook* that had detailed word-position statements, there were 45 consonants that could not occur initially and 170

Table 3.23
Featural Categories of Impermissible Word Locations for Consonants in 32 Languages

	Word initial		Word-final	
	N	%	N	%
Voiced stops	0	0	42	24.9
Voiceless stops	0	0	37	21.9
Voiced fricatives	2	4.4	18	10.7
Voiceless fricatives	4	8.9	30	17.8
Voiced affricates	0	0	3	1.8
Voiceless affricates	1	2.2	4	2.4
Glides	3	6.7	3	1.8
Liquids	18	40.0	13	7.7
Nasals	11	24.4	15	8.9
Voiceless nasals	1	2.2	0	0
Glottal stops	5	11.1	4	2.4
	45	99.9	169[a]	100.3

Source: Calculated from *Handbook* data.
[a]One sound was unclassifiable by this scheme.

consonants that could not occur finally. Table 3.23 shows the number and percentage of various feature categories which were impermissible in initial or final positions. It is apparent that initial restrictions apply mainly to liquids and nasals, and in no cases apply to the stops. This is in dramatic contrast to the final impermissibilities, which apply mainly to the stops and fricatives, less so to the nasals and liquids. From these data it could be said that the architects of language structure—proficient adult speakers—do not "like" to end words with obstruents, and that their tendencies to avoid word-final obstruents have been formalized. Incidentally, there appears to be a greater restriction on voiceless than voiced fricatives in word-final position. This effect, which is contrary to the stop pattern, is not apparent in the final omissions of children (Prather data), who appear to be about equally likely to omit a voiced or voiceless final fricative. However the ratio of voiceless-to-voiced fricatives in languages of the world, irrespective of position, is about three to one. Consequently, some numerical superiority, as in Table 3.23, might be expected on this basis alone.

As mentioned, the cross-linguistic tendency to avoid consonants is mainly a word-final phenomenon, with relatively few prohibitions against word-initial occurrence. Janda (1979) analyzed the phonetic environments of 250 word junctures from samples of written text in 20 languages. A portion of his data appears in Table 3.24. Note that an overall average of 75% of the words begin with a consonant. Notice that the place features of word-initial consonants have been "selected for." In Janda's sample, the majority were [+coronal, + palatal], followed by [+anterior, −coronal], with back consonants represented the least often in word-initial position. Later (pp. 174–178) we shall return to this preference for front consonants in word-initial position.

Phonotactics

It is obvious that however various systems are structured, there are certain vocal tract limits beyond which the requirements of a phonological or lexical system cannot go. For example, it would be extremely difficult to produce sequences of four tautosyllabic stops, and consequently such sequences are rare or nonexistent. In Greenberg's (1978) analyses of consonant clusters some interesting patterns and permissibilities have come to light. In his analysis of 53 languages with nasal + obstruent clusters, Greenberg found that 33 languages had both homorganic and heterorganic clusters, and 20 had homorganic but no heterorganic clusters; none of the languages had heterorganic but no homorganic clusters. The difficulty we would experience in saying tautosyllabic /np/ and /mt/ (without an epenthetic [p]) may be the cause of their rarity. As we will see later, even in languages in which they do occur, heterorganic clusters are statistically infrequent compared to their homorganic equivalents.

Table 3.24
Percentage of Occurrence and Features of Word-Initial Consonants in 20 Languages

		Features		
	Occurrence	[+coronal] [+palatal]	[+anterior] [−coronal]	[+back]
Hungarian	63	28	24	10
Finnish	76	40	22	14
(Uralic Mean)	(70)	(34)	(23)	(12)
Latin	72	32	23	16
Catalan	74	41	22	11
French	75	45	21	10
Italian	72	43	20	9
Rumanian	82	53	22	6
Spanish	69	48	12	9
(Romance Mean)	(74)	(44)	(20)	(10)
Dutch	74	34	23	18
Old English	83	44	14	25
Middle English	72	36	23	13
Modern English	73	36	22	15
Middle High German	76	50	14	11
New High German	74	44	17	12
Gothic	79	41	19	18
Old Norse	71	30	18	23
(Germanic Mean)	(76)	(39)	(19)	(17)
Czech	84	54	27	2
Polish	82	48	29	4
(Slavic Mean)	(83)	(51)	(28)	(3)
Swahili (Bantu)	90	43	21	26
Yoruba (Kwa)	67	40	17	11
(Niger-Congo/Kordofanian Mean)	(78)	(42)	(19)	(18)
(Overall Mean)	(75)	(42)	(20)	(13)

Source: Based on Table 1 in Janda (1979).

Greenberg also studied the incidence of shared voicing within consonant clusters. His data appear in Table 3.25. Overall, there was shared voicing in 88–91% of the clusters. In the 9–12% of the cases where there is a voicing shift, it also is of some significance that the unvoiced–voiced clusters occurred in the

Table 3.25
Consonant Clusters in Languages Reported by Greenberg (1978) Sharing or Not Sharing Voicing, as a Function of Word Position

	Word initial (N = 1030)		Word final (N = 683)	
Unvoiced–unvoiced	66.70 }	88.35	78.62 }	91.21
Voiced–voiced	21.65 }		12.59 }	
Unvoiced–voiced	10.68 }	11.65	2.05 }	8.78
Voiced–unvoiced	.97 }		6.73 }	

initial position about five times more often than they occurred word finally; the voiced–unvoiced clusters occurred finally nearly seven times more often than they occurred in the word-initial position. These statistics for consonant clusters are very much in conformity with predictions based on aerodynamic principles.

Small Inventory Systems

In previous pages I have documented a number of similarities in the structure and the segment inventory of adult and child phonological systems. And this is remarkable in itself, for the number of segments and the degree of elaboration differ obviously (and by definition) in the systems of these populations. What common characteristics do we find when the segment inventories are similarly small? In a small inventory system, does one see a "childlike" set of consonant segments?

One might suppose that languages originate with highly natural articulatory movements, and that only with external pressures (e.g., increasing cultural complexity) toward an expanded segment base do less natural articulations and units become a part of the system. One might view the small inventory system as equivalent in some sense to the early and still highly natural system. Were that so, one would expect that the very young child's preferences for certain segment types and feature classes (i.e., articulatory movements) might be readily apparent in the small inventory systems of adults. Such a relationship has been imagined since at least the turn of the century, when child speech was compared to that of "primitives" (Chamberlain, 1900, p. 167) or Polynesian peoples (Johnston, 1896).

We saw in Maddieson (1980) that the typical or modal language has about 22 consonants. In my analysis I selected 17 languages from Ruhlen (1976) having 10 or fewer consonants. From Leonard *et al.* (1980) I obtained the segment inventories of 10-month-old children having a dozen or fewer consonants. Figure 3.3 shows the relative frequency of the various feature classes which were common to both populations. In the small inventory languages there is a clear preference for stops, followed by nasals, fricatives, glides, liquids, and affricates. In the child system, stops were even more predominant, followed also by nasals, fricatives, and glides, with some affricates but no liquids. In general, small languages look like small children.

This is in bold contrast to the feature patterns of large inventory systems. From Ruhlen (1976) I selected 6 languages having 53 (Agul) to 84 (Margi) consonants ($\bar{X} = 64$) and tabulated the relative frequency of segments in each of the feature categories examined above. I discarded implosives, ejectives, and clicks, which amounted to 1, 11, and 14% overall. Figure 3.4 shows the relative frequency of the remaining feature classes, arrayed—as in the small inventory systems of Figure 3.3—from stops to nasals, fricatives, glides, liquids, and

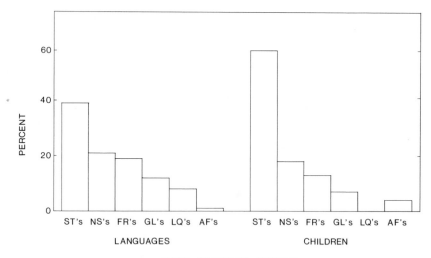

Figure 3.3. *Featural distribution of consonants in languages and in children with small segment inventories (stops, nasals, fricatives, glides, liquids, affricates).*

affricates. However, in the large systems it is evident that such a pattern no longer holds, for the predominant category is fricatives followed closely by stops but with a considerable drop in frequency for affricates, nasals, liquids, and glides. There were fewer than three nasals and two liquids for each of the six large inventory systems. So the expansion of the segment base was created not by drawing equally or proportionately upon the available categories, but by selecting disproportionately from the fricative and affricate categories. I suspect, though it probably is impossible to prove, that the late sounds in developing

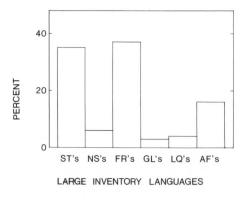

Figure 3.4. *Featural distribution of consonants in languages with large segment inventories (stops, nasals, fricatives, glides, liquids, affricates).*

children also were incorporated at a relatively late stage in the phylogeny of many languages.

Lexical Avoidance in Adults

If there is a relationship between the ease of acquisition of sounds and their universal representation, one might suppose there is a mechanism that allows adults to avoid difficult phonetic elements. Perhaps the most extreme, though—ironically—also the most subtle, way of revealing one's desire to avoid difficult elements is to avoid saying the words that contain them (if such words ever were created "in the first place"). It has been suggested that lexical avoidance occurs in children (Ferguson & Farwell, 1975; Ingram, 1978), but do adults avoid phonologically troublesome words as well? Or do adults merely mutilate and modify, forced by semantic and social constraints to muddle through? Or is the whole question moot as adults have the capability to produce all words in their language and, therefore, no need to avoid?

Ferguson and Farwell (1975) commented that "there are probably different degrees of effort with which an adult acquires new vocabulary items of different phonetic shape; and adults may systematically—even consciously—avoid words difficult to pronounce [p. 434]." I believe Ferguson and Farwell are correct, for there are several different sources of evidence which support their contention. Some of the evidence on adult avoidance is statistical, some is historical, and recently I have obtained empirical evidence from the "confessions" of normal adult speakers.

There is prima facie evidence for adult avoidance in the phonological universals data (Table 3.20), where it is clear that some phonetic elements have been passed over in the construction of segment inventories. There is a similar evidence in the lexical frequencies of consonant sounds in various languages. As we will see in Chapter 4, words containing English /b/ are plentiful, words containing English /ʒ/ are few. Such facts indicate phonological selectivity in the composition of lexicons, hence in the construction of individual words. Beyond this, I will point later to a relationship between lexical frequency in standard languages and phonological mastery in children (Table 4.1). With certain exceptions, the more frequently appearing a sound in the English lexicon the more accurate that sound in children's speech. This implies that languages (i.e., normal adults) and children are inclined to favor and to disfavor the same sounds or movements.

If there is statistical evidence for avoidance in adults, there must be a mechanism for lexical avoidance, and historical evidence of its application by human speakers. Though Malkiel (1964) studied this briefly, the primary work on lexical avoidance in adults, historically, is due to Dworkin (1977, 1978, 1979,

1980). Dworkin specifically identified "phonotactic awkwardness" as the source of a word's disuse and eventual loss from a language. In phonotactic awkwardness, speakers find that because of a sound change, they are left with phonetic sequences that either violate the constraints of their language or are difficult to say. For example, Dworkin pointed to Old Spanish *ruá* ('street') which derived from RUGA when the G was dropped. Though *ruá* was an accepted form in the thirteenth and fourteenth centuries, it faded in favor of the synonymous *calle*. Dworkin attributed the demise of *ruá* both to the phonotactic awkwardness of *uá* and to the availability of a "handy substitute."

The testimony of language teachers also seems to support the existence of an avoidance strategy in adults. For example, teachers have reported the illusion that a class was rather easily developing a mastery of English, only to discover that their students had not yet used certain language structures. This was investigated by Kleinmann (1978), who asked Arabic and Spanish (or Portuguese) students to describe pictures and real-life action sequences in order to elicit their knowledge of four English structures: passives (e.g., *the car was hit by the bus*), infinitive complements (e.g., *I told Mary to leave*), direct object pronouns (e.g., *I told her to leave*), and the present progressive (e.g., *the man is running*). Through separate testing, Kleimann determined that both groups could comprehend the four structures adequately.

On the basis of contrastive analyses of English and the other languages, it was predicted that Arabic speakers would have the most difficulty with passives and present progressives, whereas the Spanish and Portuguese speakers would experience the greatest difficulty with infinitive complements and direct object pronouns. Most of these predictions were realized, for the Arabic students produced significantly fewer passives than the Spanish and the Portuguese subjects, who in turn produced significantly fewer infinitive complement sentences and direct object pronouns than the Arabic speakers. Kleinmann concluded that "second language learners resort to an avoidance strategy that cannot be attributed to a lack of knowledge of the avoided structure [p. 165]."

Recently I broached the question of word avoidance with normal adolescent and adult speakers (Locke, 1982b). Specifically, interviewees were asked to identify any words they avoided because the words were awkward or hard to say. In such cases, subjects also were asked to indicate whether they deployed such "handy substitutes" as abbreviations and synonyms.

A phonological analysis of over 80 avoided words revealed clear and consistent patterns. In fact, the words distributed almost equally into four phonotactically distinctive categories. An /m–n/ category included such words as *seminary, animal,* and *minimum*. Apparently, speakers disturb the order of the bilabial and alveolar nasals. An /r–l/ category contained words such as *burglar, auxiliary,* and *behavioral*. A third category of avoided words was rich in multiple fricatives, including *hypothesis, surrepetitious,* and *thesaurus*. A fourth category contained words with consonant clusters such as *statistics, specific,* and *tachistoscope.*

It would be hard to determine whether words in the four featural categories are less frequent in English conversational speech than words of similar function but of different form. However, one assumes that a speaker avoids *animal* because he has had previous failures with it, perhaps catching himself before, during, or after a production of [aemɪnl]. If so, these feature categories for avoided words ought to be useful in categorizing adult slips of the tongue.

An inspection of Fromkin's (1973) corpus of errors shows that adults do indeed make slips on words similar to those discussed here. Where I found avoidance of /m–n/ words, Fromkin's data include such items as *dynamics →* *dymanics* and *terminus → ternimus.* Where my subjects reported a tendency to avoid words containing /r–l/, Fromkin's corpus includes slips such as *pro-* *toplasm → plotoprasm* and *peculiarity → pecuriality.* Where my subjects avoid-ed a number of multiple fricative words, Fromkin's list of slips includes *Athabaskans →* [æskəbæɵkənz], *philosophy → phisolophy,* and *paraphasias →* *farapasias.* Finally, the consonant cluster category is also represented in Fromkin's corpus of slips, e.g., *fixed →* [sɪkst], *whisper → whipser,* and *discon-* *tinuous constituent → disconstinuous.* Consequently, it appears that normal adult speakers observe the malfunction of their vocal tract, identify the words associ-ated with such malfunction, and consciously strive to avoid its recurrence by eliminating the use of such words.

4

The Phonetic Nature
of Phonemic Segments
and Phonological Rules

In Chapter 3 we saw numerous correspondences between the phonetic patterns of infant babbling, child phonological development, and the speech of adults who represented a number of disparate languages in a variety of speaking conditions. The adult evidence included field studies of conversational speech habits and laboratory analyses of careful speech. It included the characteristics of special populations, such as the brain injured; special conditions, such as inebriation; and special modes, such as glossolalia. The adult evidence also included the context-sensitive rules of contemporary languages and the patterns of sound change documented historically.

The Phonetics of Phonologies

As there is so much congruity of surface patterning—across so many different populations and conditions—it would seem that speakers' underlying phonetic forces are powerful enough to be reflected, additionally, in the present structure of languages considered from *within*. That is, if adult speakers "prefer" stop consonants to the extent that all known languages have them (Table 3.19), then it would be ironic indeed were stop consonants used only sparingly in the lexicons of the individual languages that do have them.

It is understood that following the devoicing of final obstruents most of the dialects of German no longer had *any* words that ended with voiced obstruents.

But what of the languages that underwent no devoicing? Might they still not have "disfavored" such contrasts, either "originally" or over the centuries of their history? One assumes that phonetic forces, however subtle at any given point in time, are always present (as *physiological* forces), and are potentially telling. The net effect of such perpetual forces ought to be a skewing in human languages, and in directions predictable from a knowledge *either* of language ontogeny in the child or language phylogeny in social communities.[1]

I assume that what Dworkin (1979) documented in a few cases—complete loss of a word purely due to phonetic "awkwardness"—is true on a less dramatic but more general scale. Certain constructions, rather than being totally expunged from the lexicon, probably were never created in the first place, or having been invented, are few in number and steadily diminishing. Whatever the precise reasons, such separate or interactive forces are revealed—by implication—in the structure of the current lexicon of a language. If my assumptions are correct, the developmental implications are considerable. For if phonological segments and rules can be so "natural," it must be difficult indeed to know when a child has "acquired" a rule, "learned" an articulation, or "avoided" a word. Such phonological naturalness may blur the separate contributions of biologically innate mechanisms, environmental stimulation, and their modes of interaction.

Avoidance

The term *avoidance* has been used (cf. Ingram, 1978) to label or to explain a child's apparent lack of attempts at words containing sounds he seems unable to produce. For example, between the ages of 1:4 and 1:10 Daniel Menn attempted no words whose standard forms contained fricatives, though he did produce words containing other consonants (Menn, 1971). Tacitly, it is assumed that Daniel knew about words containing fricatives and intentionally avoided saying these words because he knew he could not say fricatives. It also is possible that Daniel knew about words that contained fricatives, but did not know *enough* about them to attempt a replication. As far as I know, this perceptual hypothesis

[1] I am not arguing that all aspects of every phonological system are to be understood in phonetic terms, that there is no arbitrary sense to segment inventories and phonotactic rules. Even if the sound system of a language were phonetically natural in the formative stages, a variety of nonphonetic changes would occur to obscure and to reduce the naturalness. In fact, this may be the fate of all languages. Frishberg (1979) has observed a number of changes in the gestural units of American Sign Language from the early part of this century to today. She concluded that "in general, when signs change, they tend strongly to change away from their imitative origins as pantomimic or iconic gestures toward more arbitrary and conventional forms [p. 70]." We also know of "natural" sound changes which, according to phonetic theory, ought to occur with great frequency but for some reason do not (Houlihan, 1982).

has received no consideration, nor has any conceptualization of avoidance either been reasoned or tested.

Before we can explain why avoidance occurs we must document it more carefully in additional cases.[2] In order to do this we will need reliable methods for determining what the child knows. In this regard, it may be helpful to ask what the child has been exposed to. A start may be to ask, how well represented are fricative words in the *adult* lexicon?

I will develop this question further in a moment, but first let us consider another group, the 3–6-year-old deaf children whose babbling was analyzed by Sykes (1940). They had a very marked "preference" for certain sounds and an equally apparent "avoidance" of others. But since they could not hear, hence, target for specific sound patterns, one assumes they merely produced movements that were kinesthetically pleasurable or motorically natural. They might not have attempted certain articulations, but they need not have *avoided* them not to have produced them. Columns 1–3 of Table 4.1 show the syllable-initial frequency data reported by Sykes. I have listed the consonants in descending order in four groups of six each. The most frequent 6 consonants account for 78% of the total, the most frequent 12 consonants for 97%. One may note that with the exception of /h/, which has questionable *articulatory* status, the fricatives sum at less than 3%, compared to 54% for the stops and 18% for the nasals. The data in column 4 suggest that hearing children prefer to *say* what deaf children prefer to *babble*. It is apparent, from these data reported by Olmsted (1972) on the speaking of normal children, that some sounds (i.e., words containing certain sounds) are attempted frequently, others only rarely. Moreover, it is apparent that the six most frequent sounds in deaf children's babbling also are less avoided (16%) than the second (21%), third (29%), and fourth (34%) sets of consonants. In the following column one can see that this increasing tendency to avoid is associated with a decreasing tendency to produce sounds correctly. So whatever motivates the child's avoidance, it is apparently not pursued with great consistency or vigor, as certain highly avoided segments such as /v/ are produced inaccurately when they are *not* avoided.

We come now to the last and most interesting columns of Table 4.1, which report the corresponding word-initial data for English. The first of these two columns shows the number of monosyllabic words in the English lexicon in which each sound occurs word initially, and the second lists the number of different words of any syllable length in which each sound occurred word initially in discourse elicited from an adult speaker (with over 10,000 words in the corpus). As one looks down these columns, with the decrease in babbling and the increase in avoidance one also sees a fairly regular diminution in lexical representation. Words beginning with /b/ are not avoided by children and they have

---

[2]The paradigm used by Leonard *et al.* (1981) may be more helpful than naturalistic studies.

Table 4.1

Phoneme Frequency in Deaf Children's Babbling, Percentage "Avoidance" in Normal Children, Percentage Correct in Normal Children, Number of Monosyllables in English Lexicon, and Number of Different Words in an English Speech Sample

Sound	Deaf babbling		Percentage avoidance	Percentage correct	English monosyllables	Adult corpus
	N	$\%$				
b	483	36.9	14.3	83.7	711	392
m	184	14.1	26.7	65.4	491	438
j	128	9.8	64.3	22.4	218	78
d	81	6.2	20.4	70.4	492	567
h	75	5.7	15.3	66.3	555	342
w	69	5.3	43.9	44.9	582	257
	$\Sigma X =$	78.0	$X = 30.82$	58.85	508.17	345.67
			$\% = 16.35$	43.44	34.75	32.11
g	68	5.2	45.9	44.9	337	126
l	61	4.7	39.4	29.3	538	344
n	47	3.6	42.9	46.9	329	206
p	41	3.1	34.7	43.9	540	448
t	20	1.5	26.5	48.0	480	272
f	15	1.1	42.9	47.9	458	398
	$\Sigma X =$	19.2	$X = 38.72$	43.48	447.00	299.00
			$\% = 20.53$	32.10	30.57	27.78
k	9	.7	9.2	71.4	571	722
v	8	.6	92.9	3.0	186	148
ð	6	.5	15.3	9.2	44	36
θ	5	.4	74.5	4.1	100	52
r	5	.4	91.3	2.9	586	636
ŋ	1	.1	43.9	19.4	110	12
	$\Sigma X =$	2.7	$X = 54.52$	18.33	266.17	267.66
			$\% = 28.92$	13.53	18.20	24.86
s	1	.1	29.6	31.6	529	624
tʃ	1	.1	65.3	12.3	244	105
ʤ	0	0	61.2	15.3	288	108
z	0	0	88.8	4.1	87	4
ʃ	0	0	42.9	25.5	289	105
ʒ	0	0	99.0	0	8	39
	$\Sigma X =$	.2	$X = 64.47$	14.80	240.83	164.17
			$\% = 34.20$	10.93	16.47	15.25

Source: Data for deaf babbling from Sykes (1940, Table 5), for percentage avoidance from Olmsted (1972, Tables 38 & 44), for percentage correct from Olmsted (1971, Tables 38 & 44), for English monosyllables from Moser (1969), and for adult corpus from Roberts (1965).

Note: All sounds were in initial position, except /ŋ/ and /ʒ/.

not been avoided by adults, that is, by the language. Words beginning with /θ/ are avoided by children and they also have been avoided by adults. For monosyllabic words in the English lexicon, the percentage representation goes from 35 for the six more frequent consonants to 31, 18, and 16. For all words in the corpus of the adult speaker, the percentage representation goes from 32 to 28, 25, and 15.

As child accuracy declines with lexical representation, one might expect to find a series of correspondences between the patterns of children and the patterns of language. For example, we know that in child language singletons are more frequent than clusters, stops exceed fricatives, final voiceless stops are more common than voiced stops. Are these trends also embodied in the internal structure—the "phonostatistics"—of languages? Is there a degree of isomorphism between what speakers would physiologically "like" to do and what their language phonologically insists that they do?

Final Consonant Deletion

Surely one of the more compelling patterns in the babblings of infants, the speech of children, and the structure of the world's languages involves the preference for open syllables. Where there are closed syllables, final weakening processes (cf. Hock, 1975) tend to be constantly at work to increase the stock of vowel-final words.

ENGLISH

In English, the monosyllabic lexicon contains at least 13,907 entries (Moser, 1969). Of these, over 90% begin and end with a consonant, so we surely cannot claim that open syllable words are more common than closed ones. But there are some subtle effects. There are 660 words that end with a vowel but 556 that begin with one. For the 19 consonants that can begin or end English words (and allow, therefore, for direct comparisons), the data show a marked favoring of CV over VC syllable shapes. If we look separately at the 7 consonants that serve as grammatical suffixes (/r, l, d, t, s, v, z/) and, therefore, inflate /C#/ figures, we see that the initial and final means for these consonants are nearly identical at 414 and 409, respectively. The remaining 12 consonants are considerably more frequent in the word-initial ($\bar{X} = 367$) than in the word-final ($\bar{X} = 211$) position. But we have already seen that just slightly more words end in vowels than begin with them, so what kinds of sounds make up the difference in initial and final consonants? Obviously, it has to be consonant clusters, and in fact there are 175 different word-final clusters in Moser's monosyllabic lexicon, and just 52 different word-initial consonant clusters.

The Moser data are not supported by Roberts's (1965) tabulations of his adult speaker, in whom the number of different VC syllables exceeded the number of different CV syllables by nearly two to one (from his Table 5). This discrepancy between Moser and Roberts is a discrepancy between monosyllabic words and words of all lengths. One may extrapolate a bit and assume that truly final (i.e., word-final) position is more likely to be open than syllable final–word medial, which is logical on phonetic grounds.

FRENCH

Tabulations of the frequency of French consonants and vowels (Juilland, 1965) show that in running text vowels constitute 70.4% of the word-final sounds but only 16.4% of the word-initial sounds. The ratio of *consonants to vowels* is 5.08 to 1 in the word-initial position; the ratio of *vowels to consonants* is 2.37 to 1 word finally.

GERMAN

King (1966) drew 5000 phonemes from each of three German texts and determined the frequency of each "sound." From his word initial and final data, I calculated the absolute and relative frequency of consonants and vowels. Though the trend is less dramatic than French, the results showed that German consonants favor the word-initial position over the final by a ratio of 1.08 to 1. Vowels favor the final position over the initial by a ratio of 1.13 to 1.

Cluster Reduction

The tendency for infants to produce singletons over clusters is well known (Oller *et al.*, 1976). In the babbling of 3–6-year-old deaf children, Sykes (1940) counted 1438 singletons and just 6 clusters (and 5 of these were consonant + glide clusters). The tendency for children to "simplify" or to reduce clusters is very powerful and traceably cross-linguistic (Chervela, 1981).

ENGLISH

Of the consonant-initial English monosyllables, 66% begin with a singleton, 34% with a cluster. In word-final position, clusters predominate, but this is only due to suffixing of grammatical markers (t, d, s, z). When clusters ending in these sounds are isolated from the lexicon and only stem-final comparisons are made, 82% of the monosyllabic words are seen to end in singletons, 18% to end in clusters.

Roberts (1965, Table 5) lists the 21 canonical forms which represent 75% of all the words in his sample. It is apparent from his syllable shape tabulation that singletons have only a slight edge over clusters in word-final position (51 versus 49%) but greatly predominate in word-initial position, where they represent 93% of all consonant-initial forms.

FRENCH

Working from the "Dernier Diphone" tabulations of Appendix II of Juilland (1965), I calculated that 73.7% of the French words ending in a consonant terminate in a singleton, compared to 26.3% which end in consonant clusters. In French, the marking system requires no suffixing, so these figures should represent stem-final consonants in all cases.

Malécot (1974) surreptitiously recorded 50 half-hour conversations and achieved a tabulation of 64,976 consonant singletons and 7910 consonant clusters in initial and final word positions. According to my calculations, 88% of the word-initial consonants were singletons, as were 92% of the word-final consonants.

CHEREMIS

Some consonant singleton and cluster tabulations are available (Ristinen, 1960) on Eastern Cheremis, a language of the Uralic family spoken in east central Russia. According to my calculations, there were 12,038 consonant singletons in the sample, but only 174 initial and final clusters (abutting medial consonants were considered sequences rather than clusters). Singletons, then, constitute 98.6% of the consonants in the sample. If medial sequences (1569) are counted as clusters, singletons constitute 88% of the consonants.

Initial Voicing

The tendency of children to voice (or deaspirate) initial voiceless stops is well known, having been documented both in English (Macken & Barton, 1979) and in Spanish (Ferguson, 1975). At the earliest stages of acquisition, phonemically voiced and voiceless stops are produced with a short lag (Kewley-Port & Preston, 1974), as are nearly all the syllable-initial stops of prelexical infants (Enstrom, 1982). This tendency of children to voice initial stops is more apparent for bilabial than for alveolar and for velar places of articulation, as our earlier analyses of Olmsted's (1971) data showed.

My inspection of the English lexicon (Moser, 1969) and French text frequencies (Julliand, 1965) has shown similar trends for the initial position of standard lexical items:

	Bilabial			Alveolar			Velar		
	/b/	/p/	%/b/	/d/	/t/	%/d/	/g/	/k/	%/g/
English	711	540	57	492	480	51	377	571	37
French	111	187	37	723	2766	21	138	1398	9
Prevoicing			(56)			(50)			(39)

From these data it is apparent that both languages have a trend for more voicing of bilabials relative to alveolars and to velars, even though French is less inclined toward stop voicing than is English. Just below the French figures I have placed in parentheses the percentage of word-initial /b/s, /d/s and /g/s that were *prevoiced* in Smith (1978a). The figures nearly match those from the English lexicon, and further serve to illustrate the compatibility between phonetic factors and phonological structures.

Final Devoicing

We have seen throughout the earlier portions of this book that the tendency toward devoicing of final obstruents is exceptionally common whether in children, brain-damaged adults, or in the allophonic rules and historical developments of established languages. And the sensitivity of this to articulatory place parallels the trends indicated in the preceding paragraph for initial voicing: /g/ devoices more frequently than /d/ and /b/. This tendency is reflected in the relative frequencies of these word-final segments in the French lexicon (Juilland, 1965) which, unlike English, is uncontaminated by the grammatical suffixing of stops:

Bilabial			Alveolar			Velar		
/b/	/p/	%/b/	/d/	/t/	%/d/	/g/	/k/	%/g/
62	105	37	492	2503	16	59	1101	5

A position-independent analysis of such place patterns show how strong the bilabial–alveolar–velar trend is across languages. Table 4.2 shows relative frequency data from six languages. The data represent text or conversational frequency rather than dictionary frequency. In Bengali (Ferguson & Chowdhury, 1960, see also Chatterji, 1926) the trend is strong for both the unaspirated and the aspirated stop series. Across all six languages, the mean percentage voiced is labial–58, alveolar–38, velar–19. There can be little doubt that the phonological structure of languages reflects the anatomy and physiology of the human vocal tract!

Stopping

The tendency toward the stopping of fricatives and affricates is common developmentally and in the error patterns of phonologically disordered children.

Table 4.2
Stop Frequency (in Percentages) in Six Languages, and Percentage of Each Articulatory Place Occupied by Voiced Items

	/b/	/p/	%/b/	/d/	/t/	%/d/	/g/	/k/	%/g/
Bengali									
Unaspirated	4.40	1.73	72	2.82	3.87	42	2.83	6.54	22
Aspirated	.84	.21	80	.42	.52	45	.25	2.06	9
Spanish	4.54	3.59	56	3.35	3.83	47	.72	3.83	16
English	3.24	3.07	51	5.70	9.88	37	2.02	5.30	28
Japanese	.94	0	100	1.30	6.19	17	.13	4.20	3
Kaiwa	5.08	4.69	52	2.58	3.46	43	.25	3.42	7
Swedish	1.30	1.40	48	5.10	6.70	43	1.70	3.50	33
$\bar{X}$	2.91	2.10	58	3.04	4.92	38	.99	4.12	19

Source: Data for Bengali from Ferguson and Chowdhury (1960), for Spanish from Motley (1975), for English from Mines, Hanson, and Shoup (1978), for Japanese from Bloch (1950), and for Kaiwa and Swedish from Sigurd (1968).

In babbling, Oller *et al.* (1976) found that 91% of all initial obstruents were stops. In deaf children's babbling (Sykes, 1940), 95% of all syllable-initial obstruents were stops, though in final position 51% were fricatives. Ingram (1978) recognized stopping as the third stage of fricative acquisition, coming between segment omission and continuant substitution. All four Japanese 5-year-olds seen by Nishimura (1980) were consistently guilty of stopping. Among the 438 normally developing children seen by Snow (1963), the ratio of word-initial to word-final stopping was, by my calculations, roughly two to one.

Among adults, on the other hand, there is much less of a tendency to stop fricatives in the word-initial position. But in final position there frequently is some tendency toward the reverse, that is, toward "spirantization." It is of interest, therefore, to witness *both* tendencies in Table 4.3. This table shows the conversational proclivities of word-initial and word-final stops and fricatives for French (Malécot, 1974) and for English (Roberts, 1965). In the French data, it is clear that stops exceed fricatives in word-initial position, but the reverse is true

Table 4.3
French and English Conversational Frequencies for Initial and Final Stops and Fricatives

	Stops	Fricatives
French		
Initial	21,138	15,011
Final	4033	9466
English		
Initial	2527	1367
Final	1384	1081

Source: French data from Malécot (1974); English data from Roberts (1965).

finally. This, then, is consistent both with child and adult sound change patterns. The English trends reveal more stops than fricatives in both positions, though the ratio is larger initially (1.8:1) than finally 1.3:1).

Fronting

Oller *et al.* (1976) observed that among the nasals and obstruents in the babbling of normal infants, there were 351 apicals but only 83 dorsals. Deaf children's babbling (Sykes, 1940) also shows a preference for sounds produced in the front of the mouth over middle and back sounds. The data from Sykes (1940) for voiced stops, voiceless stops, and nasals are remarkably regular:

	Bilabial	Alveolar	Velar
Voiced stops	493	81	68
Voiceless stops	48	20	10
Nasals	228	58	4
Total	769	159	82
Percentage	76	16	8

In children's errors, there are—in truth—few cases where a bilabial replaces an alveolar, so the designation "fronting" is too undifferentiated as it stands. I have listed in Table 4.4 two frontings involving the stops, two involving fricatives, and one involving nasals. Each is fairly common at one stage or another in normal children's acquisition of English, and each may persist as part of a pattern of disorder. In the five columns of the table are the relative frequencies of the

Table 4.4
Conversational Frequency of Intruding and Target Consonants, as Occur in Children's Fronting Errors, in Five Languages

	German (%)	French	Japanese	English (%)	Czech
t/k	8.152/2.073	10,242/8196	617/418	9.88/5.30	3616/2739
d/g	4.593/2.399	8085/1069	130/13	5.70/2.02	2157/160
s/ʃ	3.313/1.726	12,293/891	252/189	7.88/.95	2720/988
z/ʒ	2.133/0	4133/3508	22/0	4.70/.15	1296/839
n/ŋ[a]	10.432/.493	5566/31	347/130	11.49/1.85	4114/1681
$\bar{X}$	5.725/1.338	8064/2739	274/150	7.93/2.05	2781/1281
Ratio	4.3:1	2.9:1	1.8:1	3.9:1	2.2:1

Sources: German data from King (1966), French from Malécot (1974), Japanese from Bloch (1950), English from Mines *et al.* (1978), and Czech from Kucera and Monroe (1968).
[a]In Czech, the closest equivalent to /n/ is /ɲ/.

nearest equivalent sounds in German, French, Japanese, English, and Czech. In all 25 comparisons, the intruded consonant is more frequent in conversation than the replaced consonant, and the overall ratios of intruders (alveolars) to targets (postalveolars) varies from 1.8 to 1 for Japanese to 4.3 to 1 for German.

Gliding

The phonological pattern termed "gliding" (or, sometimes, "liquidation") refers to the replacement of liquids (/r, l/) with glides (/w, j/). It is exceedingly common in children, with [w] replacing both /r/ and /l/ and with [j] replacing /l/. But, unlike our previous cases, in adult languages there appears to be a *preference* for the liquids, or at least a form of /r/. Recall, first, that Maddieson's (1980) modal inventory (p. 141) included all four sounds, that is, did not exclude the liquids. Second, for English, both conversational (Mines et al., 1978) and lexical (Roberts, 1965) counts show /r/ to exceed /l/, /w/, and /j/, which take that order. Many other languages do not have all four sounds, so complete comparisons are not always possible. But Bengali (Ferguson & Chowdhury, 1960), Kaiwa and Swedish (Sigurd, 1968), Cheremis (Ristinen, 1960), Indonesian (Altmann, 1969), German (King, 1966), and Chontal (Yegerlehner & Voegelin, 1957) all show a greater frequency for their variant of /r/ than whichever of the other three sounds they may have.

This adult preference for /r/ is even observable in the neologisms of aphasics and the output of glossolalians. Table 4.5 shows the relative frequency of the liquids and glides in English, and in the neologisms of two monolingual English aphasics; corresponding data are presented for conversational French and for "neologistic French." In the sixth column is shown the relative frequency of the liquids and glides in the glossolalia of a monolingual English speaker. In all

Table 4.5
Frequency of Liquids and Glides in English; in the Neologisms of Two Monolingual English Aphasics; in French; in the Neologisms of French Aphasics; and in the Glossolalia of a Monolingual English Speaker

	English	English aphasics		French	French aphasics	English glossolalic
		K.C.	B.F.			
/r/	6.61	19.71	9.28	12.93	14.5	13.40
/l/	6.21	9.74	7.51	10.13	9.5	4.02
/w/	4.74	3.67	1.03	2.09	0	.18
/j/	1.87	1.22	0	2.99	5.5	.16

Sources: English frequencies from Mines *et al.* (1978), French from Malécot (1974); frequencies for K.C. from Butterworth (1979) and for B.F. from Buckingham and Kertesz (1976); French aphasic frequencies derived from Lecours and Lhermitte (1972, Figure 9); English glossolalic frequencies calculated from transcriptions in Motley (1975).

Note: I am indebted to Jodi Feiner for assistance in the tabulation of neologistic data.

cases it is evident that the frequency of /r/ is increased over the modal conversational values, and that the frequency of /r/ exceeds that of /w/, its most common intruder in child language.

So we have a glossolalian who apparently had a normal vocal system, and who observably produced an exceptional range of phonetic forms. And we have several aphasics, in two languages, who may have had a freedom of phonological "choice" not enjoyed by the more lexically constrained nonaphasic. From these cases, one gets the impression that left to their own resources, adult speakers really would rather say /r/. This, to a lesser extent, is what their language encourages them to do anyway.

Consonant Harmony (Assimilation)

Consonant harmony and contiguous assimilation have been observed in the developing phonological systems of children acquiring English (Menn, 1971; Smith, 1973) and a variety of other languages (Lewis, 1936; Vihman, 1978). Though Vihman doubts Smith's statement that consonant harmony is developmentally "universal," she does allow that it is "widespread." In contrast, Vihman has pointed out that consonant harmony in adult languages is relatively rare. Of the 850 rules in the Stanford *Handbook,* only 4 have anything to do with harmony (Drachman, n.d., has also referred to this child–adult disagreement). I should like to suggest that this is because the lexicons of adult languages already reflect considerable "built-in" consonant assimilation.

PRENASALIZED STOPS

We may start by examining the incidence of homorganicity in languages that have prenasalized stops, such as /^{m}b/, /^{n}d/, and /^{ŋ}g/. Of the 700 languages in Ruhlen (1976), I found 68 that have prenasalized stops. Table 4.6 shows the breakdown by place of articulation. In general, the prenasalization of voiced stops is considerably greater than the prenasalization of voiceless stops, the ratio

Table 4.6

Distribution of 230 (Homorganic) Prenasalized Stops by Place of Articulation; Drawn from 68 (about 10%) of the Languages Reported by Ruhlen (1976)[a]

	Bilabial	Alveolar	Palatal	Velar	Labiovelar[b]	Uvular
Stop						
Voiced	^{m}b 64	^{n}d 64	^{ɲ}ɟ 15	^{ŋ}g 56	^{ŋm}gb 8	^{N}G 1
Voiceless	^{m}p 4	^{n}t 7	^{ɲ}c 4	^{ŋ}k 7		
	68	71	19	63	8	1

[a]There also were some prenasalized affricates (e.g., /^{n}tˢ/, /^{n}c/) and two prenasalized fricatives (/^{m}v/, /^{m}ʃ/).
[b]Actually, four labiovelars were listed as /^{ŋm}gb/, four as /^{mŋ}gb/.

ranging from 4 to 1 up to 16 to 1. That in itself may be a form of assimilation, or at least bespeaks a "harmonious" relationship. But more directly to the point is the high incidence of homorganicity. Of the 233 prenasalized stops, 230 (98.7%) were homorganic. The only exceptions were /ᵐt/, /ᵐd/, and /ᵑʔ/, the last of which lacks a homorganic potential.

PLACE ASSIMILATION: NASAL + NONNASAL CONSONANT CLUSTERS

Chervela (1981) observed that in the acquisition of medial consonant clusters by Telugu (a south Dravidian language) children, the homorganic nasal + stop clusters (/mb/, /nt/, /nd/, /ŋk/) are the earliest to be mastered. For a language to have mainly homorganic clusters, then, would be developmentally optimal. This is true of English. In Moser (1969) there are 321 word-final nasal + stop clusters involving /m, n, ŋ/ and /p, t, k/:

Homorganic		Heterorganic			
/mp/	81	/mt/	0	/mk/	0
/nt/	126	/np/	0	/nk/	0
/ŋk/	114	/ŋp/	0	/ŋt/	0
	321		0		0

All 321 of the nasal + stop clusters are homorganic, leaving literally nothing for a place assimilation process to apply *to*. In the Roberts's (1965) data, I examined the incidence of homorganicity in nasal + stop, nasal + fricative, nasal + liquid, and nasal + glide clusters (or sequences) occurring intervocalically both within and across syllable boundaries. This is a strict test of structural assimilation (i.e., assimilation already present in the system), for there is less reason to expect that assimilative processes will apply with full strength across syllable boundaries as tautosyllabically. Table 4.7 shows the clusters and their frequency in the corpus as listed in Roberts's Table 20. Of the 1051 total clusters, 982 (or 93.4%) are homorganic.

EPENTHESIS

Historically, a number of cases of consonant epenthesis have brought about more or less permanent changes in the lexicon of various languages. Some examples (due to Hans Hock), involve the change of pre-Greek *amrotos* and *anros* to *ambrotos* and *andros,* respectively; the OE form þymle became þymble (which even later became ME *thimble*). This tendency for nasal + liquid clusters

Table 4.7

Homorganic and Heterorganic Nasal + Nonnasal Consonant Clusters and Sequences Occurring Intervocalically in English Discourse

Homorganic				Heterorganic	
nd	265	md	1	ŋd	1
nt	303	mt	2	ŋt	0
ns	153	ms	5	ŋs	0
nz	5	ms	0	ŋz	1
nl	37	ml	7	ŋl	8
mb	45	nb	1	ŋb	0
mp	81	np	5	ŋp	0
mw	2	nw	5	ŋw	0
ŋg	17	mg	0	ng	6
ŋk	25	mk	1	nk	31
nj	49	mj	0	ŋj	0
	982		22		47

Source: Taken from Roberts (1965, Table 20).

to undergo epenthesis has a phonetic explanation; in the transition from the nasal to the liquid the velum is elevated too quickly, and a homorganic stop is the (logical) result. This being so, in English we should not be surprised to find more /mbr/ than /mr/ clusters, more /mbl/ than /ml/ clusters, and so forth, even though three-consonant clusters are less frequent than two-consonant clusters in general. Table 4.8 shows the number of nasal + liquid and nasal + stop + liquid clusters (or sequences) in Roberts's (1965) for the intervocalic location. As you can see, whereas the nasal + liquid clusters number only 24, the nasals + stop + liquid clusters number 37 for the voiced stops and 143 for the voiceless stops; overall, they are over seven times greater in frequency than the nasal + liquid clusters. It is not clear why voiceless stop epenthesis should exceed voiced stop

Table 4.8

Nasal + Liquid and Nasal + Stop + Liquid Clusters Occurring Intervocalically in English Discourse

		Nasal + stop + liquid			
Nasal + liquid		Voiced stops		Voiceless stops	
mr	2	mbr	8	mpr	22
nr	7	ndr	9	ntr	38
ml	7	mbl	6	mpl	50
nl	0	ndl	8	ntl	29
nr	0	ngr	5	nkr	2
nl	8	ngl	1	nkl	2
	24		37		143
			180		

Source: Taken from Roberts (1965, Table 20).

epenthesis at all, much less by such a wide margin (nearly 4 to 1), though see Javkin (1979a) for an illuminating discussion of the /ls/–/lts/ and /lz/–/ldz/ problem.

VOICING ASSIMILATION: TWO OBSTRUENT CLUSTERS

I have located all two-obstruent (stop + fricative, stop + stop, fricative + fricative, and fricative + stop) clusters in the intervocalic data of Roberts (1965) and examined the extent to which the participating obstruents had the same voicing. Of the 660 cases, 616 (or 93.3%) shared voicing. It is difficult to imagine how in English one might reveal a tendency toward contiguous voicing assimilation when the contiguous consonantal candidates, in 93% of the cases, already have the same voicing.[3]

DISCONTIGUOUS VOICING ASSIMILATION

Voicing assimilation is strong enough to have produced, in English words, adjacent consonants with shared voicing. But child and adult speakers are known to produce discontiguous effects, particularly regressive ones, in which final sounds (in monosyllables, at least) affect initial ones. Does the structure of the English lexicon also reflect such discontiguous effects? Are words ending with voiced consonants more likely to begin with voiced consonants? The data in Table 4.9 were extracted from English (Moser, 1969) and French (Juilland, 1965) lexical inventories in an attempt to answer these questions. The English data show the number of monosyllabic words that begin and end with each of the six stops. For example, 11 words begin with /p/ and end with /p/, 16 words begin with /p/ and end with /t/, and so forth. The overall probability of a word ending in a voiceless stop, for these data, is 211/331 = .64. The probability of a word ending in a voiced stop, irrespective of initial voicing, is 120/331 = .36. The overall probability of a word beginning with a voiceless stop is 181/331 = .55. The probability of a word beginning with a voiced stop is 150/331 = .45. I have calculated the probability that words will end with stops of a certain voicing given the voicing of their initial stop, and the probability that words will begin with stops of a certain voicing given the voicing of their final stop. Table 4.10 shows these probabilities, with the "harmonious" cases in parentheses. For the English data, it is clear that there is a greater probability of a final stop being voiceless if the initial stop is voiceless (.69 to .58), and that there is a greater probability of an initial stop being voiced if the final stop is voiced (.53 to .41).

The French data in Table 4.9 represent the monosyllables (37) and the final

---

[3]Readers wishing to know more about voicing assimilation at the phonetic level may wish to consult Westbury (1979), who reports acoustic measurements of voicing and voicing assimilation for abutting word-medial stops.

syllable of polysyllabic words (1265) that begin and end with a stop. Unlike the English entries then, "initial" and "final" refer not to the location of stop consonants in words, but to syllable position. Hence, the /pit/s of *pite, épite,* and *décrépite* contribute equally to this analysis.

The French trends agree with the English pattern. Table 4.10 shows that there is a greater probability of a final stop being voiceless if the initial stop is voiceless (.90 to .80), and that there is a greater probability of an initial stop being voiced if the final stop is voiced (.41 to .24).

These data suggest that voicing harmony is built into the structure of English and French words. This is true in spite of spectrographic findings that in adults' CVC(C) forms, initial voiceless stops are *more voiceless* when final consonants are *voiced* (Weismer, 1979; Port & Rotunno, 1979). The reasons for this relationship are not clear, though it appears that initial and final voicing characteristics may be mediated by the intervening vowel. Port and Rotunno found that long

Table 4.9
Monosyllabic English Words (Moser, 1969) and Word-Final French Syllables (Juilland, 1965) That Begin and End with Stop Consonants

English

Initial consonant		Final consonant								
		p	t	k	ΣX	b	d	g	ΣX	$\Sigma\Sigma X$
p		11	16	16	43	1	12	6	19	
t		10	13	16	39	4	7	5	16	
k		10	17	15	42	9	11	2	22	
	$\Sigma X =$	31	46	47	124	14	30	13	57	181
b		3	28	14	45	6	12	9	27	
d		7	10	4	21	7	10	4	21	
g		6	11	4	21	4	9	2	15	
	$\Sigma X =$	16	49	22	87	17	31	15	63	150
	$\Sigma\Sigma X =$				211				120	331

French

Initial consonant		Final consonant								
		p	t	k	ΣX	b	d	g	ΣX	$\Sigma\Sigma X$
p		16	86	45	147	0	46	0	46	
t		21	164	368	553	6	0	7	13	
k		38	111	13	162	8	30	2	40	
	$\Sigma X =$	75	361	426	862	14	76	9	99	961
b		0	45	42	87	7	19	10	36	
d		4	87	47	138	2	1	5	8	
g		7	41	0	48	4	15	5	24	
	$\Sigma X =$	11	173	89	273	13	35	20	68	341
	$\Sigma\Sigma X =$				1135				167	1302

Table 4.10
Probability of Final Stop Voicing as a Function of the Voicing of the Initial Stop, and Probability of Initial Stop Voicing as a Function of the Voicing of the Final Stop

English		Final stop will be: Voiced	Voiceless
If initial stop is:	Voiced / Voiceless	(.42) / .31	.58 / (.69)
		If final stop is: Voiced	Voiceless
Initial stop will be:	Voiced / Voiceless	(.53) / .47	.41 / (.59)

French		Final stop will be: Voiced	Voiceless
If initial stop is:	Voiced / Voiceless	(.20) / .10	.80 / (.90)
		If final stop is: Voiced	Voiceless
Final stop will be:	Voiced / Voiceless	(.41) / .59	.24 / (.76)

Source: Based on data reported in Table 4.9.

vowels, irrespective of final consonant voicing, are associated with reduced initial stop VOTs. Through application of the voicing–vowel length rule, final stop voicing may indirectly affect initial stop voicing. Whatever the precise mechanism, the harmony data reported above imply an overriding or offsetting process which works to equate the voicing of initial and final stops.

DISCONTIGUOUS PLACE ASSIMILATION?

The data in Table 4.9 also are useful in examining the possibility that place assimilation is structurally built into the English lexicon. I calculated the number of cases in which initial and final stops share one of three places of articulation and compared these figures to the cases in which place is not shared. The data are shown in Table 4.11. Overall, it is clear that there are fewer place sharings ($\bar{X} = 28.0$) than place changes ($\bar{X} = 41.2$). Why is place assimilation not reflected in the structural composition of English words? In slips of the tongue, there is a strong tendency to modify articulatory place (Shattuck-Hufnagel, 1975), though it is not obvious that such changes increase or result in consonant harmony anymore than they work to disrupt whatever harmony already exists.

Actually, the fact that there are relatively few place sharings in lexical structure, and that place changes are frequent in slips, suggests that speakers may be creating harmony with their slips (they are at least not likely to be reducing it).

Table 4.11
Place Sharings between Word-Initial and Word-Final Consonants

Bilabial–bilabial:	(21)	Alveolar–alveolar:	(40)	Velar–velar:	(23)
Bilabial–alveolar:	68	Bilabial–alveolar:	68	Bilabial–velar:	45
Bilabial–velar:	45	Alveolar–bilabial:	28	Alveolar–velar:	29
Alveolar–bilabial:	28	Alveolar–velar:	29	Velar–bilabial:	29
Velar–bilabial:	29	Velar–alveolar:	48	Velar–alveolar:	48
ΣX	170		173		151
$\bar{X}$	42.5		43.3		37.8

Source: From Moser (1969) data.

But if slips create harmony—which, at this point, is a matter of conjecture—why is it that these tendencies have not become a property of English word structure? The answer may be that there are articulatory advantages in the avoidance of place assimilation. For example, faster rates of speech are achievable because coarticulation is possible. I believe one typically is able to say *pocket* faster than *pop-up*; in diadochokinesis, there may be more total syllable productions per unit of time of [pʌtʌkʌ] than of the sum of [pʌ], [tʌ], and [kʌ] said individually (cf. Lass & Sandusky, 1971).

On the basis of what we have seen so far—the greater voicing than place harmony in English monosyllables—one should be able to predict that slips of the tongue will more frequently involve place changes than voicing changes. This is dramatically so; the leading slips on English consonants uniformly involve place changes with voicing preserved. The only exception is intrusions of /k/ for /g/ (Shattuck-Hufnagel, 1975, p. 133). On structural grounds alone, the greater statistical probability is that place errors will *create* place harmony, and that voicing errors will *disrupt* voicing harmony. Perhaps this is why the former predominate.

MANNER ASSIMILATION

There is little evidence that a word is more likely to begin and end with consonants of the same manner. In English, stop–vowel–stop words number 331, as we saw in Table 4.9; there are 127 fricative–vowel–fricative sequences. By way of comparison, stop–vowel–fricative and fricative–vowel–stop sequences number 251 and 173, respectively. I believe there also is no evidence that words beginning with a nasal consonant are more likely to end with one, and vice versa.

The Anterior-to-Posterior Progression

Phonologists have observed in the speech of very young children a tendency for word-initial consonants to be predominately of anterior vocal tract origin, and for word-final consonants to originate from more posterior constrictions (Ingram, 1974). Figure 4.1 shows the expanding phonological system of a young (11–14 months) child, T, based on the first syllable of polysyllabic words (Figure 5 in Shibamoto & Olmsted, 1978). It is evident that syllable-initial segments describe a broad spectrum of places of articulation, with an apparent preference for anterior constrictions. Velar and glottal articulations seem to appear late and inconsistently. Much the same pattern is evident in the three other children (12–22 months) whose data were analyzed by Shibamoto and Olmsted; their Table 24 indicates that in about 64% of the monosyllabic words, the final consonant was produced farther back in the vocal tract than the initial consonant; in only 6% of the cases was the final consonant produced in a more anterior location.

I have analyzed all the word statistics reported for the four children in Shibamoto and Olmsted (Tables 7–10), and it becomes evident when polysylla-

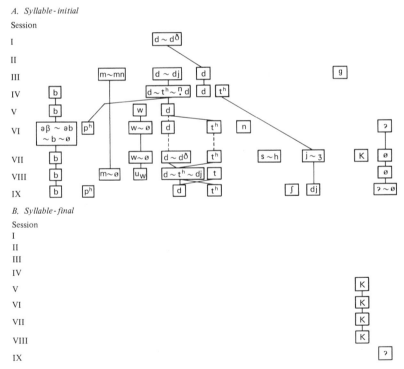

Figure 4.1. *Phone tree depicting the early phonological development of a child, based on the first syllable of polysyllables [from Shibamoto, J. S., & Olmsted, D. L. (1978). Lexical and syllabic patterns in phonological acquisition.* Journal of Child Language, 5, *417–446; with permission from Cambridge University Press].*

bles are included that three anatomical sites correlate fairly well with three word positions. The distributions, in percentages, are as follows:

	Initial	Medial	Final
Labial	(50)	40	26
Alveopalatal	45	(47)	10
Velar	5	13	(64)

A similar pattern was present in the segment inventory data reported on a 16–18-month-old American child by Taymans (1976, p. 292). For stops and nasals, the percentages were as follows:

	Prevocalic	Intervocalic	Postvocalic
Bilabial	(56)	33	29
Alveolar	29	(38)	9
Velar	15	29	(62)

A Czech child of almost identical age (15–17 months) was described by Pačesova (1968, p. 121). For stops and nasals, I have calculated his percentages by articulatory place and word position to be:

	Initial	Medial	Final
Labial	(47)	33	23
Alveopalatal	41	(46)	26
Velar	12	21	(51)

The data on the English- and Czech-learning child are inventory data. They say nothing about errors. But as both children produced more alveolars than velars in the word-initial position, and more velars than alveolars in the word-final position, it seems to follow that children's tendencies toward "velar fronting" must occur more commonly initially. Indeed, in word-initial position a velar seems quite out of its element, practically a "sitting duck" for the alveolar intruder, though it is quite secure in final position. Snow's (1963) data show that there is indeed a greater incidence of velar fronting initially than finally, and of alveolar backing finally than initially:

	Word-initial	Word-final
Velar → Alveolar (d/g, t/k)	34 (59%)	24 (41%)
Alveolar → Velar (g/d, k/t)	5 (19%)	21 (81%)

The anterior-to-posterior progression seen in children also is a structural characteristic of English. According to Table 4.11, there are more bilabial–velar words (45) than velar–bilabial words (29). There are *not* more alveolar–velar words (29) than velar–alveolar words (48), but there is no place for a velar-initial progression to go except to a more anterior site. From the standpoint of intelligibility, it is fortunate that children's tendency to perform regressive velar assimilation has relatively few candidates.

The front-to-back progressions evident in English words also proceed modestly one place at a time, for the most part. There are more bilabial–alveolar words (68) than bilabial–velar words (45), and in the reverse order, there are more velar–alveolar words (48) than velar–bilabial words (29). It appears, insofar as lexical structure is representative of phonetic tendencies, that speakers prefer an articulatory change to an articulatory repetition, and prefer a minimal articulatory excursion to a maximal one.

I have somewhat more information on the phonotactic sequences of French which—unlike English—is unaffected by the grammatical suffixing of /t–d/. Table 4.9 shows the monosyllables (37) and final syllables (1265) that both begin and end with a stop, a sample of 1302 syllables. As the three articulatory places were of unequal frequency, I have indicated the number and the percentage of syllables beginning or ending at each place:

	Initial	Final
Bilabial	316 (74%)	113 (26%)
Alveolar	712 (52%)	645 (48%)
Velar	274 (33%)	544 (67%)

These data are clear. In French, bilabials occur more frequently (may I say more "naturally") in the syllable-initial position, alveolars are "at home" in either position, and velars seem to occur more naturally in final position.

Vowel Height and Final Voicing

We saw earlier (p. 164) that French has more voiceless than voiced obstruents in word-final position. The same is true of English. And in English I have observed a very striking regularity to this preference for voicelessness; it is sensitive to the height of the preceding vowel. I obtained from Moser (1969) the number of monosyllabic English words that end in each of the four bilabial and velar stops and are preceded by each of 10 vowels. I then calculated the number of voiced and voiceless stops preceded by each of the vowels, and I determined for each vowel the proportion of following (i.e., final) stops that were voiceless. Figure 4.2 depicts these values. As the figure indicates, final stops are more likely to be voiceless than to be voiced in every vocalic context. But when the preceding vowel is high, the preference for voicelessness is even stronger.

The vowels of English, of course, vary not merely in height, but also in intensity, frequency, duration, lip configuration, and other parameters. But from the known facts of vowel intensity, duration, and lip configuration it appears that none could have produced the pattern in Figure 4.2, at least in isolation. Whatever evidence one could marshal in favor of fundamental frequency, which varies with duration (cf. Lehiste & Peterson, 1961; Lehiste, 1976), would seem to be unconvincing, even if F_0 contour also varies (Gruenenfelder & Pisoni, 1980).

One thing that raising the tongue does is to make vowels very slightly more like obstruents and cause intraoral pressure to increase. Schwartz (1972) measured intraoral pressure in 16 adult speakers during repetitions of /p/V syllables where the vowel was /i/, /u/, /æ/, or /a/. Though Schwartz was interested only in comparisons between a whispered and a vocalized condition, it is apparent from his data that in both conditions the mean oral pressures (in cm/aq) were higher for /i/ and /u/ than they were for /æ/ and /a/.

/i/		/u/		/æ/		/a/	
vocal	whisp.	vocal	whisp.	vocal	whisp.	vocal	whisp.
6.7	4.5	6.7	4.9	5.7	4.0	5.5	4.1

If there is more oral pressure for high vowels than for low ones, perhaps high vowels would be in greater danger of devoicing. Jaeger (1978) found that of the

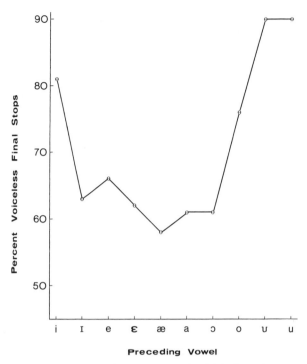

Figure 4.2. *Proportion of English words ending in voiceless bilabial or velar stops as a function of the preceding vowel.*

languages in the Stanford Archive some 24 had both voiced and voiceless vowels. Of these, in 20 the voiceless vowels were predominantly or exclusively high. If the oral pressures of high vowels are great enough to cause their devoicing, as Jaeger surmised, imagine what such pressures could do to the voicing of immediately following (and final) obstruents. These elevated pressure levels would exist in the vocal tract at the time of consonantal closure, which would cause even further buildups of intraoral pressure. In the interaction, without special subglottal compensations voiced obstruents would lose some of their voicing. Enough, perhaps, to be heard as voiceless.

It is, of course, also conceivable that the natural compatibility between high levels of intraoral pressure and voicelessness is such that proportionately fewer high vowel–voiced obstruent sequences would have been introduced into the lexicon in the first place. Whatever the historical facts, the natural compatibilities seem now to be present in, and a property of, English. To a degree, they also are characteristic of French, the only other language I have detailed vowel–obstruent *dictionary* frequencies for (as opposed to the less desirable text or conversation figures). In French (Juilland, 1965), there are proportionately more words ending in /p, t, k/ than in /b, d, g/ when preceded by /i, y, ø, o, u/ vowels, the proportion being .82. For /ɛ, œ, ɑ, a, ɔ/ vowels, the proportion, like the height of vowels, is lower (.74).

In our lab we have obtained some evidence for a vowel effect in children. Plevyak (1982) found that 3-year-olds were significantly more likely to devoice final /g/ when preceded by /i/ and /u/ than when preceded by /æ/ and /a/. The effect was weaker and nonsignificant for /d/ and /b/. Parrucci (1983) obtained no evidence for a vocalic effect in adults, but argued that mature speakers compensate for devoicing tendencies. It also is possible, as Javkin (1979b) suggested, that high vowels are associated with more turbulence, which listeners assume is correlated with voicelessness. Hence, the pattern in Figure 4.2 may be the result of an interactive process with some devoicing or frication by the speaker and some misinterpretation of the speaker's intentions by the innocent listener.

The Phonetic Nature of Phonological Rules

In a classic study of developmental morphology, Jean Berko (1958) asked children to pluralize various contrived, or nonce, words. For example, she showed them a drawing of a novel creature, saying "This is a wug." Then she directed the children's attention to a drawing of two such creatures saying "Now there is another one. There are two of them. There are two _____." In supplying the missing form, the child revealed his knowledge of the appropriate morphological rule. In the test for plurals, most items had English-appropriate endings of /-z/, as in *wugs, luns,* and *tors,* or /-ɪz/, as in *tasses, gutches,* and *nizzes.* There was one possible /-s/ item, *heafs,* though many of the adult controls called it *heaves.*

It is interesting that children did fairly well on this task, generally adding /-s/ and /-z/ appropriately. Specifically, 85% of the children added /-z/ to *tor,* 82% added /-s/ to *heaf.* Berko thought the children deserved some developmental credit for knowing that "a final sibilant makes a word plural," but assumed that the choice of /s/ or /z/ was, in a sense, *made for them.* She pointed out that in English once a stem-final voiceless stop has been said, "even if the speaker intended to say /-z/, it would automatically devoice to /-s/ [p. 175]." In this connection, we saw earlier (p. 171) the predominance of shared voicing among intervocalic stop–fricative clusters.

In the Berko study there were 56 children of 4–7 years of age, and the nonsense items to be pluralized ended in nine different sounds. More recently, a master's thesis was completed at the University of Alberta using 120 children of ages 2–7 who attempted to pluralize syllables ending in 24 different sounds. Analyses were reported in a paper by Baker and Derwing (1982), and the findings generally support but also extend Berko's conclusions. One finding of Baker and Derwing was that many children were less likely to add either /s/ or /z/ if the stem terminated in /θ/, /ð/, /f/, or /v/. The authors suggested, in a broader formulation than Berko's, that "a final fricative makes a word plural [p. 217]." However, as children were extremely unlikely to add /z/ to -/ð/ syllables, some adding /ɪz/, it might be necessary to rule out *articulatory* difficulties before specifying the precise nature of the plural form. But, in general, it appeared that even children who added /s/ and /z/ forms appropriately may have had only the /z/ form underlyingly. This morpheme was expressed phonetically as [z] except when it was added to forms ending in /p, t, k, f, θ/. In these cases, Baker and Derwing assume that progressive assimilation caused the underlying /z/ to appear at the surface as [s]. As the rule for adding /ɪz/ to sibilant-final forms presumably requires more in the way of learning, this was the last form to be mastered.

In English there are other morphological forms that are phonetically conditioned, or that can be stated in phonetic terms. Skousen (1975) has discussed some of these cases, referring mainly to examples from Finnish, but also pointing to the English use of the indefinite articles *a* and *an*. The English rule, of course, is [ə] before consonant-initial words and [æn] or [an] before vowel-initial words. There is a somewhat analogous situation with respect to the definite article, which typically is pronounced [ðə] before consonants and [ði] before vowels (cf. Roberts, 1965, p. 19). In yet another example, Berko's child subjects also scored at better than 80% by adding /-s/ and /-z/ appropriately to form the possessive, as in *bik's* and *wug's*. In the formation of past tense, Berko's subjects transformed *bing* to *bang* or *binged* and added /-t/ to the form *rick*.

My point in bringing up these cases is that one may acquire and use forms without necessarily *learning* their precise surface characteristics. In fact, if young children pick up a particular structure very easily, one might even suspect some sort of phonetic accident, with little evidence that the child is aware of the rule in question. Exactly such a lack of awareness was found by Healy and Levitt (1980) in a study of *adults'* ability to learn "rote" associations between nonsense syllables ending in a voiced or voiceless obstruent (e.g., /æp/, /aid/) and fricatives of either voicing. If the fricatives were /s/ and /z/ the subjects were able to learn the associations, which conformed to English pluralization rules. If the fricatives were /f/ and /v/, however, subjects performed no better than if the associations were completely arbitrary. Healy and Levitt concluded that "the voicing distinction is not accessible for use in learning tasks [p. 113]."

Such results would seem to argue for the generally unconscious nature of the English pluralization rule and—by extension—the hypothesis that the rule is phonetically determined. However, in our view a better test would be to compare the estimated awareness (based on performance on some sort of learning or categorization task) of adults for two rules, one demonstrably phonetic, the other not demonstrably phonetic. Differences in performance *might* be useful in distinguishing between phonetic and nonphonetic rules. But one is justified in being cautious on this point. A study by Jenkins, Foss, and Greenberg (1968) found that adults were not quick to learn a simple paired-associate task in which the syllables differed only in voicing (e.g., /pa/–/ba/, /ta/–/da/). Only those explicitly told to "mouth" the syllables turned in a reasonably convincing performance.

Implications for Phonological Development

Earlier, a variety of compatibilities was seen to exist between the structural characteristics of standard languages and the phonetic dispositions of children and adults. It was observed that the "architects" of English have avoided many of the same consonants that are eschewed by the child speakers of English and disfavored by the deaf children who babble sounds but speak no language. The phonological processes of children were found to correspond to the phonostatistics of French, English, and other languages; child tendencies to omit final consonants, reduce clusters, voice initial stops, devoice final obstruents, all were reflected in the lexical inventories of standard languages. The child's penchant for place assimilation was paralleled by an exceptionally high incidence of homorganicity in English clusters, and by the lack of consonant harmony rules in the Archive. The articulatory "slippage" that causes nasal + fricative clusters to be rendered epenthetically by all speakers was observed to agree with the English preference for nasal + stop + fricative clusters. Anterior-to-posterior consonantal progressions are a feature of child speech and English words. These correspondences make it clear that as the young child begins to function in a linguistic mode, *he will be asked by his language to do certain things he already was doing;* things he—naturally—would continue to do as long as articulatory activity was, in some sense, valued by him. As might be imagined, there are a number of implications here for the child's phonological development and how it is most properly interpreted.

Developmental Assessment

In general terms, one is thought to have acquired something when he "gets" that thing. This assumes that the acquisitor has "gotten" the thing from some*where* and in some *way*. When a child acquires language, it is tacitly assumed that he got it from his environment, and according to some general laws of acquisition which include a variety of learning processes. Thereafter, children (mysteriously) become able to create, lie, and joke with language; to think in it and to think about it. One assumes that children have a special ability to "get" language merely because they do it with such apparent ease and universality, but whether they are born with even the smallest element of language knowledge is disputable.

On the other hand, it is exceedingly clear that the environment plays a large and demonstrated role; children born in Germany tend to speak German, children reared in closets tend to speak no language. But they do vocalize, and that is precisely the point. Children exposed meaningfully to no speech still produce sounds that adult listeners recognize (and symbolize, if asked to do so) as elements in their own linguistic system. The child is not born with anything of "ours"; rather, we share something with him—similar sensory functions and motor tendencies. It is no more of a coincidence that he sounds like us than it is a coincidence that adults sound like him!

As the infant approaches his first "true" words, that he sounds increasingly like us is no evidence that he is acquiring language, or that he is learning anything. He is, in addition to more cognitive changes, altering patterns of respiratory and laryngeal and articulatory movement in accordance with the dictates of an innate maturational schedule. This occurs whether the child is hearing or deaf, of normal intellectual capability or mentally retarded (Smith & Oller, 1981). With this sort of change, one is inclined to use terms such as "development" or "emergence" or "unfolding," which imply that the mandate for *and the direction of* change are genetically determined.

We have seen similarities between the babbling patterns of infants and the phonological patterns of languages. Perhaps it should not surprise us, then, that the transition from babbling to speaking tends to be smooth and continuous. It is a genetically foregone conclusion that infants will say bilabial nasals in syllable-releasing position and produce low vowels, open syllables, and reduplicated patterns. Therefore, to say *mama* requires no accommodations of any type; no attention, no memory, no planning and, most important, no departures from whatever internal codes as might exist. The child's first *mama* may suggest some sort of a development, but is it a language development? Has something been acquired? Is the child *using* his repertoire toward some environmental end or is he merely behaving (i.e., dealing with internal states)?

From deaf children's babbling it is apparent that some "sounds" (i.e., movements) simply are not in the developmental scheme of things. At 6 months, deaf infants do not say [dʒ], nor do they say it at 2 years, or at 3, 4, 5, or 6 years. There is something about [dʒ], one might conclude, that is motorically unnatural. It is, metaphorically speaking, buried at the bottom of the child's phonetic deck. And some special circumstances are needed to bring it to the surface; the child has to want to say a word that contains it. And he is not alone. The /dʒ/ sound has largely been ignored by the languages of the world (some 60% do not have it), not excluding English, in which it ranks twenty-first (among 24 consonants) in conversational frequency (Mines *et al.*, 1978).

Consider [d], on the other hand. It is made at nearly every age by infants—hearing and deaf—and grows in frequency as they develop. It is high in babbling frequency as the child begins to speak, and high in accuracy in the child's first words. Except for the first months of life, it is essentially correct to say there is never a time that [d] is *not* produced. It also is the leading replacer of /ʤ/. Significantly, [d] usually survives various forms of brain damage. Unlike /ʤ/, the /d/ sound has been coveted by the languages of the world (over 71% have one); in English it ranks sixth in conversational frequency.

Do we give the same credit for [d] as for [ʤ]? If so, it may be necessary to argue–precariously, in my view—for a nonphonetic basis to phonological development. If [d] is to be given less credit, does this not offer de facto recognition of the functional link between babbling and speech, between biological and social bases of phonology?

But the issue goes considerably beyond /ʤ/ and *mama*. For the fact is that practically every inherent tendency of the child to alter the phonetic form of words is reflected in the statistics of the system. The tendencies to reduce clusters, to voice initial stops, to devoice final obstruents, to alter voicing in a place-sensitive fashion, to stop (mainly initial voiced) fricatives, to front a variety of consonants—all these transformations are *more rewarded and less penalized* than they would be in a truly arbitrary system.

I submit that a child can, and that all children do, *blunder* into the sound pattern of English or Maori or Portuguese. This is made possible by the fact that the child's system is more or less like those phonological systems. But "blundering" is unlikely to win acceptance among scholars as a formal mechanism of language acquisition. So we have a choice. If we reject the child's [m]s and [d]s as "unacquired," to study phonological acquisition we will have to untangle that which might have been acquired from that which probably was not. To do this, we must begin the study of a child's phonological acquisition during the later (prelexical) periods of babbling. To treat [m] and [d] as "acquisitions," we will have to show either that they (*a*) did not exist at a prior time, meaning we will still have to begin our observations in the later periods of babbling, or (*b*) underwent physical change in the transition from babbling to speech. Then we could say these segments were not inherited from babbling, and that their presence says something about the child's phonological development. But as a practical matter, it may ultimately be that language and communication development are fostered by *perceived* phonological progress. As long as [mama] is taken to be /mama/ (gloss: maternal caretaker), the child's phonetic play may (rightly) be perceived by the child as communicatively useful, therefore regarded by the scholar as linguistically admissible. So it seems that from a cognitive perspective of phonological development, [m]s and [d]s should be given little or no credit as "acquisitions." But by its very (phonetic) nature, much of phonology is not all that cognitive.

Consider a nearly analogous dilemma in the writing of linguistic grammars. Dinnsen (1980) questioned how many of the observed facts of vowel nasalization need to be incorporated into phonological descriptions:

> It appears that low vowel nasalization is necessary (probably a physiological necessity), an unavoidable consequence, and thus is universal. However, if low vowel nasalization is a universal, it need not be represented in the grammar of any particular language. Furthermore, if low vowel nasalization is a necessary consequence of constraints on human physiology, then it is not even clear that it is a linguistic matter at all. [This quote is reprinted from Dinnsen, D. A. (1980). Phonological rules and phonetic explanation. *Journal of Linguistics*, p. 183, with permission from Cambridge University Press; p. 183.]

It is obvious that a proper phonological description (i.e., a complete one) could be performed by a single statement of universal phonetics followed by a series of parochial statements about the particular system being described. Were this logic applied to phonological development, many young *speakers* still would not have evidenced any phonological development, for descriptions of their phonological systems would differ little from descriptions of their prelexical phonetic systems. Formal analyses would show they were doing very little that was different.

Comparative Ease of Acquisition

From what we have observed about the correspondence between child tendencies and language structure, it follows that some phonological systems must be easier to acquire or "emerge into" than others. Let us, for the moment, return to Dinnsen's point. Imagine that one has an immense catalog of natural phonetic patterns that are characteristic of all or most known languages, one that includes specifications such as "vowels before final nasal consonants tend to be produced nasally." Imagine further that some languages have—and need to have—only a small number of additional statements. One could consider these languages to be maximally aligned with the productive capabilities of the human vocal tract. In contemporary terms, they would be highly "natural." Would it not be the case that they also would be comparatively easy to acquire and to use? Could we not construct an idealized phonological system that ought to be relatively easy to blunder into—maximally receptive to the child's inherent phonetic tendencies, minimally restrictive on his inherent tendencies? And having constructed such a system, might we not use it as a yardstick for measuring the "acquisitive naturalness" of human languages?

We would expect to find that those systems that were high in "acquisitive naturalness" also would be acquired earlier, ceteris paribus. Unfortunately, it is impossible to test this hypothesis with existing data, which are scant and methodologically nonuniform in the extreme. But there are promising indications from studies of developmental syntax (Peters, 1981), and hopefully the critical cross-linguistic studies will someday be done in phonology.

Error or Mismatch?

If 'mama' is to be considered evidence for a correct /m/ in pre- and inter-vocalic position, what are we to make of 'duh' for *truck?* If we can give no segmental credit for the /tr-/ and the /-k/, then we must assume the child *accomplished* more in saying 'mama' than in saying 'duh'. But both forms are directly traceable to patterns that would have been evident in babbling. Is it not the case, more realistically, that just as some *languages* may be more "natural" than others, within languages there are some *words* that are more adapted to the child's production abilities than are others? If so, these "preselections," more than any child-internal factor, might account for the success of early lexical production. From a purely phonological point of view, in scoring the child "correct" for saying [mama] one is giving a ("naturalness") point to the language spoken by his parents. In "counting off" for the child's production of 'duh' for *truck* the analyst is unwittingly discrediting the language. The point is that 'mama' and 'duh' are both "natural" for the child, probably motivated and constrained by similar principles of vocal and articulatory function, and it is mainly in the matching or mismatching of these principles to the ambient language that the concepts of "correct" and "incorrect" derive their applicability. This argues—for error analysis in particular, and for phonological development more generally—that one must observe the interaction between the demands of the lexicon and the capabilities of the child: The language and the child must both be in the equation, as each is under scrutiny.

Lexical Determination

Correspondences between the "neologisms" of the child and the "logisms" of the language make it hard to know when the child is targeting for a particular form that he has heard other people produce. Consider the Japanese girl described by Nakazima (1970) who

> uttered /papa/ not only in various articulatory forms, but also in various situations. At first she pointed at her father's picture and uttered /papa/ sounds, then she uttered them pointing at a male adult picture on a newspaper, and even at a microphone, at a tooth brush, at a toy dog, etc. She uttered them rather actively when she was playing alone and without relations to any particular objects. When she was fourteen months old, her father came home. Transfer from the relation of /papa/ with father's picture to the relation with father himself was easily done.

After that she uttered /papa/ sounds to a male adult other than her father, and even to her mother and to her maid [p. 27].

According to Rūķe-Draviņa (1976) in the children of Latvian parents who used the terms *męmmę* and *tętę* to refer to 'mother' and 'father', "syllable sequences of the type *męmęmęm* and *tętętę* can be found already during the 'babbling exercises', and these were interpreted by the adults as the primary word units for 'mother' and 'father' [p. 161]." That children are naturally inclined to produce sequences such as 'papa' and 'mama' is *part* of the problem in lexical determination. The other, a neglected part, is that languages happen to include such items in their lexicons.[4] Perhaps the first to call attention to this was Edmund Noble, who wrote in an 1888 issue of *Education* that "Herr Bushmann found the sounds PA and TA (AP and AT) to predominate as names for 'fathers' in a large number of languages examined by him, while the forms for 'mother' were in the largest proportion of the cases MA and NA (AM and AN) [p. 118]." Noble went on to suggest that the reason for these particular forms was the fact that they were the easiest to produce, and that humans acted in accord with "the general law of preference for easy sounds." He gave no clear reason for the appropriation of these patterns for use in parental designation, and considered the specific choices within the 'easy' set by any particular language to be due to "the particular circumstances of each case."

This question was revisited nearly 80 years later by Roman Jakobson (1960) in an article entitled "Why 'Mama' and 'Papa'?" Jakobson had more extensive data than Noble, namely, the 1072 parental words gathered by Murdock (1959) in his cross-linguistic study of kinship terms. Murdock had observed some striking regularities in maternal and paternal names. From my own analysis of Murdock's data (his Table 1), I have obtained the following percentages:

Labial and dental	'Mother'		'Father'		
	N	*%*	*N*	*%*	Sum
Nasals	283	78	81	22	364
Nonnasals	95	22	343	78	438

These data represent the labial and dental forms, which constitute 75% of all the kinship terms in the sample (some contained only vowels, aspirates or clicks and vowels, etc.). There is complete symmetry, with 78% of the maternal names containing nasals, and 78% of the paternal terms nonnasal consonants.

[4]It has been documented (Brooks-Gunn & Lewis, 1979) that children are likely to use appropriately the name *daddy* more frequently than *mommy*. Elsewhere, I have argued that this difference may reflect phonetic factors (Locke, submitted).

In what must surely be the "strong form" of motherese, Jakobson speculated that adult speakers have in some cases "deliberately adapted" their speech to conform to the infant's own pattern, causing a "specific infantile layer in standard vocabulary [p. 539]." The use of nasals to represent 'mother' was thought by Jakobson (1962) to involve her role as *la grande dispensatrice:*

> Often the sucking activities of a child are accompanied by a slight nasal murmur, the only phonation which can be produced when the lips are pressed to mother's breast or to the feeding bottle and the mouth is full. Later, this phonatory reaction to nursing is reproduced as an anticipatory signal at the mere sight of food and finally as a manifestation of a desire to eat, or more generally, as an expression of discontent and impatient longing for missing food or absent nurser, and any ungranted wish. When the mouth is free from nutrition, the nasal murmur may be supplied with an oral, particularly labial release; it may also obtain an optional vocalic support [p. 542].

That the "dispensing" capability of mothers may be linguistically significant also is suggested by Schieffelin's (1979) description of the Kaluli people of Papua, New Guinea. She observed that Kaluli children were not credited by their parents with "first words"—even if they had already begun to speak—until the children used two critical words: [nɔ] 'Mother' and [bo] 'breast'.

That parents derive inspiration for naming (or renaming) from their children's speech, as Jakobson speculated, also had been suggested by Leopold (1949) in studies of his daughter Hildegard's nonstandard words ("mostly carried over from babbling"). He attributed the genesis of nonstandard words to the child's persistence in using them, and also to the family's

> passive aid . . . the adults were willing to understand them in the meaning which was associated with them. This kind of "invention" probably plays a part in every infant's linguistic development. The extent to which such "words" take root in a child's language depends on the reaction of the environment. It is natural for the family to take up such words and use them actively [p. 71].

An illustration of such tendencies is the "Comanche Baby Language" reported on by Casagrande (1964). At one time, in Comanche there was a rich and formalized vocabulary or sublexicon that was used only in talking to children. The apparent purpose of this vocabulary was to ease the young child into the use of oral language. It was begun "when the child was old enough to understand [p. 245]," at about 1 year, and discontinued at about 3 or 4 years. In most of the examples, which number about 60, the typical pattern of a baby word is disyllabic with a long, stressed second syllable ending in a glottal stop. There is considerable reduplication and a small stock of labial and stop consonants and cardinal vowels. Two sounds, [x] and [m:], are used only in baby words.

What Casagrande described was baby "language," but there also is baby "talk," called *language enfantin* by the French and *lallwort* by the Germans. Baby talk refers to adults' attempts to pronounce standard lexical items in a childlike manner for the benefit (?) of the child listener. A number of scholars have investigated baby talk, most notably Ferguson (1956, 1964) and Kelkar (1964). Based on a review by Paradis (1979), it appears that at least 17 languages have some sort of baby talk, for as many as that have been described. Such studies are potentially of value to developmental theory, for they show what adults *believe* are the difficult structures for children and, therefore, where adult speakers might naturally be inclined to make phonetic changes in their speech to children. For example, Ferguson (1964) reported that in baby talk there frequently is cluster reduction, replacement of /r/ by /l/, a glide, or apical stop, velar fronting, and various commutations involving sibilants, affricates, and stops. If a parent wishes to provide his child with helpfully lucid targets, he might—in mirror image—be expected to disproportionately "clean up" his articulation of *these* segments.

It appears that there will be correspondences between what the baby babbles and what the adult says, and the reason is that the baby goes by physiologic impulse and the adult speaks a language in which such phonetically based forms are, to a degree, built into the system. Tuaycharoen (1977) observed that a Thai infant's responses "matched the models in cases where the models were imitations *of the baby's vocalizations* and where the models had no complexity in terms of articulatory differentiation [p. 81; emphasis mine]."

From the 'mama'–'papa' evidence, the invented words of Hildegard Leopold, the Comanche baby language, and the adult imitations noted by Tuaycharoen, it appears that there is a tendency for adults to incorporate into language structure, by intent or unwittingly, items that will maximally accommodate the phonetic capabilities of infants and children. As adults have many of the same tendencies, I do not wish to imply that such "accommodations" are purely of the selfless and child-centered type.

Table 4.12 shows a developmental consequence of this. Note by looking down the first column the rich variety of meanings represented by the early lexical items of children. The second column shows the languages these examples were drawn from. The third lists the child's phonetic forms as they were supplied in the original report. Note how similar the forms are in their syllable shape, tendency toward reduplication, and favoring of stops and nasals. I do not doubt that the child in many cases *meant* what he seemed to, but it also is striking that his early meanings (i.e., words) are so phonologically constricted. In some cases, the child may have been awarded lexical credit he did not deserve. In other cases, the child may have been using a variety of "words" but the only identifiable ones were the CV syllables with stops and nasals and reduplicated patterns.

Table 4.12
Early "Words" in a Variety of Languages

Gloss	Language	Child's form[a]	Source
uncle	Pokat	mamá	Fleming, 1981
goodbye	Afrikaans	tata	Locke
food	Polish	papa	Olstuscewski, 1897
dog	French	wawa	Taine, 1877
this	Czech	toto	Pačesova, 1968
how	Egyptian Arabic	ʔaya	Omar, 1973
mom	Slovenian	mam	Kolarič, 1959
beard	Estonian	habe	Vihman, 1976
door	Garo	tu	Burling, 1959
beat	Chinese	pah	Lin, 1971
dog	Hindi	tu:tu:	Srivastava, 1974
bite	Dutch	ap	Elbers, 1980
give me	Luo	miya	Blount, 1969
dancing	German	taketake	Bateman, 1917
to poke	Bulgarian	boc	Gheorgov, 1905
sleep	Spanish	nana	Jespersen, 1964
to eat	Thai	manm	Tuaycharoen, 1977
I want	English	awəu	Scollon, 1976
father	Russian	dadada	Noble, 1888
mother	Carib	bababa	Noble, 1888
grandfather	Zuñi	naʔna	Kroeber, 1916

[a]In some cases, the child's version is an alternative to the standard form.

Phonetic Exposure

It is commonly accepted in teaching that one should spend a disproportionate amount of time and attention on the poorly or partially developed skills. One of the developmental implications of our phonostatistical analysis is that children are systematically exposed the most to sounds they least need to hear. The two most frequent sounds in English conversations (Mines *et al.*, 1978) are /n/ and /t/. The two least frequent are /ʒ/ and /tʃ/. This seems maladaptive, for /n/ and /t/ are among the earliest sounds of child speech, /ʒ/ and /tʃ/ are among the latest sounds to be mastered.

It is likely that /n/ would be early and /ʒ/ would be late regardless of their conversational frequency—or their "functional load." But it also seems plausible that adult frequency works to exacerbate the inherent ease and difficulty of these sounds.

Intelligibility

The unequal phonetic load referred to here also may benefit the child by increasing his intelligibility. For he not only hears more /n/s than /ʒ/s, he also will be called upon to make more /n/s than /ʒ/s. And since he can do quite passable /n/s in his earliest speaking (and before), he should appreciate a net gain in intelligibility, and have at his disposal a small but workable vocabulary while his phonological development is still far from complete.

The Determination of "Avoidance"

Ingram (1978) has claimed that the acquisition of fricatives may involve as many as five separate stages, and that children start with an avoidance of the words that contain them. He remarked that "adult words with /v-/, /z-/, and /ɵ-/ remained infrequent in the speech of children throughout the first two years. Words with /f-/ and /s-/, however, occurred frequently [p. 71]." But if we look at the conversational frequency of these sounds in stressed English syllables (Denes, 1963) it becomes apparent that /f/ and /s/ words are also more frequent in adult speech (mean percentage: 4.26) than are /v, z, ɵ/ (mean percentage: 1.50). As we saw earlier (pp. 159–160), a fair amount of avoidance is built into the system. All that is needed for the *appearance* of avoidance, rather than a "true" avoidance *strategy,* is for the child to be less than loquacious. This will produce a small sample, and a small sample of adult speech is likely to include few sounds in the /v, z, ɵ/ category. Therefore, an additional implication of phonostatistics is that children occasionally will be misdiagnosed as "avoiders" when they are merely a bit reticent. If avoidance was defined in relative rather than absolute terms, all children would be misdiagnosed as avoiders even when speaking freely.

In discussing this relationship between adult (systemic) avoidance and child avoidance, I am reminded of an observation of Kroeber's (1916) with respect to the Zuñi use of the word *tu'tu* ('drink', where ' = ʔ). Kroeber developed "the impression that the Zuñi mentioned water less frequently than we in connection with the act or desire of drinking. . . . their word for drink is much easier for a child to form than their word for water, *ky'awe,* in which the initial sound is both glottalized and heavily palatalized [pp. 531–532]."

Babbling Drift

As mentioned in Chapter 1, Roger Brown's (1958) use of the term *babbling drift* implies a form of *learning* represented by the drift of infants' sound making toward the values of their environment. As I have indicated, there appears to be little or no formal evidence for this position, and a considerable amount of negative evidence. However, a developmental implication of phonological naturalness is that infants will be heard to babble increasingly like adults "babble." This is no accident, but it does not have an environmental explanation such as learning. In fact, as infants progress into the later—but still arguably prelexical—stages of babbling, their phonetic repertoire becomes increasingly rich.

Oller (1980) has called this "variegated" babbling in recognition of the diversity of sound patterns that are evident. It will sound more like English than babbling ever did before. It also will sound more like Burmese, Greek, Hungarian, and Macedonian. If there is any "drift" involved here it is a drift toward the vocal tract capabilities (and pleasurabilities) of that stage of development. Even the babbling of 5-year-old deaf children is "more English" than the vocal play of 5-month-old hearing children.

Implications for Phonological Usage and Change

The implications of isomorphism are not limited to problems of phonological development, but include aspects of phonological execution in adults and changes in sound systems over time.

Slips of the Tongue

I pointed out earlier (pp. 171–173) that the initial and final consonants of English words tend to share voicing, but not place, and that slips of the tongue (cf. Shattuck-Hufnagel, 1975) tend to violate place but not voicing. These mirror-image phenomena suggest that the probability of a within-word feature exchange may be a function of the speaker's phonetic programming *and* the availability of eligible forms. If speakers were disposed to assimilate voice, there would be relatively few candidates, and for that reason alone the incidence of voice slips would be low (at least where target and source segments are in the same word). English words are likely to begin and end with consonants of *different* place of articulation. This suggests that even if speakers' tendencies toward place assimilation were no stronger than their tendencies toward voice assimilation, the former would predominate.

Context-Sensitive Rules

There is an interesting paradox with regard to context-sensitive rules. They are often interpreted as indices of phonetic tendency. However, they also are the raw material for more lasting sound change. If sound change is complete, there must be a loss of phonological rules, for they then would have no forms left to apply to. Therefore, to find *no* phonological rules of a particular type in the world's languages can mean that a phonetic tendency is *so strong* that there is no need for the rules. Earlier (Table 4.8) we observed that in English there are over seven nasal + stop + liquid clusters for every nasal + liquid cluster. Though the small number of nasal + liquid clusters probably are epenthesized frequently, their rarity is such that the need of a formal implementation rule might not be readily appreciated.

Functional Load

The concept of "functional load" has been around for most of this century, though very little seems to have come of it. King (1967) defined functional load as

> a measure of the number of minimal pairs which can be found for a given opposition. More generally, in phonology, it is a measure of the work which two phonemes (or a distinctive feature) do in keeping utterances apart—in other words, a gauge of the frequency with which two phonemes contrast in all possible environments. [From King, R. D. Functional load and sound change. *Language, 43,* p. 831; with permission from Linguistic Society of America.]

Various linguists have asserted the importance of functional load in historical sound change, claiming that the most heavily loaded contrasts were the least likely to undergo change. Jakobson (1931/1972) said that "the low frequency and the weak functional load of a phonological difference naturally favors its loss [p. 131]."

The functional load concept is essentially the same, in different terms, as the "pressure to avoid homonymy," for the collapse of a working contrast will obviously create more homonyms than the collapse of an inactive contrast. King (1967) tested three different variants of the functional load construct with several cases from historical Germanic. None proved to be especially powerful, but more pertinent to our present purpose is the *interest* in functional load.

That a hard-working contrast would be resistant to collapse is entirely logical when phonology is considered as a communicative code, operating in the service of lexical transmission. But one needs to ask, as well, how the hard-working contrasts *became so* in the first place. Is it not conceivable that heavily loaded contrasts are loaded because of their lexical frequency, that is, the more frequent two sounds (in a word position), the more likely that they will contrast? If so, the conditions would be present to encourage a perhaps spurious construct such as functional load when sound change might more nearly be under the control of phonetic naturalness. That functional load would prove to be a mediocre predictor of sound change would only reflect the imperfect relationship between the controlling (mostly phonetic) factors and minimal pair contrastivity. This speculation is supported by Table 4.13, which shows the number of words in English dialogue that contain each singleton consonant (all word positions included; data from Roberts, 1965, Tables 17–19) and the number of minimal pairs in English that involve that consonant (from Denes, 1963, Table 7). Note that as lexical frequency declines so, in general, does minimal pair frequency.

Table 4.13

Lexical Frequency and Frequency in Minimal Pairs of English Consonants

Lexical frequency		Minimal pair frequency		Lexical frequency		Minimal pair frequency	
/l/	1501	235		/b/	592	129	
/r/	1290	168		/w/	536	204	
/n/	1272	283		/z/	499	144	
/s/	1224	305		/v/	468	74	
/d/	1221	270		/h/	368	158	
/k/	1157	179	(39.0%)	/ʃ/	350	117	(22.4%)
/t/	1112	308		/dʒ/	303	61	
/m/	886	255		/g/	230	75	
/ŋ/	809	31		/tʃ/	189	88	
/p/	755	164		/ө/	90	56	
/f/	648	200		/ð/	85	115	
/j/	630	62	(27.6%)	/ʒ/	31	10	(11.0%)

Source: Data on lexical frequency from Tables 17–19 of Roberts (1975); data on frequency in minimal pairs from Table 7 of Denes (1964).

Table 4.13 also shows that most of the stops and all of the nasals—but few of the fricatives—are among the more frequent consonants (and I continue to be chagrined, as a developmentalist, by the frequency of the liquids!).

Implications for the Study of Acquisition and Change

I have tried in this chapter to show that phonological systems are phonetically nonarbitrary in a variety of ways. As a consequence of this fact, developmental progress frequently will include pseudoacquisitions, even a role for serendipity as the child's vocal meanderings take him perceptibly into certain *linguistic* structures, with the child receiving credit which perhaps should be shared with his language. It might prove beneficial for historical linguists to consider how and with what cognitive and sensorimotor mechanisms children approach acquisition, for these factors affect the learnability, hence the long-term viability of linguistic units. Likewise, it might be advantageous for developmental linguists to turn their attention more directly to the nature of systems children are expected to attain, weighing the relative "naturalness" of each of the segments and sequences and rules to be mastered. As Wang (1978) has pointed out, many of the phenomena in both domains, even the explanations to which they are susceptible, are essentially the same.

5

Developmental Effects
of Adult Variability

In Chapter 3 we examined a number of distortions and reductions which occur so commonly in the day-to-day speech of adults that they have been catalogued and formally described by linguists, essentially gaining the status of American English "properties." We saw that even when adults were speaking carefully, there were frequent cases of final obstruent omission and devoicing, expression of /t/ as glottal stop or flap, elimination of initial /ð/, and so forth. In general, our focus was on the adult speaker as a phonetic animal, constrained by the design characteristics of his own vocal tract and—to a degree—subject to many of the same mechanical limitations as children.

As the adult speaker also is a listener, it is not surprising that special processing strategies have evolved that are effective in decoding fast or casual speech. With such strategies adults are able to listen through the acoustic mess, and to posit phonemes where there seem to be no phones. For example, in Shockey's (1974) research, a lengthening of the /n/ in *warn a guy* caused it to be heard as *warn the guy*, a strategy that compensates for speakers' tendency to drop word-initial /ð/s and lengthen the preceding consonant. This works very well for adults, but what of the child? What besides casual speech is heard in the home? How is the child to know that [n:] can mean an omitted /ð/? Could it be—as Linell (1979) suggested—that some words are produced so variably that "it may take considerable time before the child becomes acquainted with the most precise pronunciations [p. 217]." If this is true, how are phonologists to evaluate the child's (imperfect) forms in the meantime?

That children must form their conception of the ambient language from the samples to which they are exposed is obvious, and it should be just as evident that variability and deviancy in a child's models are not without developmental consequences. In one case (Klinger, 1962), a Spanish-speaking child, John, learned English from his cousin, who happened to have a cleft palate. Like his model, John's English—though not his native Spanish—was characterized by hypernasality and nasal emission. As John had heard no other English, he presumably had no way of knowing where "English" started and "cleft palate" stopped! Likewise, Edwards (1979) described a first-grade boy who represented the meaning of standard English *just* with the syllable *cet* (usually pronounced [sɛt]). His younger sister evidently learned this novel form from him; she produced *cet* in all the cases where *just* would fit both semantically and syntactically. In another case, Peters (1983) described a child who called elephants "intits." To phonologists who compare children's utterances to standard forms, there is quite a bit of explaining to do here. How does *elephant* get reduced to "intit"? But the child's mother was very perceptive (Clark, 1977), and she happened to recall the original transaction:

MOTHER: *That's an elephant, isn't it? What is it?*
CHILD: *Intit.*

What Is the "Child's Linguistic Environment"?

Although children acquire phonology from speakers in their environments, most existing theories of acquisition are devoted exclusively to children's utterances—as compared to the formal properties of a standard or 'dictionary' system.[1] In the first part of this chapter, I illustrate with actual cases some of the pitfalls of this approach and argue that we must know more about children's phonetic environments. Then I examine the prospects that adult variability may negatively affect phonological development in children.

Steinar's [s] for /z/

When we wish to characterize a child's linguistic input, do we need merely to know the properties of the local dialect or must we be familiar with the child's immediate environment? Consider the case of Steinar, a native speaker of Icelandic who emigrated to the United States at the age of 6 years. In looking at

---

[1]Consider the statement by Aslin and Pisoni (1980) that "phonologically irrelevant contrasts . . . are obviously not presented to the infant [p. 79]." In reality, infants are exposed to a variety of phonetic patterns that have no status in formal linguistic descriptions (cf. MacKain, 1982) and are not exposed with great frequency to some elements that are formally described in grammar.

Steinar's acquisition of English, Hecht and Mulford (1982) were unable to explicate certain of his phonetic patterns because they could not rule out environmental influence. Steinar perceptibly devoiced 54% of the final /z/ sounds in the sample, which the authors expected because Icelandic has final /s/ but not final /z/, and because final obstruent devoicing is a frequent developmental error irrespective of linguistic experience. But additionally, Hecht and Mulford observed that final /z/ devoicing "is an acceptable American English pronunciation in some phonetic contexts and speech styles [p. 322]." To understand Steinar's error patterns, the authors assumed they would need to know more about what Steinar had been exposed to:

> Peer speech clearly would have to be described in order to assess its possible influence on Steinar's pronunciations. In addition, his other main sources of English (e.g., his schoolteacher, adult "playmates," and parents) would have to be documented. The more completely the range of variability can be described in each of the L2 models the second language learner hears, the better we can evaluate the potential influence of modeled forms on the variability of the child's own speech patterns [p. 325].

In Hecht and Mulford one sees investigators hampered in their study of interference from a first language because there was too little information about the second language as it actually is spoken to the child. Fortunately, Hecht and Mulford were aware of the problem. But what if the researcher is not aware that standard and actual forms may be quite different? One might think that a child was suffering from a phonological learning problem, or an anatomical defect, as in Klinger's (1962) description of "pseudo-cleft palate speech." One might underestimate the role of experience by confusing phonemic with phonetic (Aslin and Pisoni, 1980). If ambient patterns of stimulation are unknown, one might also make the mistake just narrowly averted by Macken and Barton in their study of Spanish-learning children's "allophonic" spirantization.

Spirantization in Spanish

According to Harris (1969), Spanish has an allophonic rule which converts /b, d, g/ to [β, ð, ɣ] in certain phonetic environments. The stops occur following nasals and in absolute utterance-initial position; in careful speech, they may also occur word initially. The fricative cognates occur elsewhere. Macken and Barton (1980a) set out to observe the acquisition of this spirantization rule in seven young children being reared in California homes where Mexican Spanish was spoken predominantly. Three of the children were 2 years of age, the others were 4 years old. The testers employed by Macken and Barton were native speakers of Mexican Spanish, two monolingual in that language, the other bilingual in Mexican Spanish and English.

In the recording sessions, the children were encouraged by the experimenters to talk about some familiar objects whose names began with the six Spanish stop consonants. An average of just over 450 tokens per child were analyzed for their continuancy. As expected, the voiceless stops—which, according to Spanish rules, are not eligible for spirantization—were produced as stops in 98–99% of the cases. Macken and Barton refer to the 1–2% produced as spirants rather than stops as "the margin of error that could be expected with children, or speakers who do not have perfect articulatory control. [This quote and subsequent quotes from Macken & Barton, 1980a, are reprinted from Macken, M. A., & Barton, D. (1980a). The acquisition of the voicing contrast in Spanish: A phonetic and phonological study of word-initial stop consonants. *Journal of Child Language, 7*, p. 447; with permission from Cambridge University Press.]"

Macken and Barton received quite a surprise with respect to the voiced stops. First, though, it is necessary to understand that most of the stops (*a*) were in utterance-initial position, due to a large number of one-word sentences; and (*b*) were produced in careful (andante) speech. Therefore, nearly all of the tokens *should* have been produced, according to the rules of Spanish, *as stops*. Add to this the overwhelming tendency of children in the 2–4-year age range to replace fricatives with stops, and there is even greater reason to have expected that the voiced stops—like the voiceless ones—would be produced *as stops*. Thus, the investigators were quite surprised to discover that the voiced stops were spirantized by 45.7% of the 2-year-olds and by 31.4% of the 4-year-olds. And this occurred despite the fact that "the two-year-olds produced /f, s, x/ as *non*continuants throughout nearly all of the study [p. 447]."

What could possibly explain this developmental anomaly? It occurred to Macken and Barton that the Spanish spirantization rule might not be as Harris had described it. Upon examination, they learned that "during the recording sessions our experimenters produced spirant phones in absolute utterance-initial position: examination of eighty minutes of tape recording per experimenter revealed that *these adults produced from 30% to 40% of all utterance-initial /bdg/ phonemes as spirants* [p. 456; emphasis mine]." Turning to other data (Hammond, 1976) on adult-to-adult discourse in (Miami-Cuban) Spanish, they found similar evidence of spirantization of voiced stops in 'illegal' environments. On the strength of their own adult-to-child data, and Hammond's adult-to-adult data, Macken and Barton accepted the "interesting possibility that *the spirantization patterns in the four-year-old data are in fact relatively adult-like and that, moreover, the conventional analyses of adult Spanish are incorrect* [p. 457; emphasis mine]."

Macken and Barton are to be commended for their keen insights and analyses. Harris (1969), after all, is a trusted reference on the phonological structure of Mexican Spanish. I note, however, that his sample was limited to "a few Mexican friends whose speech [he] believed to be typical of educated speakers from Mexico City [p. 3]."

Variation in Maya

There are other cases in which developmental puzzles of various sorts have betrayed an insufficient knowledge of adult speech. Straight (1976) studied the acquisition of Maya phonology among children in the Yucatan Peninsula of Mexico. The children and their parents resided in the same sector of a small village. Although Straight included 22 children in his sample, the "adult norm" to which their speech was compared was derived from *one* native speaker from the village. Straight observed that "phonology acquisition proceeds in a relatively piecemeal and idiosyncratic manner [p. 216]," whereas he discovered later that the children's variations may actually have corresponded to variations in the adult speech of their different homes:

> I may have been too hasty in attributing the patterns of variation among the children I studied to strictly idiolectal factors . . . the observed variations might instead have their roots in *adult* variation . . . the "failure" of the children . . . to adhere to the adult norm . . . may actually have been due to my failure to base the latter on an adequately varied sample of adult speech. It now appears that my best course of action would have been to subject the adult sub-population to the same extensive set of elicitation instruments as their children were given. In this way variations in the children's speech might even have proved to be directly attributable to the patterns of contact (and emulation) which they had with particular adults in their linguistic environments [p. 218].

Is it not odd that the last place we look, in attempting to explain child speech, is at the speech to which children are exposed! And when we look at adult speech (cf. Chapter 3), we find an immense variety of phonetic smudges and smears. Does this, as Linell (1979) hinted, delay phonological development? What happens when a child, who would "like" to devoice, is exposed to the speech of others, who frequently *do* devoice? And what of "motherese"? Does it function at the phonological level; if so, does it make developmental matters easier or more complicated?

This may be more than one can effectively undertake at present. But we can start by asking some very preliminary questions about the nature of phonetic *variability,* and how it does or might affect the language-innocent child. Fortunately, nature has provided an interesting natural laboratory for the study of the developmental effects of adult variability. That natural laboratory is *language death.*

Language Death

Language death refers to the demise of a language, usually because it is dominated by a stronger, competing language. Examples—and there are many—

include most of the American Indian languages. Currently, Gaelic and Welsh are in danger of being extinguished by English, as is Breton by French.

Though there is something sad about the death of a language, it does provide an opportunity to understand more about language change. Dressler (1972) studied Breton, which is spoken in the Brittany region of France. Dressler was struck by the "fluctuations and uncertainties" of the speakers of Breton; he observed that uncertainty "results in free variation," which—in turn—"render[s] perception rather difficult." Dorian commented that in East Sutherland Gaelic, certain obligatory rules were becoming optional (1977), and certain features were becoming "sporadic" (1978).

Some of this variability occurs where the dying language does not overlap with the victorious language, as might be expected. Other points of variation were considered "weak points" by Swadesh (1948), and Dressler (1972) observed that certain rules are more vulnerable to loss, especially the less natural ones ("Those mutations or submutations which can be lumped together as a switching rule are better preserved than those which cannot [p. 451]").

It is interesting that the speakers themselves are not especially aware of the specifics of the decline. Dorian (1973) discovered that whereas her Gaelic speakers were mindful of lexical loss, only "sporadic note is taken of certain phonological developments [p. 414]."

When these "less natural" rules become more variable, they also become less likely to develop in the succeeding generation. According to Dressler, "if a rule is optional with the older generation which has a full and varied command of a still vigorous language system, it is lost in the disintegrating language of a younger generation [p. 452]."

This transgenerational view was reinforced by Knab and Knab (1979) who studied the demise of Aztec in the central highlands of Mexico (the Valley of Puebla). They observed five distinct stages of language death. In the first stage, there is some curtailment of the language. For example, it may be used mostly at home, along with the to-be-victorious language. In the second stage, most of the speakers are over 30 years of age, and the younger ones—"semi-speakers" in Dorian's terminology—are limited in their use of the language. In the third stage, most of the fluent speakers are now over 50, the language is no longer spoken in the home and according to Knab and Knab "children fail to learn the language [p. 473]." Only those referred to as "rememberers" are left in the fourth stage; all the fluent speakers have disappeared. In the fifth stage the language is dead. As Knab and Knab point out, the duration of each stage is 20–30 years, "or approximately one generation [p. 473]."

When a language or *any part of a language* becomes variable in adults it tends to be lost in their children. But it seems the parents may not trace the loss to themselves, back to their own speech. As Miller (1971) observed in the speakers of Shoshoni in Utah and Nevada, "Older speakers sometimes comment unfavorably on the corruption of the language by younger speakers who interlard English words and phrases, or who have a meager vocabulary and incomplete Shoshoni grammar. But these same people also interlard their Shoshoni with English words and phrases [pp. 119–120].'' Miller seemed to make that statement incidentally, in passing, and yet I believe he identified what is a major obstacle to theorizing in child phonology. We simply have not considered the possibility that the adult's speech might be a *source* of the child's phonological errors.

I think this is why it has not occurred to us to study the contributions of adult speech to child errors. Always knowing our own lexical and phonological targets it is natural that as speakers we concentrate mainly on the smooth execution of the appropriate motor commands. We pay relatively less attention to the allophonic variations which, in my judgment, would be communicatively maladaptive and cognitively difficult. Therefore, both adult speaker and adult listener are likely to be seduced by the *constancy* of it all, where I suspect the child hears something more like what we see in spectrograms, the *variability* of it all.

How Does Variability Function?

From the studies of language death, it appears that where variability exists in the adult system there is a reduced probability of acquisition by the children of those adults. But what do we know of the nature of this effect? From studies of language acquisition it would appear that we know very little, though one encounters occasional statements that children may become "confused" by highly variable language environments (e.g., homes in which three or four languages are used "indiscriminantly").

There have been a number of psychological experiments in which stimulus variability has been studied, mainly for its effects on the acquisition of visual concepts (cf. Posner, Goldsmith, & Welton, 1967; Posner & Keele, 1968, 1970; also see the excellent review in Wickelgren, 1979). I believe this work tells us something about what may be going on in phonological development, or at least provides a model for specific studies in that area.

In most experiments there is a prototype pattern which subjects, depending upon the experimental design, may or may not be allowed to see. Typically, the prototype pattern is constructed of dots that describe a recognizable "concept" such as a shape or a letter. Degrees of distortion are systematically introduced in the prototype; at extreme levels of distortion, patterns look very little like the prototype. Merely creating distortion automatically creates variability among the instances within a category.

It has been found that subjects can learn the prototype without ever having seen it, from exposure to its variants. But, as one might expect, the more distorted and variable the instances, the slower subjects are to learn the categories. There is, however, a trade-off. The more varied the instances or examples of the prototype, the greater the generality of the concept. One learns a new concept more quickly if exposed only to examples that strongly resemble the prototype, but the concept is less useful if future items to be categorized stray increasingly from the prototype.

One can envision the parallel with phonological development, where the phoneme is the prototype. If the child is reared by a single individual, who speaks in a careful and uniform manner (e.g., motherese), it is likely that the child will learn quickly. That is, he will discover (correctly posit) the functional units and their proper surface implementation with relatively little exposure. However, he may have some difficulty in understanding the speech of other individuals, and a variety of dialects and registers in which the "production constancy" of his original caretaker is violated.

When such "distortions"—and the phonetic variations they allow—are abundant, one can imagine the child (like Posner's research subjects) waiting for enough examples of the prototype to make his own matching attempt (i.e., effectively qualifying for a developmental stage, that of avoidance) or confidently targeting for (what will later turn out to be) an allophonic variation. Might this be the beginning of a pattern of development error? According to Stein (1981), the conditions that favor (historical) sound change are those in which "there is already a range of permissible realizations of some content (typically a variable situation) and that range is gradually and minimally extended [p. 178]."

Under ideal circumstances, this searching for the critical cues would occur at a relatively early stage of the child's acquisition. But when a language is in the developmentally nonideal process of change—as all languages are—the child is exposed to fluctuations (distortions of the prototype) and even in (what would otherwise be) later stages he may still be trying to infer the critical components and the range of variation about them.

But even in raising these concerns I have put a positive face on the situation, for I have treated lexical cues as though they were unitary, and of course they are not. What if fluctuations disproportionately involved a single segment in a word, with the remaining phones produced in more stable fashion? What is to tell the child that the variations he hears are *of* something? How does he know they represent a functional phonological *unity*, with which the speakers are taking liberties, as opposed to a number of different unities? With complex stimulus configurations the subject has to discover structure on the basis of cue *saliency* (cf. Kintsch, 1970, pp. 350–352), and how salient will he find the output of "optional rules"? How quickly and easily will the German child develop an internal representation for *geb-en* ('to give'; 'we/they give') from its phrase-final realizations in "everyday" German speech as ['ge:bɛn, 'ge:bən, 'ge:bm, 'ge:m, 'gem, 'gɛm], or for first-person singular *geb-e* from ['ge:bɛ, 'ge:bə, 'ge:βə, 'ge:p, 'gɛp, 'gɪp, 'gi:b, 'gi:p, gip] (Dressler & Wodak, 1982)?

According to Gibson (1969), stimulus enhancement may be achieved by physically exaggerating the distinctive features or by eliminating nondistinctive features. Either modification results in better performance on a variety of learning and sorting tasks than is obtained with normally appearing stimuli. Perhaps speakers' (unconscious) awareness of this enhancement effect is behind what has come to be known as "foreigner talk" and the "clear speech" that commonly is directed to the hearing-impaired adult (Chen, 1980). It follows that there ought also to be a form of *phonological motherese*. Surprisingly, the evidence on this is just emerging, though there is an abundance of studies on syntactic complexity, utterance length, and a variety of lexical and semantic factors (cf. Snow & Ferguson, 1977). The few articulation studies that have been reported suggest, variously, that mothers make no adjustment at the phonetic level when talking to their children (Baran, Laufer, & Daniloff, 1977), that they tend to enhance their phonetic values (Bernstein, 1982) though not consistently (Malsheen, 1980), and that they reduce their articulatory clarity (Shockey & Bond, 1980; Bard & Anderson, 1983).

One hopes the tangle will eventually be sorted out. In the meantime, phonetic variability among adults must be seen as a theoretically important factor in children's phonological development, the precise proportions to be worked out in future research.

6

Developmental Rephonologization

In the first three chapters, I attempted to show that infants, children, and adults speak under the influence of a variety of physiological, anatomical, and aerodynamic factors. Infants were seen to possess a clearly defined sound (or movement) system, shaped almost exclusively by these factors. Adult speakers were assumed to be operating within a more arbitrary (learned) system, but one that was subject to erosion and subperceptual shifting as the result of phonetic forces. In Chapter 4, I showed that the phonological systems of standard languages actually are less arbitrary than one might have supposed, with segment inventories and sequences susceptible to phonetic rationalization. In Chapter 5, phonetic variation in the adult system was assessed for its developmental consequences, and found to be potentially a source of delay in children's mastery of the contrasts in variation. As the monograph has developed, the focus has increasingly shifted toward the *cognitive* implications of *phonetic factors*. It is appropriate, in this regard, that we now consider a developmental theory in which phonetic and cognitive components *interact*.

Dephonologization, Phonologization, and Rephonologization

Dephonologization Historically

Jakobson (1931/1972) was among the first to address significantly the process of dephonologization. The dephonologization of a phonological contrast presumably results in its complete loss, with no trace remaining at the phonetic level. This process often takes place gradually (Chen & Wang, 1975), and in the previous chapter we saw some dramatic cases of dephonologization in which a dying contrast was cast into extreme variability before its extinction.

In most cases of historical sound change, the phonetic space occupied by the altered realization of a phoneme already is in systemic use, and the loss is therefore of a phonological distinction. As I illustrated some examples of this in Chapter 3, I will not review the truly historical cases here. I will, however, examine the ongoing dephonologization of one English phoneme, namely, the loss of /hw/ to /w/.

/hw/ → /w/

Due to the linguistic atlas project conducted in the United States in the 1930s and 1940s by Hans Kurath, something is known about the distribution of the voiceless glide /hw/, at least in the eastern part of the country (Kurath & McDavid, 1961; McDavid & McDavid, 1952; McDavid, 1950). At that time, words such as *whip* and *wheelbarrow* were pronounced with a [w] in England (treating it as a cluster, Trnka (1968) has stated that [h] cannot precede [w] in British English) and in three reasonably distinct regions in the United States. Those regions were (*a*) along the New England coast from Boston north; (*b*) a triangular area whose base extended from Albany, New York, to Baltimore, Maryland, and whose apex lay just east of the Ohio River; and (*c*) along the South Atlantic coast from Georgetown, South Carolina, to St. Augustine, Florida. Elsewhere, at least in the eastern portion of the United States, most *wh* words were pronounced [hw]. McDavid (1950) thought it unlikely that the /hw/ form would spread to other parts. On the other hand, he observed

> some indication that the pronunciations without /h/ are spreading. They are well established, though not exclusive, in the cultured speech of many metropolitan areas, not only along the Atlantic seaboard but farther west. In communities of divided usage the pronunciations without /h/ seem to be favored by younger and better-educated speakers and by speakers from the old, established cultured families of those communities [p. 459].

Whereas the 1952 edition of *Webster's Dictionary* shows only /hw/ pronunciations for *which, where, when, wheel*, and so on, the 1961 edition lists both /hw/ and /w/, in that order, but indicates neither is the preferred pronunciation. What is the status of /hw/ today? A direct answer might be difficult to find, but I believe there is evidence to indicate that /hw/ is almost totally dephonologized.

In French, Carter, and Koenig (1930), telephone conversations were monitored in order to count the frequency of words and sounds in conversational speech. Tabulations represent a total sample of 79,390 words. My own analyses of their data indicate that there were 10.3 *w* words to every *wh* word (excluding *who* and other such words). In their word-initial sound count, there were 10.3 /w/s to every /hw/. This can only mean that French *et al.* listed what they took to be the "correct phonemes" for each word, not the actual sounds heard. And, in fact, the authors stated that the standard of correctness used was "the typical pronunciation heard in reasonably enunciated conversation among educated persons in New York [pp. 310–311]" (the conversations were monitored in New York City). As New York City was a /hw/ region in the 1930s, according to the linguistic atlas project, and the dictionaries of the day carried /hw/ as the only correct pronunciation, we may be confident that all *wh* words were counted as /hw/.

In Mines *et al.* (1978), the conversations of 26 speakers from all over the United States were tape recorded so that an *allophone* count could be made. There were over 100,000 consonants and vowels in the sample. Their tabulations show a total of 2536 [w]s in word-initial position, and just 43 initial [hw]s. The ratio of [w] to [hw] is 59 to 1. As the ratio of /w/ to /hw/ in French *et al.* was 10.3 to 1, it is apparent that the Mines *et al.* speakers produced many more [w]s and many fewer [hw]s than were required by the lexical standards for educated New Yorkers in the 1930s. As [w] is not known to substitute for other sounds in adult speech, and /hw/ may be represented either by [hw] or by [w], one may take it that the speakers in Mines *et al.* were saying /hw/ words with a [w] pronounciation. I believe even the frequency of this may reasonably be estimated. There were 2579 words that began either with [w] or [hw] phones. By the 10.3 to 1 prescriptive ratio, there should have been 250 [hw]s. The observed number, 43, represents a *wh* → [w] conversion of 82.8%.

Why has /hw/ dephonologized to /w/? There may be several reasons. First, /hw/ occurred in a fairly restricted set of words, mainly functors of very high predictability. Second, /hw/ and [hw]-like sounds are not prominent either in the languages of the world or in infant sound making. Of the 197 languages in the Stanford Handbook, 167 have a /w/; only 27 have a /hw/. Of the 167 languages having a /w/, 25 have a /hw/ also, hence possibly a /w/–/hw/ contrast. So there are 142 languages with only a /w/, and 2 languages with only a /hw/. Among 12-month-old infants, Fisichelli (1950) heard 300 [w]s and no [hw]s. In Irwin (1947) at 11–12 months the ratio of [w] to [hw] was 40 to 1. There were similar ratios between [w] and [hw] in the deaf populations described in Chapter 1.

It may also be true that many adult speakers have derived their [hw]s from *underlying* /w/ by application of what Henning Andersen (1973) has called adaptive rules (or A-rules). According to Andersen, A-rules are needed where the standard system has been inadequately analyzed: "A-rules enable the individual speaker to adhere to the received norms of his speech community even if his phonological structure does not correspond to these norms [p. 782]." A-rules apply stylistically, in certain speaking situations, to a small and decreasing number of words. Adult speakers whose own A-rules permit them to derive [hw] from underlying /w/ would consider children's [wɪs]]s and [wɪp]s natural simplifications, to be tolerated rather than corrected.

/hw/ to the New Generation

Given the relative weakness of [hw] in the babbling of babies and in the speech of their parents, one can imagine developmental studies showing a less than convincing performance on the part of child speakers. Of the 384 children whose articulation patterns were analyzed by Cairns, Cairns, and Blosser (1970), there were 120 children whose only "error" was [w] for /hw/ in *wheel*. Templin's (1957) data show that the /hw/ was said correctly by 25% of the 4-year-olds, but at age 8 it was correct in only 8% of the children (the next to the lowest, /z/, was said correctly by 75% of the 8-year-olds. In Prather *et al.* (1975), /hw/ was said correctly by 70% of the children at 40 months, but by only 52% of the 4-year-olds (Prather's raw data show that all /hw/ errors involved [w] replacements). One wonders if these children, like Jacob (in Menn, 1976, see my p. 211), heard and tried to achieve in their own speech what later turned out to be an irrelevant variation. If so, perhaps we should assign them sensory credit for noticing the very occasional [hw]s in their environment, and give them cognitive credit for learning, later, to ignore them!

For the last several years I have questioned and tested a number of college students as to their production and perception of *wh* words. The majority, of course, say [w]. However, I have found that they *accept* both [w] *and* [hw] as correct representatives of the initial sound in *wheelbarrow*. The same students accept only [w] as the correct way to begin *wagon*. It appears either that the internal representation for *wh* words includes both voiced and voiceless forms, or that /hw/-less speakers have two internal representations, one which prescribes their own output values and a second which operates receptively for the speech of others.

Given the indeterminate status of /hw/ in American English, one might suppose that this particular sound is ignored on tests of children's speech articulation. It is not. Most of the leading tests contain /hw/, usually with the same weighting in the articulation score as English phonemes, though the sound typically is not said by the *examiner!* Perhaps this is why there is less interobserver agreement on children's /hw/ productions than there is on truly functional units (Norris, Harden, & Bell, 1980).

Dephonologization Developmentally

Do children ever "devalue" a phonological contrast? Consider the fate of word-final stops in English. The child—from birth—has produced syllables, but nearly all of them have ended in vowels. As he turns his attentions to the speech of adults, he hears adult speakers omit, release, flap, check, glottalize, devoice, and merge their word-final stops with adjacent consonants. Is it not logical that a child, under such circumstances, might conclude that whatever it is that occurs at the end, it (or they) cannot be terribly important? The child's "failure" to produce this dazzling array of phonetic forms may well be a *principled* action on his part—as if he were drawing, as King (1969) suggested, "too much of the right conclusion from the data presented to him. [This quote and subsequent quotes from King, 1969, are reprinted from King, R. D. (1969), *Historical linguistics and generative grammar*. Englewood Cliffs, N.J.: Copyright 1969 by Prentice-Hall, Inc; p. 88.]"

There are scattered throughout the literature in child phonology cases of what sometimes are called "progressive phonological idioms" (cf. Moskowitz, 1980). These occur when young children utter a word with a proficiency that seems to exceed their level of phonological development at that time. Undoubtedly the most frequently cited of these idioms is Hildegard's (Leopold, 1947) early and adultlike production of the word *pretty*, which later became reduced to [pɪtɪ]. Presumably, Hildegard did not lose the articulatory ability to produce /pr/, but in the interim developed a phonological system that carried no provision for such sequences. Or, it may be the case that *pretty* was for Hildegard an unanalyzed unit; what appears to observers as a regression might in fact be an equilibrating of a phonological system that contains certain instances of "pseudoprogress."

Other dephonologizations that occur developmentally may not represent a true abandonment of a phonological distinction. The child may not be aware of a contrast in the ambient language, and therefore may not have internal representations that correspond to those of adult speakers. A phonological distinction also may be obliterated when a young child with an appropriate internal representation takes articulatory aim and misses his anatomical target, or hits one that happens to be wrong. In either case his articulators land someplace else, and, if that other place is routinely used by the standard language, to the listener there will be a merger and to the analyst there will be an *apparent* dephonologization. Careful diagnostic testing is necessary to discern these cases from true dephonologizations.

Phonologization Historically

Perhaps the first to address significantly the process of phonologization was Baudouin de Courtenay (1895–1972) followed by Jakobson (1931/1972), and more recently by Jeffers and Lehiste (1979), Hyman (1975), and Anderson (1981). All agree that phonologization has occurred when, as Hyman puts it, "a phonetic process becomes phonological [p. 171]." In all cases, the source of a systemic property is a lower level articulatory behavior which is inducted into the system and begins, then, to carry a functional load. Consider the well-known tendency for speakers to front velar consonants before high front vowels, as in English [ki]. According to Hyman, in the Luganda language this fronting tendency has become a phonological requirement, in the form of "a particularly noticeable palatal offglide. . . . /ekikopo/ 'cup' is pronounced [ek^{y}ikopo] [1975, p. 171]." According to Jeffers and Lehiste, in the Latvian language this fronting tendency also has become a phonological requirement. Syllables such as [ki] were advanced to the more palatal [ci], but, additionally, the (independent) vocalic shift of [ai] to [i] left Latvian both with /ki/ and /ci/. What began as an innocent articulatory effect—probably both unintended and unconscious—became a working linguistic unit, capable of performing lexical service.

Pointing to a single case, the palatalization of velar stops, may give readers the impression that phonologization is a rare process. Just the opposite is true. All human speech contains phonetic artifacts that are not intended by the sophisticated speaker. Many of these artifacts are due to coarticulation, a fundamental property of speech. The fact that coarticulation may not be consciously intended says nothing of its usefulness, for coarticulation is perhaps as important to speech perception as it is to speech production. Coarticulation may arise from constraints on the speech motor system, but it becomes, as a critical "constant" in the system of phonetic cues, significantly entrenched in the speaker-hearer's cognitive system.

Perceived in this way coarticulation has two logical consequences. One is that phonological systems have a "naturalness" about them, that is, are describable in universal phonetic terms. We have seen that languages (i.e., adult speakers) prefer singletons over clusters, initial over final consonants, and voiced bilabials over voiced velars. I think this is because the structure of phonological systems is largely due to the phonologization of phonetic operations. The other logical consequence of coarticulation—the raw material of phonologization—is a developmental one. How is the language-innocent child to know which are the phonological units and which are the phonetic artifacts?

Phonologization Developmentally

How is a child to sort through the complex distribution of noises and come up with the *important* noises? Not knowing which are the critical sounds—or even that there is a difference between "-emic" and "-etic"—would the child not echo *everything* he could?

If an engineer were to design a system for communicating thoughts with vocal sounds, he probably would create one level of organization. But if a second phonetic level somehow crept in, our engineer would at least control the degree of variation. He would shove it into an insensitive region of our auditory curve.

He would specify that only the robust contrasts could be the phonological ones. But engineers do not design speech, and there are levels of organization, and the physical and psychological magnitude of phonetic contrasts says very little, if anything, about their linguistic significance. This leads to problems for the acquisitor of the system. The problem for the Russian child, according to Shvachkin (1948/1973), is that "the distinction in the Russian Language between the prelingual and postlingual *r* can be clearly perceived by ear, but it does not serve to distinguish word meanings. At the same time, the much finer acoustic distinction between palatalized and unpalatalized *r* does serve this function [p. 95]."

Baudouin de Courtenay (1895–1972) considered that such "neophonetic alterations" as the palatalized and unpalatalized /r/s were noticed by children, who incorporated them into their own speech, and even *embellished* them:

The tendency to develop new divergences is, on the whole, much more typical of the speech of children than that of adults, whose language represents the linguistic norm. What is only embryonic in the latter can become apparent and palpable in the speech of children [1972, pp. 209–210].

Menn (1976) observed a consequence of allophonic variation in the speech of a boy named Jacob, who learned to produce some "-etic" variations while merging other contrasts which are "-emic" for adults. In fact, Menn observed at one point, Jacob

often seems to match phonetic detail which is subphonemic for English speakers and yet at the same time fails to show any production response to distinctions which seem very salient to us: compare the absence of distinction between initial /r/ and /w/ with this reaction. . . . to the difference between the "light" palatal [lˆ] of the word 'light' and the 'dark' velar [lˋ] of the word 'roll' [p. 112].

I am not sure Jacob's differential failure to achieve these contrasts was purely an organizational problem, but it could have been. And this possibility prompted Menn to comment that "there is no measure of magnitude of phonetic difference which predicts in advance that differences less than such-and-such will be subphonemic and differences greater than such-and-such will be phonemic [p. 112]."

Fry (1972) observed in a British child the tendency to express /tr/ and /dr/ clusters as [tʃr] and [dʒr]. In their study of 510 British children, Anthony *et al.* (1971) found that for the /tr/ *train*, 21 children said [tʃ] and 20 said [tʃr], though none palatalized the /t/ in *tent*. It is conceivable that some children phonologize the affrication produced in [t]–[r] transitions. That this might be so is suggested by children's spelling errors.

Spelling Errors

There are indications (Read, 1975; Barton, Miller, & Macken, 1980) that children's production of affricates for stop + liquid clusters may be an example of developmental phonologization. Read studied the misspellings of children who were enrolled in beginning reading programs. He found that about 17 or 18% of his young spellers represented /tr/ words as *chr* or *ch* and /dr/ words as *jr*. Hence *try* was spelled *chrie* and *dragon* was erroneously spelled as *jragin*. Read placed a number of such children in an ingenious experiment which required them to categorize these sounds. Specifically, he showed the children pictures of objects such as a tie, a tree, and a chair, and asked them which of these began with the same sound as the word *train*.

Much of the time, Read's subjects properly selected other /tr/ words as matches for *train*. Of interest is the number of *other* words they also judged to match *train*. The first column in the following chart shows the percentage of consistent selections of a *stop* + /r/ *cluster and an affricate* (e.g., /tr/ and /tʃ/). The second column shows the percentage of consistent selections of a *stop* + /r/ *cluster only* (e.g., /tr/). The third column shows the percentage of consistent selections of a *stop* + /r/ *cluster and a stop* (e.g., /tr/ and /t/). It is evident from these data that Read's kindergarten subjects were slightly more likely to assign stop + /r/ clusters to the affricates than to the stops. Eliminating the middle column, in about 53% of the classifications the /tr/ and /dr/ words were thought to be more like the affricate words than the stop words:

	Stop + /r/ and affricate	Stop + /r/ only	Stop + /r/ and stop
/tr/	42	22	36
/dr/	43	17	40

As spelling does not require speech articulation, spelling errors represent an invaluable source of information as to children's phonological organization. They appear to be relatively free of the confounding of immature speech–motor programming (though there could be a kinesthetic component in spelling, as Read recognized). Consequently, when Read observed spellings such as *cwnchre* for *country,* he suggested that "what such spellings as these really show is that the children who created them have yet to learn that /t/ is regarded as the underlying form or, in traditional terminology, the affricated [t] belongs to the phoneme /ṭ/ [p. 53]."

Read, incidentally, explored a number of other cases of apparent phonologization, as indicated by the spelling of intervocalic /t/s as *d*s. The children spelled *pretty* as *prede*, *bottom* as *bodom*, and *better* as *bedr*. Such "mistakes" speak eloquently to a variety of linguistic and developmental issues, and it is clear that systematic studies of children's misspellings could reveal even more about children's underlying representations and phonological categories.

Physical Effects of Phonologization

Little is known of the physical effects of phonologization in children. As it is generally assumed (Anderson, 1981, p. 58; Hyman, 1975, p. 172) that phonologization causes *exaggeration* of the originally phonetic effect, one might suppose that children's (incorrect) phonologizations would give their speech a somewhat unnatural quality. Indeed, there is evidence from several quarters (Krause, 1980, 1982b; Simon, 1978) that children do exaggerate certain secondary cues while phonetically shortchanging the primary ones. It is not known what the perceptual consequences of these exaggerations might be for the adult listener, but an interesting question is suggested by this situation: Might the child accidentally *phonologize the environmental effects of a contrast and dephonologize the contrast itself?*

To overly value coarticulatory effects—while undervaluing the segment that is their source—is to perform what has been termed a rephonologization. In a moment I will examine some evidence on developmental rephonologization, but first it is appropriate to consider some of the historical evidence on this restructuring process.

Rephonologization Historically

Rephonologization involves a shifting in which one segment loses its contrastivity and another, typically an adjacent segment, gains contrastive potential. There are perfectly logical reasons why this should happen, and certain linguistic places where rephonologization should be likely to occur. Because the speaker's articulatory programming of phonetic units affects the production of other sounds in the immediate vicinity, from a perceptual point of view each sound is *multiply cued*. In most cases, the strongest cue or set of cues to a segment will be intrinsic to that segment. However, secondary cues will be contained in the coarticulated segments, with the most salient typically residing in the immediately adjacent segments. This perfectly natural condition provides for some interesting sound change possibilities. One is that the primary cues are technically free to weaken, and may be more susceptible to weakening—at least if listeners are aware of the secondary cues—without a resulting loss in surface distinctiveness. As it is generally assumed that homonymy is a threat to communication, at least when its level becomes intolerably high (cf. Locke, 1979a), language users would be released from this usual "pressure to avoid homonymy" where secondary cues are available. Wang (1978) has depicted the situation as follows:

$$\text{XE}' \text{—————————————} \rightarrow \text{XE}'$$
$$\text{YE}'' \text{—————————————} \rightarrow \text{XE}''$$

Time 1   Time 2

Due to coarticulation, the vowels following initial consonants X and Y are produced distinctively. At Time 2, the consonants X and Y are merged, but the following vowels retain their earlier distinctiveness. As this distinctiveness can no longer be traced to consonantal differences, it must now be intrinsic to the vowels. Hence, the consonantal contrast has been dephonologized, the vocalic contrast has been phonologized, the entire process constituting a rephonologization. The number of contrasts in the system remains the same.

There are many examples of rephonologization historically. They include languages in which initial /s/ + C clusters have lost their /s/ but retained their distinctiveness from singleton cognates. How was the distinctiveness retained? Laboratory analyses show that /sm/, /sw/, and /sl/ clusters typically are rendered with a voiceless or partially voiced nasal, glide, or liquid. Hence, the loss of /s/ from *sna*—as it is still written in Tibetan—left speakers of Modern Burmese with /nḁ/ 'nose' (Greenlee & Ohala, 1980).

Perhaps one of the most interesting examples of rephonologization historically is the sequence of events leading up to the formation of tones in languages such as Chinese, Vietnamese, and Thai.

Tonogenesis

As the result of an excellent paper by Hombert, Ohala, and Ewan (1979), a great deal is known about the evolution of tones in languages that had previously been nontonal. Most of what I say about tonogenesis was learned from their paper.

Hombert *et al.* show with the data of earlier studies and with their own measurements as well, that there is a systematic relationship between initial stop consonant voicing and the fundamental frequency of the following vowel. Specifically, voiceless stops are associated with somewhat higher fundamental frequencies than their voiced cognates. For English (male) speakers, the frequency difference is about 18 Hz at the beginning of the vowel, and it persists—though at a declining level of magnitude—for at least 100 msec. Hombert *et al.* also found that these voicing effects on fundamental frequency occur in tone languages. In a study of two Yoruba speakers, the authors observed what appears to be a more robust effect, though for shorter vocalic durations. High tones were substantially lowered by voiced stops and low tones were significantly elevated by the presence of a preceding voiceless stop. The high tone frequency difference for voiced and voiceless cases was equal to more than 40 Hz at vowel onset.

Hombert *et al.* provided a vocal cord tension hypothesis for the frequency effects they observed. According to this hypothesis, there would be more horizontal vocal cord tension during the production of voiceless stops, to inhibit accidental voicing. This tension would not immediately dissipate upon the release of the consonant, and would raise the frequency of vowels following voiceless stops. This elevated fundamental frequency would decline gradually over the course of the vowel.

To test the perceptibility of frequency differences similar in magnitude to those measured earlier, Hombert *et al.* synthesized 10 instances of an [i]-like vocalic pattern with starting fundamental frequencies of 110 or 130 and a variety of slopes before stabilizing at 120 Hz. Various combinations of the tones were then presented in pairs to subjects whose task required them on each trial to match the second tone to the starting frequency of the first. Subjects were able to perform this task with accuracy when the slope from the initial fundamental frequency to the steady state portion of the vowel was 60 msec or more. As the frequency differences observed earlier in English speakers lasted for at least 100 msec, it appears that consonantally conditioned vowel frequencies are different enough to be phonologized as tones.

Hombert *et al.* also showed that a possible factor in tonogenesis could be the offset of vowels. Specifically, they observed that vowels ending in [h] were systematically lower in frequency than vowels ending in [ʔ], that this difference begins at least 70 msec before vowel offset and is well within the limits of detectability. All that is required to complete the explanation of tonal development are certain facts, namely, that the languages in question underwent sound change that merged the source segments (the voiced and voiceless stops in initial position, the [h] and [ʔ], in final position). Hombert *et al.* present evidence that the source segments were indeed merged. As a consequence, having lost the primary consonantal cues, speakers (wishing to maximize or to retain lexical distinctiveness) began for the first time, presumably, to try to produce different vocalic frequencies. And listeners began to listen for pitch variations. Fundamental frequency was thus phonologized as "tone."

The Role of Redundancy in Rephonologization

As previously mentioned, in tonogenesis, and in other cases of rephonologization, the primary cues weaken in favor of secondary cues residing, usually, in an adjacent segment. Consequently, one might be inclined to look upon rephonologization as a serendipitous event: When secondary cues "happen" to be immediately adjacent, they can accommodate the to-be-abandoned contrast, and a transfer of phonological function is possible. Indeed, if one wished to predict *where* rephonologization might occur, a perfectly reasonable approach might be to explore the cue system of a language, noting the cases of unusually perceptible coarticulation. But is such coarticulation present purely by accident, or is it there for a reason? Might it be that the threatened segment is threatened for a phonetic reason, for example, that it is physiologically difficult to achieve? If so, it is logical that speakers would need to anticipate the difficult segment more than would be necessary for easier movement patterns, and perhaps speakers would need to invoke and to coordinate additional motor operations. If these operations and the states they induce do not dissipate readily, sound patterns whose production requires extreme deviation from "normal" vocal tract routines might be disproportionately represented in the segments on either side. Initial voiceless stops would perturb the following vowel, final voiced stops would perturb the preceding vowel. That there was a salient cue in a segment, then, would be prima facie evidence that a difficult and therefore potentially threatened segment lay nearby.

There is another reason why the existence of a heavily conditioned segment might spell the demise of a source segment, quite independent of their physiological relationship. That reason has to do with the *internal redundancy* that such a relationship provides. The listener can get the information he needs in several different places. As the listener also is a speaker, he knows that when he talks his listeners can get the information they need from several different segments. He is, therefore, free to allow the weakening of the more difficult segment. This generally will be the source segment (the initial voiceless stop, the final voiced stop) rather than the affected segment, for reasons noted in the preceding paragraph.

Christie (1979) has described the redundancy hypothesis, and speculated on how redundancy might permit sound change to take place:

> At one stage in the history of the language certain features are distinctive and others are not. At this stage the nondistinctive features are free to change without any danger of disruption in the communicative system. There follows a shift in categorization (not in the sounds themselves) through which certain features that were previously nondistinctive become distinctive. Now the previously distinctive features are free to change, again without a disruption in the process of communication. The net result is the possibility of a complete change in the articulatory and auditory characteristics of the phonemes without any threat of a disruption in communication [p. 4].

The "complete change" referred to by Christie is, of course, what I have been calling rephonologization. That *internal* redundancy might be so powerful is suggested by the degree to which articulation is influenced by *external* redundancy. Lieberman (1963) found that speakers articulate a word with increased intensity, greater duration, and improved intelligibility when the word appears *nonredundantly* in sentences (e.g., "The number that you will hear is *nine*") than when it appears in redundant or predictable contexts (e.g., "A stitch in time saves *nine*").

Rephonologization in History and in Childhood

The abundance of phonetic cues and the redundancy they provide are potential problems for the child who is attempting to discover the structure of the system. One of his tasks will be to determine that there are entities such as "words," a task made difficult by the fact that speech is delivered not in word-sized chunks but in longer and less determinate stretches. As Chiat (1979) observed,

> Only a minority of words, typically only when they perform certain functions, are commonly used in isolation even in adult-to-child language—nouns used with a naming function; sentence adverbs like *yes/no, there;* question words; odd adjectives like *good.* The majority of words will only be encountered in combination with other words which may be unfamiliar to the child and from which they must be abstracted [p. 598].[1]

While the child is attempting to isolate words, he must also make some structural decisions regarding the status and preferred form of word constituents, the segments, which I indicated in Chapter 5 may vary considerably. Not coincidentally, these variations may be the greatest for segments that are likely to be difficult for the child for physiological reasons. If the child assumes that the wildly fluctuating information is the least important, and the more nearly stable and invariant information is the most important, he frequently will come to exactly the wrong conclusion. His conception of the structure of his parents' system will differ from their own conception of it.

A cognitive source of such errors is possible because the child actively hypothesizes—before he discovers—the structure of the system he must simultaneously use and learn. That children do this ordinarily is suggested, extraordinarily, by the collected evidence on creolization (Bickerton, 1982). If children can convert a pidgin to a creole, they have the ability (if not, perversely, the desire) to create a linguistic organization that differs from that of their parents.

[1] In 1971, Waterson suggested that children perceive and attempt to reproduce whole utterances, not merely their lexical parts. Since that time, Moskowitz (1980), Vihman (1982), and especially Peters (1983) have drawn our attention to the abundance of 'formulaic' patterns in the speech of children (as well as adults). As Peters points out, young children cannot know exactly what the units of language are, so they are not likely to uniformly select *words* as the units. Rather, they may target frequently for such larger-than-word patterns as 'all gone' or 'that's mine', quite unaware of standard morpheme boundaries. One of the interesting aspects of these developmental idioms is the implication that children's internal representations can be quite different from those of adults (see also Aitchison, 1972; Aitchison & Chiat, 1981; Aitchison & Straf, 1981).

In what follows, I will examine several cases of rephonologization that have occurred historically and that I believe may also act to delay the rate and alter the course of phonological development in children. Each involves a shift of functional status from word-final consonants to their preceding vowels.

Vowel Nasalization Historically

The process of regressive nasal assimilation is well known and reasonably well understood (cf. Ohala, 1975). In producing a word that ends with a nasal consonant, speakers anticipate the need to lower their velum while producing the preceding vowel, which as a result takes on nasal resonance itself. This phonetic effect occurs in most of the world's languages. However, in Ruhlen's (1978) analysis of 706 languages, some 155 (or about 22%) have *phonemically nasal* vowels. The evidence in Ruhlen, and in Entenman (1977), is that the assimilative effect was phonologized when final nasal consonants were lost in these languages. Perhaps one of the more familiar cases of nasal vowel rephonologization is French, in which language *bon* is expressed phonetically as [bɔ̃] prepausally and before most consonants but as [bɔn] before vowels (e.g., [bɔnæpətit]). Tranel (1981) has argued persuasively that nasal vowels are now lexical, that is, exist underlyingly.

It is apparent that the amount of nasal resonance produced in a vowel by a following nasal consonant, that is, the normal assimilatory effect, is perceptible enough to have figured into its phonologization. Ali, Gallagher, Goldstein, and Daniloff (1971) clipped the final nasal consonants and consonant transitions from the syllables of a Midwestern speaker, and played the remaining portions to a number of native American English listeners. Ali *et al.* found that nasal resonance, as produced through this normal assimilative process, was sufficiently detectable to be used as a cue in word recognition. Indeed, in some experiments with synthetic speech and splicings of real speech, Malécot (1960) found American listeners eminently able to discriminate words such as *camp, hint,* and *bunk* from *cap, hit,* and *buck* purely on the basis of nasal resonance in the vowel. In his spectrographic measurements, Malécot observed that the nasal consonants had surprisingly short durations. When they were excised and inserted into words with oral vowels (e.g., transferring the [m] from *ample* to *apple,* on about 80% of the trials the nasal consonants were not even noticed by Malécot's listeners. Malécot concluded that

> phonetically, there is almost always a vestigial nasal consonant segment present, clearly perceptible in *hunt* and *hint,* for example, but usually so short as to be practically insignificant; in most cases, its suppression does little more than detract somewhat from the naturalness of the utterance. In its place, we have come to rely for manner information primarily on the nasality that the vowel has acquired by anticipation of the nasal consonant. Vowel nasality is thus the principal distinctive

feature . . . . [This quote is reprinted from Malécot, A. (1960). Vowel nasality as a distinctive feature in American English. *Language*, 36, p. 229; with permission from Linguistic Society of America.]

Vowel Nasalization Developmentally

There are a number of cases in which English-learning children have been observed to omit final nasal consonants but nasalize the preceding vowel. It is as though the children—like the French—had the nasal consonant as an underlying form. Leopold's (1947) daughter Hildegard omitted word-final nasals while nasalizing the preceding vowel, hence [ã, æ̃] for *on, an, man, hand* at the age of 1:5–2:1. Olmsted's (1971) American children made a total of 89 errors on /n/. Of these, 28 involved omission of /n/ with nasalization of an adjacent vowel. Anthony *et al.*'s (1971) British children commonly deleted nasals while nasally resonating the preceding vowels. Examples, using the authors' notational system, included:

$$stamps \rightarrow {}^{\sim}ps \ (13)$$
$${}^{\sim}\text{?s} \ (\ 2)$$
$$monkey \rightarrow {}^{\sim}k \ (\ 5)$$
$$pencil \rightarrow {}^{\sim}s \ (\ 2)$$

There are several reports of child speech that contain phonetic transcriptions of the spontaneous or elicited speech of young children. Table 6.1 shows a portion of the transcriptions for three children from Maxwell (1981) and one child from Elbert, Dinnsen, and Weismer (forthcoming), who were not preselected because of any particular penchant for deleting final nasals. The entire sample for each child indicates that all four subjects omitted final nasals frequently; I have shown some of the words in which the preceding vowel was nasalized. This was the typical case, and it was exceedingly common.

There is other evidence in Maxwell's transcriptions. A.B. reduced all oral consonant clusters, but some final nasal + obstruent clusters were preserved in:

skunk	[dʌŋk]	*lamp*	[æ̞əmp]
shrimp	[wɪmp]	*find*	[band]

These cases suggest that tautosyllabic nasal + obstruent sequences were not candidates for cluster reduction because to A.B. "the nasal" was not a consonant but a resonance on the vowel. I assume that Maxwell would have been inclined to perceive A.B.'s productions as *nasal + consonant* obstruent clusters because Malécot (1960) found that a nasal vowel typically *is heard as* a nasal consonant if followed by a tautosyllabic stop. This explains the appearance of nasal consonants in Maxwell's transcriptions of A.B.'s [dʌŋk] for *skunk* and the other cases.

Table 6.1
Loss of Final Nasals with Nasalization of the Preceding Vowel in Four Children

A.B. (4:5)		L.S. (4:0)		J.O. (4:7)		M.B. (3:11)	
hĩ	him	ʌ̃o	under	mĩ	mean	dãi	find
wʌ̃	one	tʌ̃	come	kʌ̃mã	come on	dɛ̃i	standing
wɛ̃	when	tʃã	Tom	ɔ̃	gonna	ã	on
fɪhĩ	fishing	tsĩ	screamed	ɛ̃	them	bĩ	finished
õ	don't	mãtʃo	monster	dã	don't	õĩ	holding
ɛ̃	and	kæ̃	can't	õ	want	õi	only
kæ̃	can't	tʃɛ̃i	twenty	ʤʌ̃	jump	wʌ̃	one
bãi̯	find	pai̯omæ̃	spiderman	mã	man	dɛ̃ɪ	dentist
ĩ	in	bʌsĩ	busing	pɛ̃ʔo	pencils	õ	don't
bʌ̃ʔ	bunch	sæsĩ	crashing	nɛ̃i̯	name	wĩ	ring
kæ̃	can	dʌ̃	gonna	dʌ̃	dumb	fʌ̃i	funny
ɛ̃ibadi	anybody	tsɔ̃	turn	ĩ	in	wɛ̃	when
dĩ	stream	tʃai̯	slime	wʌ̃	one	ɔ̃	gonna
tægĩ	tagging			pwæ̃	plane	dãi	pajamas
dĩ	dream			æ̃ʔo	anchor	ĩ	in
kaĩ	climb			dɪõ	different	pʌ̃ʔn̩	pumpkin
dĩ	thin			tɛ̃ʔ	tents	ʌ̃	sun
				ɛ̃	and	ʌ̃	under
				wɛ̃i̯pou̯	rainbow	ĩə	cleaner
				tʰai̯	time	dæ̃o	camel
				grĩ	green	nomæ̃	snowman
				ʌ̃	under	pɛ̃ʔo	pencil

Source: A.B., L.S., and J.O. are from Maxwell (1981), M.B. is from Elbert, Dinnsen, and Weismer (forthcoming).

I suppose my use of cluster reduction evidence in a child is similar to Malécot's (1960) use of flapping evidence in adults. Malécot observed that the /t/ in *auntie* is subject to flapping (e.g., [æ̃ɾi], though the English flapping rule only applies intervocalically, suggesting that *auntie* contains no /n/.

From the data I have observed, including those reproduced here, it appears in *transcription* that the vowel preceding a nasal is more likely to bear the diacritic for nasalization when the nasal is missing than when the nasal is present. Whether this is because the nasal resonance is physically greater when the nasal is missing or whether it only is more conspicuous seems not to be known. As nasal vowels *not* preceding nasal consonants would violate the English listener's phonological rules, one can imagine that they would be especially noticeable.

It is not clear whether all such cases of apparent rephonologization represent true restructurings of the English rule system. All four of the children in Table 6.1 had *some* final nasal consonants. It is hard to tell from transcriptions whether the appearance of these final nasals was environmentally determined, lexically variable, or unstable for motoric or other reasons. We also know nothing of the children's receptive functioning, including whether they were aware of the contrastive potential of the final consonants.

Children's (Non)Spelling of Nasal Consonants

We are again fortunate in being able to inspect Read's (1975) evidence on the spelling and phonetic categorization of children in the first grade. Read asked his subjects to spell the word *bet*. When they had accomplished this, he asked them to spell the word *bent*. Frequently these words were spelled identically, as *bet*, though the children readily admitted that the words did not sound alike. Read then supplied the children with a triangular "pointer" and asked them to place it over that part of *bent* (spelled *bet*) that contained the difference between the two words. Then the children were asked to spell *sick* and *sink*, perform the pointer task, and to spell *pup* and *pump*, performing the pointer task once more. The 20 first-graders who performed the pointer task reliably (from an original group of 28), were easily divisible into two equal groups. One group had spelled the nasal consonant in at least two of the three cases and placed the pointer between the vowel and the final consonant in the categorization task. The other group of 10 first-graders had omitted the nasal consonant in all three of the words and consistently placed the pointer on or directly above the vowel. This result suggests that children seize upon the "accidental" vowel nasalization cue as *the* cue, much like Malécot's (1960) adult listeners, and it further confirms the developmental rephonologization hypothesis.

Vowel Lengthening Historically

There are many cases, historically, in which a consonant has been dropped with subsequent "compensatory" lengthening of an adjacent vowel (cf. de Chene & Anderson, 1979). Here I will concern myself not with those cases, but with a different situation, the lengthening of vowels before word-final voiced consonants.

In English particularly, but in a variety of other languages as well, vowels are longer when they precede final voiced consonants than when they precede final voiceless consonants. Hence, [ib] is longer than [ip], [ag] is longer than [ak], and [oz] is longer than [os]. The English evidence is too extensive to cite here, but it includes Rositzke (1939), House and Fairbanks (1953), Peterson and Lehiste (1960), and Klatt (1973). For languages other than English, a similar (though perhaps reduced) relationship has been observed in Spanish (Zimmerman & Sapon, 1958), Dutch (Slis & Cohen, 1969), Hindi (Maddieson & Gandour, 1975), Danish (Fischer-Jorgensen, 1964), Norwegian (Fintoft, 1961), and French, Russian, and Korean (Chen, 1970).[2]

The phonetic basis for the voicing—vowel length rule is unknown, though there is no shortage of hypotheses. Since Scharf (1964) found that English

---

[2]Polish (Keating, 1979) and Arabic (Flege & Port, 1981), though they have postvocalic voiced consonants, seem not to have the voicing–vowel length rule of the other languages.

speakers produce longer vowels before "voiced" sounds even in *whispering*, much of the recent speculation has been less concerned with peripheral factors than with the systemic status of the relationship. For example, Raphael's (1972) electromyographic investigation showed that vowels before voiced sounds were sustained not by passive forces, but by motor instructions to the laryngeal musculature.

Lisker (1974) provided the following summary of the hypotheses that had been entertained at the time of his article:

1) Vowels are longer before voiced and shorter before voiceless consonants according to a rule of constant energy expenditure for the syllable, longer vowels and voiceless consonants both being more costly in articulatory energy.
2) Vowels are lengthened before voiced stops to allow time for laryngeal readjustment needed if voicing is to be maintained during oral closure.
3) Vowels are shorter before voiceless consonants because those consonants are fortes [sic], and fortisness involves the earlier onset of articulatory closure.
4) Vowels before voiceless consonants are shorter because the strong closure gesture is accomplished more rapidly, again because of the fortis nature of those consonants [pp. 238–239].

Lisker reviewed the evidence for or against each of these hypotheses. The first was found wanting in that there is no accepted measure of energy or articulatory effort. The second hypothesis suggests that long vowels should need proportionately less additional time to perform the requisite laryngeal gestures than short vowels, yet data from Scharf (1962) suggest that the increases in duration are linear. The last two explanations depend upon one's acceptance of fortisness as a phonetic construct. If fortisness, by definition, means an early closure and a late release, then by calling voiceless sounds fortis one automatically implies the reason for the short vowel. But nothing has been explained. To these four hypotheses, therefore, Lisker added his own, specifying the reason

5) as to why the closure for the voiceless stop should occur not long after the devoicing gesture begins, and that is that the phonetic result would otherwise be, not a sequence of vowel + voiceless stop, but rather vowel + aspiration + voiceless stop, i.e., a phonetic sequence unacceptable as normal English [p. 241].

Javkin (1979a) pointed out that Lisker's hypothesis is incomplete, for it merely states that preaspiration is unacceptable, and does not attempt to say why it is unacceptable.[3] Second, the hypothesis makes claims only for English, though a wide variety of languages have such a voicing–vowel length rule, even if of lesser magnitude.

[3]In response to this, Lisker (personal communication, January 5, 1983) writes that "one might as well ask why an apical trill is not an 'acceptable' realization of /r/ in American English. Preaspirated stops are rather rare as single phonological elements in language. Like the question of why a French

Javkin reviewed a hypothesis due to Klatt (1975), which also attempted to account for the shorter vowels that precede voiceless sounds:

6) A slightly delayed glottal opening gesture is likely to produce a few cycles of vibration during closure, which is an undesireable cue for voicing. Since perfect synchrony of glottal and supraglottal activity is difficult, the vocal folds are normally abducted somewhat early to avoid generation of a false voicing cue [p. 698].

Javkin argues that this explanation could not be correct because languages such as Hungarian and German have both the voicing–vowel length rule *and* make phonemic use of vowel duration independently of consonantal voicing. Javkin argued that the existence of such languages flies in the face of Klatt's hypothesis, for they permit vowel length to vary across voicing environments at a potential expense to the phonemic vowel length contrast. In other words, according to the Javkin criticism, if Hungarian and German speakers are not worried about what differential vowel duration could do to the length contrast in their languages, why should English speakers worry about what a few extra cycles of vibration could do to the English voicing contrast?

Javkin presented a very different alternative hypothesis, which he then proceeded to test in several experiments:

7) It is possible that the explanation lies not in the constraints of speakers' articulatory mechanisms, but in the constraints of their auditory mechanisms. The fact that one of the characteristics of the vowel, voicing, continues into the consonant, might make the vowel appear to be longer than if voicing abruptly ended [p. 57].

Javkin conducted an experiment in which listeners were to adjust a tone to match the duration of synthetic [ɪ] vowels in [hɪs] and [hɪz]. These words, *hiss* and *his,* were synthesized such that the consonants were of identical duration. The [h] portion was 85 msec, with no formant transitions to the vowel. The sibilant portion was 120 msec, preceded by a 35-msec transition from the vowel. For *hiss* items, the voicing ended with the 35-msec transition; for *his* items the voicing continued through the 120 msec of the sibilant. The durations of the vowels were made to vary from 90 msec to 125, 155, and 185 msec, including the transition. There were, then, two voicing categories (*hiss* and *his*) and four vowel durations.

---

accented English is socially less stigmatized in some circles, while a Yiddish accented variety is, the answer is not a concern of the phonetician's.'' It seems to me, however, that preaspirated stops are rare *for a reason,* perhaps that it is motorically difficult to coordinate precisely the requisite oral and laryngeal gestures. If so, this seems to be an empirical question and a proper matter for articulatory phonetics.

Table 6.2
Synthesized and Imitated Duration (in msec) of Vowels in Hiss and His Syllables

	Synthesized vowel durations			
	85	125	255	185
	Imitated vowel durations			
Hiss	181	221	246	280
His	222	250	264	298

Source: From Javkin (1979a).

Javkin's question, of course, was whether listeners would—for *perceptual* reasons—find any particular vowel duration longer when it preceded a "voiced" final consonant.

In the task, subjects heard three of each of the eight synthetic constructions. On each trial, the stimulus was followed by a 250 Hz tone which they were to adjust, by turning a knob, to the duration of the vowel. Table 6.2 shows the results. It is apparent that the listeners were "generous" in that they perceived vowels to be longer than they actually were, even in the *hiss* items. As Javkin expected, there was a systematic effect of final fricative voicing. The *his* vowels were judged to be an average of about 27 msec longer than the *hiss* vowels.

There are less than satisfying aspects to this finding. First, 27 msec is a much smaller difference than occurs in the real speech productions of *hiss* and *his*. However, in order for Javkin's hypothesis to be confirmed, one only need observe a consistent difference in the right direction. As I indicated earlier, the act of phonologizing vowel duration might well have—and in English probably has had—the effect of magnifying the difference. The other problem is not so easily dealt with. As English listeners are users of a language that has the voicing–vowel length rule, they would be inclined to regard vowels before perceptibly voiced final consonants as *long*, just as the evidence shows that if they hear a long vowel listeners are inclined to regard the next consonant as voiced whether it is acoustically voiced or not (Raphael, 1972). Consequently, Javkin conducted a second experiment to see if this expectancy explanation could be ruled out, but this second experiment ended with a note of uncertainty which, in my judgment, left the situation pretty much as it was at the completion of the first experiment.

Vowel Lengthening Developmentally

It is worth noting that perhaps the first explicit scenario of developmental rephonologization was envisioned by a *historical* linguist, King (1969), and he had in mind the shift from final obstruent voicing to preceding vowel duration. King said, suppose in adults there is a rule lengthening vowels before voiced obstruents, and assume that an innovation devoicing every [final] /bdg/ is added at the end of the grammar. From underlying /bat/ and /bad/ the surface forms will be [bat] and [ba:t] from earlier [bat] and [ba:d]. The child exposed to these and like forms will hear only length as the distinguishing feature, and we may hypothesize that the child's grammar will have vowel length in underlying forms but nowhere /bdg/. This is a complication of the underlying vowel system, but it also represents the simplest grammar that can be constructed from the output of the adult grammar [pp. 86–87].

One of the first to observe the development of differential vowel duration, as appropriate to final voicing, was Velten (1943). Velten recorded the speech of his daughter, Joan, from her eleventh to her thirty-sixth month of age. In her twenty-fourth month, Joan's word-final voiced and voiceless consonants perceptibly were distinguished exclusively by the length of the preceding vowel:

Voiced		Voiceless	
[ba:t]	*bad*	[bat]	*back*
[ma:t]	*mud*	[nat]	*nut*
[wu:t]	*red, wade*	[wut]	*wet*
[bu:t]	*bead*	[but]	*beat*
[nu:s]	*nose*	[dut]	*goat*
[fu:t]	*food*	[dup]	*coop*

"The child's language," Velten concluded, "turns the English nondistinctive variation of vowel quantity into a phonemic difference, while still disregarding the [voicing] distinction [p. 289]."

Children's differential vowel duration and its possible phonologization, was studied systematically by Margaret Naeser in her doctoral dissertation (1970). Naeser made monthly recordings of six children from 26 to 36 months of age, and of three children from 21 to 24 months of age. The children were to produce words that ended with voiced and voiceless obstruents both in naming and imitatively. The to-be-imitated syllables had vowel durations that were normal for English, or abnormal, or at gradations in between.

Though the younger children perceptibly devoiced many of the final stops and fricatives, Naeser's oscillographic measurements showed that they nonetheless produced long vowels before *phonemically* voiced obstruents, short vowels before phonemically voiceless obstruents. That some of the phonemically voiced consonants were devoiced seemed to have little effect on the duration of preceding vowels. For example, when *bib, seed,* and *food* were correctly said by the 22-month-olds, they had a mean vowel duration of 268 msec. In cases where the final stops were devoiced, these words had the similar mean vowel duration of

248 msec. In contrast, *stick, feet,* and *boot* had a mean vowel duration of just 132 msecs. This pattern was seen throughout the ages studied by Naeser, who concluded that

> despite the incorrect production of final voiced stops, correct differential vowel duration was produced continuously from the mean age of 22 months, when vowel duration before voiceless stops was 49% of that before voiced stops. At the mean age of 34 months, vowel duration before voiceless stops was 63% of that before voiced stops [p. 16].

The latter percentage is very close to the values of the children's parents, whose vowel durations also were recorded and analyzed [absolute vowel duration values may not approximate adult values even at 9 years of age (DiSimoni, 1974)].

Naeser's analysis of responses to normal, abnormal, and graded durations of vocalic stimuli showed that, in general, children produced vowel lengths appropriate to the voicing of the final consonants. Even if, for example, *feet* and *seed* were presented with (anomalously) identical durations, the children repeated them with short and long durations as appropriate to the final consonant's voicing.

Naeser's finding that young children preserve vowel duration differences even while devoicing final obstruents was observed, as well, by Greenlee in her doctoral dissertation (1978). Greenlee had three 2-year-olds and one 3-year-old name pictures (e.g., back, bag) for oscillographic analysis of vowel duration and final voicing. Like Naeser, Greenlee found that all children produced longer vowels before phonemically voiced consonants than before phonemically voiceless consonants, even if devoicing occurred.

Based on the results of her own investigation, Naeser proposed three distinct stages in children's acquisition of differential vowel duration before voiced and voiceless consonants.

Stage 1. In the first stage, the child has differential vowel duration, as imitated from parental speech, without necessarily having control over the voicing of the final consonant. Presumably, the child at this stage might not say final obstruents at all. Naeser commented that "it is possible that differential vowel duration at this stage has a phonemic status . . . [p. 139]."

Stage 2. In the second stage, the child continues to show the differential durations of Stage 1, but now reveals control over the voicing of final obstruents. In Stage 2, the child is able to derive the appropriate vowel duration from the voicing of final consonants. This is consistent with Naeser's finding that children reproduced the abnormal and graded durations of vowel stimuli with values appropriate to English.

Stage 3. Having now shown a knowledge of the voicing—length connection such that length may be derived from voicing, the child in Stage 3 (and thereafter

as an adult) *is able to derive final voicing from the duration of preceding vowels.*
The connection is bidirectional.

Whether differential vowel duration is learned and language specific or physiologically conditioned was an issue Naeser wished to decide from her study but
felt she could not. True, children produced *long vowels before phonetically
voiceless consonants* (in their cases of final devoicing), but in Naeser's view the
children "may have initiated the motor commands necessary to produce a voiced
consonant, and even made the necessary accommodations for increased vowel
duration, but for some unknown reason, were unable to voice the final consonant
[p. 143]." If so, the motivation for the durational differences might still have
been a phonetic one.

Children's differential vowel durations also may be (and probably are)
phonemic, and this becomes all the more plausible in the face of evidence that
children are *linguistically aware* of them. Krause (1982a) found that children as
young as 3 years of age were able to discriminate word pairs such as *bip–bib,
pot–pod,* and *back–bag* from synthesized tokens in which vowel duration was
the *only* discriminant feature. This task, of course, would be a perfectly logical
one for all children who had phonologized vowel duration differences.

Historical Glottalization of Stops

Hock's (1975) analysis of final weakening reveals a number of cases in which
final stops have historically yielded to glottal stops. For example, in many
dialects of Chinese all final stops were replaced by glottals. In Finnish, final /t/
and /k/ both changed to /ʔ/.

In their chronicle of historical phonology in Chinese dialects, Chen and Wang
(1975) point to different stages in the loss of final /p, t, k/. First, the three stops
are reduced to just the /t/–/k/ contrast. Second, the alveolar stops are merged
with the velars, so that only /k/ remains. Third, the /k/ is replaced by /ʔ/.
Fourth, the /ʔ/ falls away. This leaves a vowel-final form with "the characteristically short duration of a checked syllable," according to Chen and Wang,
which "assumes a phonemic significance [p. 267]." In the next and final stage,
the vowel length contrast that had just become phonologized loses its linguistic
value, as long and short vowels are merged.

Developmental Glottalization of Stops

Data have been presented throughout this monograph on the abundance of
open syllables in the sound production of infants and the word production of
children. But children do not lose final consonants as languages (normal adult
speakers) do. Rather, children begin talking and in their speech one hears vowels
and initial consonants but no syllable-final consonants. Final consonants—es-

pecially the stops—have not made an appearance at this point, or at least have not made much of an impression on the adult listener. My hypothesis is that final consonant "nonappearance" is in many cases the result of a developmental rephonologization. Before proceeding further, it may first be helpful to briefly review certain of the facts about adult behavior.

ADULTS

Earlier (p. 103), I presented evidence from Rositzke (1943) that even under laboratory conditions, educated American speakers fail frequently to release prepausal stops. Voiceless stops, for Rositzke's speakers, were unreleased (or checked) in some 36% of the cases. The most frequently checked voiceless stop was /t/, which was produced without release 61% of the time. About 29% of the voiced stops were checked, with /d/ the most frequently unreleased. In the conversational speech of educated Germans (Bonnin, 1964), we saw earlier (p. 111–112) that about 87% of word final (voiceless) stops were produced in *lenis* fashion, with /t/ the most frequently produced in this weak mode. From Malécot (1958) we saw that the failure to release final stops is no trivial matter. When the release portion of a final stop is removed, intelligibility suffers, and when the releases from two stops are exchanged, the listener may be grossly misled. Householder (1956) found that unreleased final /p, t, k/ were misidentified by adult listeners on about 48% of the trials. In fact, the probability of listeners correctly writing *p, t,* or *k* was only about 32% greater than the probability of their writing *p, t,* or *k* when the final consonant was a glottal stop!

Though failure to release final stops is measurably harmful to lexical identification, it is nevertheless exceedingly common. So is the replacement of final /t/ by glottal stop. Among others, Foley (1973) has observed that "in English *t* becomes ʔ in strong position (after a stressed vowel and before a syllabic *l* or *n*), whereas *p* and *k* do not shift in this position [p. 55]." According to Gimson (1962), "before consonants it is not uncommon in RP to find [ʔ] alone for /t/, particularly if the following consonant is a stop [p. 137]." This tendency was documented for British English in Shockey and Bond (1980), where female speakers replaced 32% of their final /t/s with [ʔ]s. Though Zwicky's (1972) Dentdel rule refers to the *omission* of final dental stops, many of Zwicky's illustrations show /t/—more than /d/—represented as [ʔ].

The special affinity between /t/ and /ʔ/ is attested in a variety of additional observations. In Mines *et al.*'s (1978) count of American English phones, the only sound glottals coexisted with was /t/. They referred to this entity as a "dental glottal," symbolizing it as [t ˉ ʔ]. According to Smith (1978b), "/ʔ/ is indistinguishable from /t/ on oscillograms [p. 62]." Coker, Umeda, and Browman's (1973) optical studies show that the glottis may be completely closed during the production of final /t/. In Shockey's (1973) transcription of adult's casual speech, she found it necessary to use a special symbol for "simultaneous glottal closure,'' but the standard symbol that had a glottal stop placed above it was [t].

In Shockey's study, three adults—two from central Ohio and one from Brooklyn, New York—were tape recorded in casual conversation and some 5 min of their speech was phonetically transcribed. I went through the transcripts for all three speakers, noting the presence of glottal and dental glottal stops occurring in place of standard consonants. In all, there were 67 glottal stops, of which 66 replaced /t/ (the other replaced the /p/ in *equipment*). In other words, there were no voiced stops and no fricatives or affricates of either voicing that were represented as glottals or dental glottals. The distribution of these allophones of /t/ by word position was as follows:

	Initial	Medial	Final
[ʔ]	0	8	58
[t̜]	0	2	4

In Mines *et al.* (1978), the distribution of glottal and dental glottal allophones, by word position, was as follows:

	Initial	Medial	Final
[ʔ]	82	107	321
[t-ʔ]	0	9	118

The fairly high incidence of glottal stop word initially reflects, I think, the "hard attack" of many speakers for word-initial vowels, especially when the preceding word has ended vocalically.

As has been indicated, [ʔ] substitutes for /t/ more than for /d/. More generally, glottal stops replace all voiceless stops more commonly than they replace their voiced cognates. There are several reasons why this might be so. First, vowels preceding voiceless stops tend to terminate abruptly (Parker, 1974; Walsh & Parker, 1981). Should speakers wish to capture this vocalic characteristic in their utterances, glottals would be a highly efficient strategy for doing so. Second, Hombert *et al.* (1979) found that the fundamental frequency of vowels ending in a glottal stop rises at least 9–48 Hz over a time course that begins at least 70 msec before the glottal stop. This might allow final glottal stops to pass for voiceless lingual and labial stops, whose F_1 transitions are of significantly higher frequency than the transitions to voiced cognates (Wolf, 1978). So, in terms of their effect upon vowels, glottal stops act more like voiceless stops, and sound more like them as well.

From the preceding it follows that words ending in abruptly terminating vowels might be misperceived to end in glottal stops. This appears to be the case. Sapir (1933/1963) observed in his phonetics class that

> after the students have been taught to recognize the glottal stop as a phonetic unit, many of them tend to hear it after a word ending in an accented short vowel of clear timbre (e.g., *a, ε, e, i*). This illusion does not seem to apply so often to words ending in a long vowel or an obscure vowel of relatively undefined quality (ə) or an unaccented vowel [p. 58].

Sapir rationalized the behavior of his (English) students in the following way. In English, a word must terminate with a long vowel or a consonant. Words having a vowel in the /ɪ, ε, æ, ʊ, ʌ/ class typically end with a consonant. Hearing an open syllable terminate with one of these vowels, the student would believe that the word ended in a consonant. According to Sapir, the best consonantal choice for ending these words would be the glottal stop, which is "the most unreal or zerolike of consonants to an English or American ear and is admirably fitted, once its existence has been discovered, to serve as the projected actualization of a phonologically required final consonant of minimum sonority [p. 59]." Sapir also noted that one may perceive a dictated final glottal stop as /p, t, k/.

Sapir's explanation may have been the correct one, and my analysis of some data reported in Carterette and Jones (1974) supports it. Carterette and Jones recorded a number of Americans in conversation, transcribing their casual speech. Table 6.3 shows the incidence of final glottal stops, /t/s, and word boundaries that were preceded by each of the vowels shown. The fourth column shows some calculations of my own; the ratio of final /t/ to final [ʔ]. Notice that the lowest values are for /ʊ, ɪ, ε, ə/. This implies that final /t/ either is replaced by [ʔ] or is omitted more often in these environments. The transcriber hears an (inherently) abruptly terminating vowel and assumes it must be followed by a (voiceless) stop consonant. Hearing no formant transitions for articulatory place, the listener assumes that the vowel must have been terminated by a glottal stop.

CHILDREN

The replacement of oral stops by glottal stops is extremely common in young children and, as we will see, may be traceable to adult behaviors as described earlier. The incidence of final stop glottalization is demonstrably a case of rephonologization in which oral stops are dephonologized and vowel offset is phonologized.

Table 6.3
Final Word Boundaries, /t/s and [ʔ]s, as a Function of the Preceding Vowel, in the Conversational Speech of American Adults

Vowel	__#	__t	__ʔ	__t/__ʔ ratio
ʊ	0	4	19	.21
æ	2	139	185	.75
ɪ	3	202	214	.94
ɛ	4	55	47	1.17
ə	189	139	185	1.29
ɔ	5	20	14	1.43
a	44	65	39	1.67
eɪ	47	58	11	5.27
u	77	26	4	6.50
i	147	49	9	9.00
ou	190	34	3	11.33

Source: Data from Table 8.2.4 in Carterette and Jones (1974).
Note: Except for schwa, there is a perfect relationship between the __t/__ʔ ratio and the number of words ending in a particular vowel.

At 15–18 months, when Tuaycharoen's (1977) Thai subject was in the two- and three-word stage, the word-final glottal stop

> played an important role as a functional unit, and for this child, the use of the glottal stop in place of other stops in the final position is articulatorily reasonable. In Thai . . . the oral closure for the stop in the final position is accompanied by simultaneous glottal closure. The child at this stage was not fully capable of making oral closure at the same time as the glottal closure was being made, especially not in cases where the closures were close to each other, e.g., velar, glottal. Thus, only one closure *which would retain the unexploded quality of the stop* was made, i.e. glottal closure [p. 173; emphasis mine].

It is not clear from Tuaycharoen's account whether [ʔ] replaced /t/ more than the other voiceless stops, but such is obviously the case in English-learning children, as it is in the adult speakers of English. Table 6.4 shows the results of various investigations of child phonetic behavior. The *glottalization* data are as follows. The Olmsted (1971) figures are derived from the spontaneous speech of 100 children from 15 to 54 months of age. They are not broken down by word or syllable position. Neither are the data in Burton (1980), which represent the elicited responses of 16 severely language-impaired children from 4 to 9 years of age. The data from Elbert *et al.* (forthcoming) are the final glottals in the first 100 lines of phonetic transcription from their 46–50-month-old subject, M.B. The *omission* data are word final, and include, in addition to Elbert *et al.*'s transcription, Moskowitz's (1970) analysis of Mackie's spontaneous speech (cf. Albright & Albright, 1956) at 26 months, and Prather *et al.*'s (1975) analysis of approximately 41 children's elicited naming at 24, 28, and 32 months. Finally,

Table 6.4
Voiceless and Voiced Stops in Standard English Represented as Glottal Stops ([ʔ]) or Omissions (ø) in Children's Speech[a]

	[ʔ] Olmsted (1971) (N = 100) 15–54 months		[ʔ] Burton (1980) (N = 16) 4–9 years		[ʔ] Elbert et al. (forthcoming) (N = 1) 46–50 months		ø Moskowitz (1970) (N = 1) 26 months		ø Prather et al. (1975) (N = 41)[b] 24–32 months		ø Read (1975) (N = 32)[c] Under 6 years	
	N	%	N	%	N	%	N	%	N	%	N	%
p	3/89	3.3	4/42	9.5	1/8	12.5	2/7	28.6	2/44	4.5	3/142	2.1
t	37/297	12.5	36/143	25.2	72/140	51.4	33/90	36.7	9/55	16.4	24/350	6.9
k	8/140	5.7	8/41	19.5	9/29	31.0	3/16	18.8	2/51	3.9	10/287	3.5
	48/526	9.1	48/226	21.2	82/177	46.3	38/113	33.6	13/150	8.7	37/779	4.7
b	2/59	3.4	7/37	18.9	0/2	0	0/4	0	2/46	4.3	1/131	.8
d	9/112	8.0	19/77	24.7	0/44	0	4/17	24.6	5/51	9.8	10/302	3.3
g	1/62	1.6	13/65	20.0	0/16	0	0/4	0	1/52	1.9	2/78	2.6
	12/233	5.2	39/179	21.8	0/62	0	4/25	16.0	8/149	5.4	13/511	2.5

[a]Read's data show the omission of letters in children's misspellings.
[b]The N for Prather is approximate, as a different number of children responded to each stimulus item.
[c]The N for Read is for his total group; I have taken data only from subjects under 6 years of age.

Read's (1975, Appendix A) data represent omissions in the *spelling* of children under 6 years of age, irrespective of word position.

The data from Olmsted reveal two patterns in children's replacement of oral stops by glottal stops. First, glottals replace voiceless stops more than voiced stops (and voiceless fricatives).[4] Second, there is a clear tendency for glottals to replace alveolars more than bilabials and velars. The convergence of these two patterns results in a preponderance of glottalizations of /t/. In the Burton data, the alveolar predominance is again evident, although the voiced–voiceless distinction is not. The pattern of M.B., the child seen by Elbert *et al.,* strongly supports the analysis of Olmsted's data, and is based only on word-final cases.

The next two columns in Table 6.4 represent "omission" data from studies in which glottal stops never appeared word finally *in the transcriptions.* Yet the pattern evident for glottal stops is also apparent for final omissions. In Moskowitz's analysis of the Albrights' data on Mackie, one can see that voiceless stops are omitted twice as often as are voiced stops, that alveolars predominate, and that /t/ is the most often omitted. The same is true for Prather *et al.,* where the data represent elicitations of children's word-final stop articulation.

I believe that a glottal stop to one investigator may be an omission to the next, and that for this reason the data in the various columns of Table 6.4 are essentially in agreement. Sapir (1933/1963) commented on the "zerolike" nature of glottal stops, which have no phonemic significance in American English. Lacking such significance, glottals might merely be regarded as sudden termination of the vowel. In words that end with voiceless oral stops, the vowels terminate suddenly. So, in a sense, for unreleased glottal stops there is no introduction of novel phonetic elements and, therefore, no *substitution.*

The problem for the developing child is an interesting one. From the vowel length and vowel nasalization data, it is obvious that young children are very much aware of and able to reproduce the spectral and durational characteristics of vowels, even well before they reproduce the consonants that follow them. All the child needs to do to be (dis)credited with an omission of a word-final stop is to form the conclusion that the offset properties of the vowel are more important than anything that might come afterward. In the child's mimicry of such properties, some listeners will classify a substitution, others will classify an omission, but the vocalic effect is the same.

INTERNAL REPRESENTATION

If this hypothesis is correct, it follows that the child's internal representation for a word such as *bat* is of the syllable shape CV where the vowel is marked for

---

[4]Smit and Bernthal (1983) used a carrier phrase (the————away), and some of their 5-year-old final omitters "demonstrated a contrast at the end of the word by using a glottal stop for a final voiceless target and a vowel glide into the last word of the carrier phrase of a final voiced target."

its abrupt offset. The data from the final column of Table 6.4 are relevant to this question of internal representations, for they show how children *spell* words that contain voiced or voiceless stops. The pattern is quite similar to that of the child glottalizations and substitutions, for letters representing voiceless stops are more likely to be omitted in children's misspellings, and alveolars are more likely to be omitted than bilabials or velars, with /t/ predominating.

If a glottalization of /t/ is the result of rephonologization, where vocalic offset becomes internally represented, then it also ought to be the case that [ʔ] is derived mainly from /t/s in the standard language. That is, if word-final /d/s were devoiced, they would yield [t] but not [ʔ] because the vocalic offset characteristics for /d/-final words would not be tagged (+ abrupt). Table 6.5 shows the phonetic realization of word-final /t, d/ in four children: M.B. from Elbert *et al.* (forthcoming), along with three children from Maxwell (1981) whose samples include both spontaneous and elicited speech, together representing roughly the same number of utterances as the excerpt from M.B.

For /t/, in three of the four subjects there were more [ʔ]s than omissions, and there was some incidence of [t]. J.O. had fewer [ʔ]s than omissions, and had no incidence of [t]. Overall, glottal stops predominated. For /d/, none of the subjects produced [ʔ], and there were proportionately more omissions than in the case of /t/. Note the interesting case of L.S., who expressed /d/ as [t] eight times. L.S. sometimes omitted final /d/; he never said [d] and never produced a [ʔ] for /d/ though his final /t/s frequently were expressed as [ʔ]s.

Maxwell's acoustic analysis showed that L.S. had a small but nonsignificant tendency toward differential vowel duration in words such as *kit* and *kid*. Accordingly, Maxwell concluded that L.S. evidenced no final voiced–voiceless distinction either phonetically or acoustically. However, recall that L.S. fre-

Table 6.5
Phonetic Realization of Word-Final /t, d/ in the Speech of Four Children from 3:11 to 4:7

/t/	[ʔ]	ø	[t]	[d]
A.B.	20	18	7	0
L.S.	25	6	9	0
J.O.	17	28	0	0
M.B.	72	67	1	0
$\Sigma X =$	134	119	17	0
% =	49.6	44.1	6.3	0

/d/	[ʔ]	ø	[t]	[d]
A.B.	0	5	0	8
L.S.	0	4	8	0
J.O.	0	5	0	0
M.B.	0	44	0	0
$\Sigma X =$	0	58	8	8
% =	0	78.4	10.8	10.8

Source: A.B., L.S., and J.O. are from Maxwell (1981); M.B. is from Elbert *et al.* (forthcoming).

quently said [ʔ] for *phonemic* /t/ and that he never said [ʔ] for /d/ (or for the *phonetic* [t] created by devoicing /d/). I believe L.S. may have rephonologized the system.[5] Rather than attempt the voicing and vowel duration appropriate to final stops, L.S. went for vocalic offset and very nearly perfected it!

Closing Remarks: An Integrated Model of Phonological Acquisition and Change

It is evident in some ways that humans are preadapted for speech and speech systems are preadapted for those who must learn and use them. The infant comes to oral language with a number of perceptual categories and physiological proclivities already in force. The infant will encounter a system whose formal structure already contains a certain amount of phonetic patterning, which is further revealed in the speech habits of his models. The mix of these elements produces a set of heavily phonetic effects in early language development.

As the child more actively explores his physical and social environment, his linguistic needs increase, and the child listens more analytically. But the forms he needs are poorly defined, so the child must make a number of personal decisions about the structure of language, and the nature of sound categories, grammatical markers, and adult lexical constituents. As the preadaptations are imperfect, and the child's decisions are often only partially correct, and the phonetic preferences and limitations persist, there is now an even more conspicuous interaction between anatomical, physiological, and cognitive–perceptual factors. This interplay will continue throughout the life of all human speakers, its signs frequently concealed by formal conventions but revealed in casual speech, slips of the tongue, brain damage, and glossolalia.

I believe that phonological acquisition, use, and change involve dynamically interrelated properties, many not easily captured in alphabetic notation or expressed in linguistic rules. Indeed, many of the more interesting aspects of phonology may even be inelligible for such transformations, bound instead to speakers' intentions to manipulate phonological categories and phonetic operations in order to achieve all the ends for which people talk.

---

[5]Jerry Saddock has suggested to me the importance of performing lexical analyses; in cases of true rephonologization, the oral stops in some standard words should *always* be expressed as glottals. An inspection of L.S.'s data revealed that in some words (e.g., *it*), final /t/ was expressed as a glottal in several cases and omitted in others. However, all eight of L.S.'s productions of *that* were transcribed with a glottal stop. A large corpus is needed for lexical analyses to control for the variation of phonetic environment.

References

Aitchison, J. (1972). Mini-malapropisms. *British Journal of Disorders of Communication, 7,* 38–43.

Aitchison, J., & Chiat, S. (1981). Natural phonology or natural memory? The interaction between phonological processes and recall mechanisms. *Language and Speech, 24,* 311–326.

Aitchison, J., & Straf, M. (1981). Lexical storage and retrieval: A developing skill? *Linguistics, 19,* 751–795.

Albright, R. W., & Albright, J. B. (1956). The phonology of a two-year-old child. *Word, 12,* 382–390.

Ali, L., Gallagher, T., Goldstein, J., & Daniloff, R. (1971). Perception of coarticulated nasality. *Journal of the Acoustical Society of America, 49,* 538–540.

Allen, G. D. (in press). Linguistic experience modifies lexical stress perception. *Journal of Child Language.*

Altmann, G. (1969). Differences between phonemes. *Phonetica, 19,* 118–132.

Andersen, H. (1973). Abductive and deductive change. *Language, 49,* 735–793.

Anderson, S. R. (1981). Why phonology isn't "natural." *Linguistic Inquiry, 12,* 493–539.

Anthony, A., Bogle, D., Ingram, T. T. S., & McIsaac, M. W. (1971). *The Edinburgh Articulation Test.* Edinburgh: E. and S. Livingstone.

Aslin, R. N., & Pisoni, D. B. (1980). Some developmental processes in speech perception. In G. H. Yeni-Komshian, J. F. Kavanagh, & C. A. Ferguson (Eds.), *Child phonology, vol. 2: Perception.* New York: Academic Press.

Atkinson, K., MacWhinney, B., & Stoel, C. (1968). An experiment on the recognition of babbling. In *Language behavior research laboratory working paper #14.* Berkeley: University of California.

Bailey, C.-J. N. (1973). *Variation and linguistic theory.* Arlington, Va.: Center for Applied Linguistics.

Baker, W. J., & Derwing, B. L. (1982). Response coincidence analysis as evidence for language acquisition strategies. *Applied Psycholinguistics, 3,* 193–221.

Baran, J. A., Laufer, M. Z., & Daniloff, R. (1977). Phonological contrastivity in conversation: A comparative study of voice onset time. *Journal of Phonetics, 5,* 339–350.

Bard, E. G., & Anderson, A. H. (1983). The unintelligibility of speech to children. *Journal of Child Language, 10,* 265–292.

Baron, N. S. (1977). *Language acquisition and historical change.* New York: Elsevier, North-Holland.

Barton, D., Miller, R., & Macken, M. A. (1980). Do children treat clusters as one unit or two? *Papers and Reports on Child Language Development, 18.*

Bateman, W. G. (1917). Papers on language development: The first word. *Pedagogical Seminary, 24,* 391–398.

Battacchi, M. W., Facchini, G. M., Manfredi, M. M., & Rubatta, C. O. (1964). Presentazione di un reattivo per l'esame dell'articolazione fonetica nei fanciulli in eta prescolare di lingua italiana. *Bollettino della Societa Italiana di Fonetica, Foniatria e Audiologia, 13,* 441–486.

Baudouin de Courtenay, J. (1895). *Versuch einer Theorie phonetischer Alternationen: Ein Kapitell aus der Psychophonetik.* Reprinted in Stankiewicz, E., 1972, *A Baudouin de Courtenay anthology,* Bloomington: Indiana University Press.

Bean, C. H. (1932). An unusual opportunity to investigate the psychology of language. *Journal of Genetic Psychology, 40–41,* 181–201.

Berko, J. (1958). The child's learning of English morphology. *Word, 14,* 150–177.

Berman, R. A. (1979). The re-emergence of a bilingual: A case study of a Hebrew–English speaking child. *Working Papers on Bilingualism, 19,* 157–180.

Bernstein, N. E. (1982). *An acoustic study of mothers' speech to language-learning children: An analysis of vowel articulation characteristics.* Unpublished doctoral dissertation, Boston University.

Best, C. T., & MacKain, K. S. (in press). Discovering messages in the medium: Speech and the prelinguistic infant. In B. M. Lester, H. E. Fitzgerald, & M. W. Yogman (Eds.), *Theory and research in behavioral pediatrics* (Vol. 2). New York: Plenum.

Bever, T. G. (1971). Comments at a conference held in 1968 and reported in R. Hurley & E. Ingram (Eds.), *Language acquisition: Models and methods.* New York: Academic Press.

Bhat, D. N. S. (1978). A general study of palatalization. In J. H. Greenberg, (Ed.), *Universals of human language, vol. 2: Phonology.* Stanford, Calif.: Stanford University Press.

Bickerton, D. (1982). Learning without experience the creole way. In L. K. Obler, & L. Menn (Eds.), *Exceptional language and linguistics.* New York: Academic Press.

Bloch, B. (1950). Studies in colloquial Japanese, IV: Phonemics. *Language, 26,* 86–125.

Blount B. G. (1969). *Acquisition of language by Luo children.* Unpublished doctoral dissertation, University of California, Berkeley.

Blount, B. G. (1970). The pre-linguistic system of Luo children. *Anthropological Linguistics, 12,* 326–342.

Bond, Z. S., & Adamescu, L. (1979). Identification of novel phonetic segments by children, adolescents and adults. *Phonetica, 36,* 182–186.

Bonnin, G. M. (1964). Some acoustic aspects of final stop allophones in Contemporary German. *Phonetica, 11,* 65–100.

Bonvillian, J. D., Orlansky, M. D., & Novack, L. L. (In press). Developmental milestones: Sign language acquisition and motor development. *Child Development.*

Boysson-Bardies, B. de (1981). *The specificity of infant babbling in the light of the characteristics of the mother-tongue.* Paper presented at the Second International Congress for the Study of Child Language, Vancouver, August.

Boysson-Bardies, B. de, Sagart, L., & Bacri, N. (1981). Phonetic analysis of late babbling: A case study of a French child. *Journal of Child Language, 8,* 511–524.

Brooks-Gunn, J., & Lewis, M. (1979). "Why Mama and Papa?": The development of social labels. *Child Development, 50,* 1203–1206.

Brown, R. (1958). *Words and things*. Glencoe, Ill.: Free Press.

Buckingham, H. W. (1981). Where do neologisms come from? In J. W. Brown (Ed.), *Jargonaphasia*. New York: Academic Press.

Buckingham, H. W., & Kertesz, A. (1976). *Neologistic jargon aphasia*. Amsterdam: Swets & Zeitlinger.

Bühler, C. (1930). *The first year of life*. New York: John Day Company.

Burling, R. (1959). Language development of a Garo and English-speaking child. *Word, 15,* 45–68.

Burton, A. J. (1980). Phonological systems of aphasic children. *UCLA Working Papers in Cognitive Linguistics, 12,* 37–187.

Butterworth, B. (1979). Hesitation and the production of verbal paraphasias and neologisms in jargon aphasia. *Brain and Language, 8,* 133–161.

Byrne, M. C. (1959). Speech and language development of athetoid and spastic children. *Journal of Speech and Hearing Disorders, 24,* 231–240.

Cairns, H. S., Cairns, C. E., & Blosser, D. F. (1970). *Analysis of production errors in the phonetic performance of school-age standard-English-speaking children*. Final report (F. Williams, Ed.) of a grant administered through the U.S. Department of Health, Education and Welfare, Office of Education.

Carr, J. (1953). An investigation of the spontaneous speech sounds of five-year-old deaf-born children. *Journal of Speech and Hearing Disorders, 18,* 22–29.

Carterette, E. C., & Jones, M. H. (1974). *Informal speech*. Berkeley: University of California Press.

Casagrande, J. B. (1964). Comanche baby language. In D. Hymes (Ed.), *Language in culture and society*. New York: Harper & Row.

Celce-Murcia, M. (1978). The simultaneous acquisition of English and French in a two-year-old child. In E. M. Hatch, (Ed.), *Second language acquisition: A book of readings*. Rowley, Mass.: Newbury House.

Chamberlain, A. F. (1900). *The child: A study of the evolution of man*. New York: Scribner's.

Chao, Y. R. (1951). The Cantian idiolect: An analysis of the Chinese spoken by a twenty-eight-month-old child. *University of California Publications in Semitic Philology, 11,* 27–44. Reprinted in A. Bar-Adon & W. F. Leopold (Eds.), 1971, *Child language: A book of readings,* Englewood Cliffs, N.J.: Prentice-Hall.

Chatterji, S. K. (1926). *Origin and development of the Bengali language*. Calcutta: University of Calcutta Press.

Chen, F. (1980). *Acoustic characteristics and intelligibility of clear and conversational speech at the segmental level*. Unpublished master's thesis, Massachusetts Institute of Technology.

Chen, M. (1970). Vowel length variation as a function of the voicing of the consonant environment. *Phonetica, 22,* 129–159.

Chen, M. Y., & Wang, W. S.-Y. (1975). Sound change: Actuation and implementation. *Language, 51,* 255–279.

Chervela, N. (1981). Medial consonant cluster acquisition by Telugu children. *Journal of Child Language, 8,* 63–73.

Chiat, S. (1979). The role of the word in phonological development. *Linguistics, 17,* 591–610.

Christie, W. M. (1979). *Redundancy as explanation in historical linguistics*. Paper presented at the Fourth International Conference on Historical Linguistics, Stanford University, March.

Clark, R. (1977). What's the use of imitation? *Journal of Child Language, 4,* 341–358.

Clumeck, H. (1979). A parallel between child and adult language: A study in the phonetic explanation of sound patterns. *Journal of Child Language, 6,* 593–598.

Clumeck, H., Barton, D., Macken, M. A., & Huntington, D. A. (1981). The aspiration contrast in Cantonese word-initial stops: Data from children and adults. *Journal of Chinese Linguistics, 9,* 210–224.

Coker, C. H., Umeda, N., & Browman, C. P. (1973). Automatic synthesis from ordinary English text. *IEEE Transactions on Audio and Electroacoustics,* AU-21, 293–298.

Crelin, E. S. (1973). *Functional anatomy of the newborn.* New Haven: Yale University Press.

Cruttenden, A. (1970). A phonetic study of babbling. *British Journal of Disorders of Communication, 5,* 110–117.

Cruttenden, A. (1982). How long does intonation acquisition take? *Papers and Reports on Child Language Development, 21,* 112–118.

Crystal, D. (1973). Non-segmental phonology in language acquisition: A review of the issues. *Lingua, 32,* 1–45.

Crystal, D. (1975). Commentary. In N. O'Connor, (Ed.), *Language, cognitive deficits, and retardation.* Boston: Butterworth.

Cullen, J. K., Fargo, N., Chase, R. A., & Baker, P. (1968). The development of auditory feedback monitoring, I: Delayed auditory feedback studies on infant cry. *Journal of Speech and Hearing Research, 11,* 85–93.

Cutler, A. (1981). The reliability of speech error data. *Linguistics, 19,* 561–582.

Darley, F. L., & Winitz, H. (1961). Age of first word: Review of research. *Journal of Speech and Hearing Disorders, 26,* 271–290.

de Chene, B., & Anderson, S. R. (1979). Compensatory lengthening. *Language, 55,* 505–535.

Denes, P. B. (1963). On the statistics of spoken English. *Journal of the Acoustical Society of America, 30,* 892–904.

Deville, G. (1890). Notes sur le developpement du langage. *Revue de Linguistique et de Philologie Comparee, 23,* 330–343.

Deville, G. (1891). Notes sur le developpement du langage. *Revue de Linguistique et de Philologie Comparee, 24,* 10–42, 128–143, 242–257, 300–320.

Dinger, M. C., & Blom, J. G. (1973). An investigation of infant babbling. *Proceedings from the Institute of Phonetic Sciences* (University of Amsterdam), *3,* 42–50.

Dinnsen, D. A. (1980). Phonological rules and phonetic explanation. *Journal of Linguistics, 16,* 171–191.

DiSimoni, F. G. (1974). Influence of consonant environment on duration of vowels in the speech of three-, six-, and nine-year-old children. *Journal of the Acoustical Society of America, 55,* 362–363.

Dodd, B. J. (1972). Comparison of babbling patterns in normal and Down-Syndrome infants. *Journal of Mental Deficiency Research, 16,* 35–40.

D'Odorico, L. (1982). *Melodic patterns in one infant's vocalization.* Unpublished manuscript.

Dorian, N. C. (1973). Grammatical change in a dying dialect. *Language, 49,* 413–438.

Dorian, N. C. (1977). A hierarchy of morphophonemic decay in Scottish Gaelic language death: The differential failure of lenition. *Word, 28,* 96–109.

Dorian, N. C. (1978). The fate of morphological complexity in language death: Evidence from East Sutherland Gaelic. *Language, 54,* 590–609.

Drachman, G. (n.d.). *Are all universals of child-language truly universals of language?* Unpublished manuscript.

Drachman, G. (1978). Child language and language change: A conjecture and some refutations. In J. Fisiak (Ed.), *Recent developments in historical phonology.* The Hague: Mouton.

Drachman, G., & Malikouti-Drachman, A. (n.d.). *Studies in the acquisition of Greek as a native language, I: Some preliminary findings on phonology.* Unpublished manuscript.

Dressler, W. (1972). On the phonology of language death. In *Papers from the Eighth Regional Meeting of the Chicago Linguistic Society.* Chicago: Chicago Linguistic Society.

Dressler, W. (1974). Diachronic puzzles for natural phonology. In *Papers from the Parasession on Natural Phonology.* Chicago: Chicago Linguistic Society.

Dressler, W., & Wodak, R. (1982). Sociophonological methods in the study of sociolinguistic variation in Viennese German. In *Language in Society, 11.*

Dworkin, S. N. (1977). Therapeutic reactions to phonotactic awkwardness: The descendants of *alauda* in Hispano-Romance. *Zeitschrift fur Romanische Philologie, 93,* 513–517.

Dworkin, S. N. (1978). Phonotactic awkwardness as an impediment to sound change. *Forum Linguisticum, 3,* 47–56.

Dworkin, S. N. (1979). *Phonotactic awkwardness and lexical loss.* Paper presented at The Fourth International Conference on Historical Linguistics, Stanford, March.

Dworkin, S. N. (1980). Phonotactic awkwardness as a cause of lexical blends: The genesis of Spanish *cola* 'tail'. *Hispanic Review, 48,* 231–237.

Eady, S. J. (1980). *The onset of language-specific patterning in infant vocalization.* Unpublished master's thesis, University of Ottawa.

Eblen, R. E. (1982). A study of the acquisition of fricatives by 3-year-old children learning Mexican Spanish. *Language and Speech, 25,* 201–220.

Edfeldt, A. W. (1960). *Silent speech and silent reading.* Chicago: University of Chicago Press.

Edwards, M. L. (1979). 'Cet ten' or 'just pretend': A lexical mismatch transmitted from brother to sister. *Journal of Child Languages, 6,* 181–182.

Eilers, R. E., Gavin, W., & Wilson, W. R. (1979). Linguistic experience and phonemic perception in infancy: A cross-linguistic study. *Child Development, 50,* 14–18.

Eilers, R. E., & Oller, D. K. (1978). *A cross-linguistic study of infant speech perception.* Paper presented at the Southeastern Regional Conference on Human Development, April.

Eilers, R. E., & Oller, D. K. (1981). *Infant speech perception: Environmental contributions.* Paper presented at the Conference on Auditory Development in Infancy, University of Toronto, June 11–13.

Eilers, R. E., & Oller, D. K. (1982). Speech perception in infancy and early childhood. In E. Z. Lasky, & J. Katz, (Eds.), *Central auditory processing disorders: Problems of speech, language and learning.* Baltimore: University Park Press.

Elbers, L. (1980). Cognitive principles of babbling: A case study. *Psychological Laboratory Report No. 21.* The Netherlands: University of Utrecht.

Elbers, L. (1982). Operating principles in repetitive babbling: A cognitive continuity approach. *Cognition, 12,* 45–64.

Elbert, M., Dinnsen, D. A., & Weismer, G. (Forthcoming). *Phonological theory and the misarticulating child.*

Enstrom, D. H. (1982). Infant labial, apical and velar stop productions: A voice onset time analysis *Phonetica, 39,* 47–60.

Enstrom, D. H., & Spörri-Bütler, S. (1981). A voice onset time analysis of initial Swiss-German stops. *Folia Phoniatrica, 33,* 137–150.

Entenman, G. (1977). The development of nasal vowels. *Texas Linguistic Forum, 7.* Department of Linguistics, University of Texas at Austin.

Fagan, J. F. (1970). Memory in the infant. *Journal of Experimental Child Psychology, 9,* 217–226.

Ferguson, C. A. (1956). Arabic baby talk. In M. Halle (Ed.), *For Roman Jakobson.* The Hague: Mouton.

Ferguson, C. A. (1964). Baby talk in six languages. *American Anthropologist, 66,* 103–114.

Dato, D. P. (Ed.), *Georgetown University Round Table on Languages and Linguistics.* Washington: Georgetown University Press.

Ferguson, C. A. (1978a). Phonological processes, In J. H. Greenberg (Ed.), *Universals of human language, vol. 2: Phonology.* Stanford: Stanford University Press.

Ferguson, C. A. (1978b). Learning to pronounce: The earliest stages of phonological development in the child. In F. D. Minifie & L. L. Lloyd (Eds.), *Communicative and cognitive abilities, early behavioral assessment.* Baltimore: University Park Press.

Ferguson, C. A., & Chowdhury, M. (1960). The phonemes of Bengali. *Language, 36,* 22–59.

Ferguson, C. A., & Farwell, C. B. (1975). Words and sounds in early language acquisition: English initial consonants in the first fifty words. *Language, 51,* 419–439.

Ferguson, C. A., & Macken, M. A. (in press). Phonological development in children: Play and cognition. In K. E. Nelson (Ed.), *Children's language* (Vol. 4). New York: Gardner Press.

Field, T. M., Woodson, R., Greenberg, R., & Cohen, D. (1982). Discrimination and imitation of facial expressions by neonates. *Science, 218,* 179–181.

Fintoft, K. (1961). The duration of some Norwegian speech sounds. *Phonetica, 7,* 19–39.

Fischer-Jorgensen, E. (1964). Sound duration and place of articulation. *Zeitschrift fur Phonetik, Sprachwissenschaft und Kommunikationsforschung, 17,* 2–4, 175–207.

Fisichelli, R. M. (1950). *An experimental study of the prelinguistic speech development of institutionalized infants.* Unpublished doctoral dissertation, Fordham University.

Flege, J. E. (1982). English speakers learn to suppress stop devoicing. In *Papers from the Eighteenth Regional Meeting of the Chicago Linguistic Society.* Chicago: Chicago Linguistic Society.

Flege, J. E., & Port, R. (1981). Cross-language phonetic interference: Arabic to English. *Language and Speech, 24,* 125–146.

Fleming, C. A. (1981). Beliefs about speech development and communication disorders in a 'primitive' African tribe. *Journal of the National Student Speech–Language–Hearing Association, 9,* 38–49.

Fletcher, S. G., & Daly, D. A. (1974). Sublingual dimensions in infants and young children. *Archives of Otolaryngology, 99,* 292–296.

Fletcher, S. G., & Meldrum, J. R. (1968). Lingual function and relative length of the lingual frenulum. *Journal of Speech and Hearing Research, 11,* 382–390.

Foldvik, A. K. (1979). Norwegian speech error data—a source of evidence for linguistic performance models. *Nordic Journal of Linguistics, 2,* 113–122.

Foley, J. (1973). Assimilation of phonological strength in Germanic. In S. R. Anderson, & P. Kiparsky (Eds.), *A festschrift for Morris Halle.* New York: Holt, Rinehart and Winston.

Fort, B. D. (1955). *Sontaneous vocalizations of two-year-old deaf children as related to degree of hearing loss and other factors.* Unpublished master's thesis, University of Kansas.

French, N. R., Carter, C. W., & Koenig, W. (1930). The words and sounds of telephone conversations. *Bell System Technical Journal, 9,* 290–324.

Frishberg, N. (1979). Historical change: From iconic to arbitrary. In E. S. Klima, & U. Bellugi, (Eds.), *The signs of language.* Cambridge, Mass.: Harvard University Press.

Fromkin, V. A. (1971). The non-anomalous nature of anomalous utterances. *Language, 47,* 27–52.

Fromkin, V. A. (Ed.). (1973). *Speech errors as linguistic evidence.* The Hague: Mouton.

Fry, D. B. (1972). Discussion of "Cluster as single underlying consonants: Evidence from children's production," by P. Menyuk. In A. Rigault, & R. Charbonneau, (Eds.), *Proceedings of the Seventh International Congress of Phonetic Sciences.* The Hague: Mouton.

Gamkrelidze, T. V. (1978). On the correlation of stops and fricatives in a phonological system. In J. H. Greenberg, (Ed.), *Universals of human language, vol. 2: Phonology.* Stanford, Calif.: Stanford University Press.

Garnes, S., & Bond, Z. S. (1980). A slip of the ear: A snip of the ear? a slip of the year? In V. Fromkin (Ed.), *Errors in linguistic performance: Slips of the tongue, ear, pen, and hand.* New York: Academic Press.

Garnham, A., Shillcock, R. C., Brown, G. D. A., Mill, A. I. D., & Cutler, A. (1981). Slips of the tongue in the London–Lund corpus of spontaneous conversation. *Linguistics, 19,* 805–817.

Garnica, O. K. (1973). The development of phonemic speech perception. In T. E. Moore (Ed.), *Cognitive development and the acquisition of language.* New York: Academic Press.

Gheorgov, I. A. (1905). Die ersten anfänge des sprachlichen ausdrucks fur das Selbstbewusstsein bei Kindern. *Archiv für die Gesamte Psychologie, 5,* 329–404. Reprinted in W. G. Bateman, 1917, Papers on language development, *Pedagogical Seminary, 24,* 391–398.

Gibson, E. J. (1969). *Principles of perceptual learning and development.* New York: Appleton-Century-Crofts.

Gimson, A. C. (1962). *An introduction to the pronunciation of English.* London: Edward Arnold.

Goldstein, L. (1980). Bias and asymmetry in speech perception. In V. A. Fromkin (Ed.), *Errors in linguistic performance: Slips of the tongue, ear, pen, and hand.* New York: Academic Press.

Gottlieb, G. (1976a). Conceptions of prenatal development: Behavioral embryology. *Psychological Review, 83,* 215–234.

Gottlieb, G. (1976b). The roles of experience in the development of behavior and the nervous system. In G. Gottlieb (Ed.), *Neural and behavioral specificity.* New York: Academic Press.

Graham, L. W., & House, A. S. (1971). Phonological oppositions in children: A perceptual study. *Journal of the Acoustical Society of America, 49,* 559–566.

Grammont, M. (1902). Observations sur le langage des enfants. *Melanges linguistiques offerts a M. Antoine Meillet.* Paris: Klincksieck.

Green, S. (1975). Communication by a graded vocal system in Japanese monkeys. In L. A. Rosenblum (Ed.), *Primate behavior* (Vol. 4). New York: Academic Press.

Greenberg, J. H. (1978). Some generalizations concerning initial and final consonant clusters. In J. H. Greenberg (Ed.), *Universals of human language, vol. 2: Phonology.* Stanford, Calif.: Stanford University Press.

Greenlee, M. (1978). *Learning the phonetic cues to the voiced–voiceless distinction: An exploration of parallel processes in phonological change.* Unpublished doctoral dissertation, University of California, Berkeley.

Greenlee, M., & Ohala, J. J. (1980). Phonetically motivated parallels between child phonology and historical sound change. *Language Sciences, 2,* 283–301.

Gregoire, A. (1933). L'apprentissage de la parole pendant les deux premières années de l'enfance. *Journal de Psychologie, 30,* 375–389.

Gruenenfelder, T. M., & Pisoni, D. B. (1980). Fundamental frequency as a cue to postvocalic consonantal voicing: Some data from speech perception and production. *Perception and Psychophysics, 28,* 514–520.

Guy, G. R. (1980). Variation in the group and the individual: The case of final stop deletion. In W. Labov (Ed.), *Locating language in time and space.* New York: Academic Press.

Haggard, M. (1978). The devoicing of voiced fricatives. *Journal of Phonetics, 6,* 95–102.

Hammond, R. M. (1976). Phonemic restructuring in Miami-Cuban Spanish. In F. M. Aid, M. C. Resnich, & B. Saciuk (Eds.), *1975 Colloquium on Hispanic Linguistics.* Washington, D.C.: Georgetown University Press.

Handbook of phonological data from a sample of the world's languages: A report of the Stanford Phonology Archive (1979). Stanford University, Department of Linguistics.

Harris, J. W. (1969). *Spanish phonology.* Cambridge, Mass.: MIT Press.

Hayes, C. (1951). *The ape in our house.* New York: Harpers.

Healy, A. F., & Levitt, A. G. (1980). Accessibility of the voicing distinction for learning phonological rules. *Memory and Cognition, 8,* 107–114.

Hecht, B. F., & Mulford, R. (1982). The acquisition of a second language phonology: Interaction of transfer and developmental factors. *Applied Psycholinguistics, 3,* 313–328.

Henderson, J. B., and Repp, B. H. (1982). Is a stop consonant released when followed by another stop consonant? *Phonetica, 39,* 71–82.

Henry, J., & Henry, Z. (1940). Speech disturbances in Pilaga Indian children. *American Journal of Orthopsychiatry, 10,* 362–369.

Hillenbrand, J. (1983). Perceptual organization of speech sounds by infants. *Journal of Speech and Hearing Research, 26,* 268–281.

Hock, H. H. (1975). *Final weakening and related phenomena.* Paper presented at the Mid-America Linguistic Conference, Lawrence, Kansas.

Hombert, J.-M., Ohala, J. J., & Ewan, W. G. (1979). Phonetic explanations for the development of tones. *Language, 55,* 37–58.

Houlihan, K. (1982). *Is intervocalic voicing a natural rule?* Paper presented at the winter meeting of the Linguistic Society of America, San Diego, December.

House, A. S., & Fairbanks, G. (1953). The influence of consonant environment upon the secondary acoustical characteristics of vowels. *Journal of the Acoustical Society of America, 25,* 105–113.

Householder, F. W. (1956). Unreleased ptk in American English. In M. Halle, H. G. Lunt, H. McLean, & C. H. Van Schooneveld (Eds.), *For Roman Jakobson*. The Hague: Mouton.

Huber, H. (1970). A preliminary comparison of English and Yucatec infant vocalization at nine months. *Papers from the Sixth Regional Meeting of the Chicago Linguistic Society*. Chicago: Chicago Linguistic Society.

Hyman, L. M. (1975). *Phonology: Theory and analysis*. New York: Holt, Rinehart and Winston.

Ingram, D. (1974). Fronting in child phonology. *Journal of Child Language, 1,* 233–241.

Ingram, D. (1976). *Phonological disability in children*. New York: Elsevier.

Ingram, D. (1978). The production of word-initial fricatives and affricates by normal and linguistically deviant children. In A. Caramazza, & E. B. Zurif (Eds.), *Language acquisition and language breakdown: Parallels and divergencies*. Baltimore: Johns Hopkins University Press.

Irwin, O. C. (1947). Infant speech: Consonantal sounds according to place of articulation. *Journal of Speech Disorders, 12,* 397–401.

Irwin, O. C. (1951). Infant speech: Consonantal position. *Journal of Speech and Hearing Disorders, 16,* 159–161.

Jaeger, J. J. (1978). *Speech aerodynamics and phonological universals*. Report of the Phonology Laboratory, 2, University of California, Berkeley.

Jakobson, R. (1972). Principles of historical phonology. In A. R. Keiler (Ed.), *A reader in historical and comparative linguistics*. New York: Holt, Rinehart and Winston. (Originally published, 1931).

Jakobson, R. (1968). *Child language, aphasia, and phonological universals*. The Hague: Mouton. (Originally published, 1941).

Jakobson, R. (1962). Why 'Mama' and 'Papa'? In *Roman Jakobson: Selected writings. I Phonology*. The Hague: Mouton.

Jakobson, R. (1968). The role of phonic elements in speech perception. *Zeitschrift fur Phonetik, Sprachwissenschaft und Kommunikationsforschung, 21,* 9–20. Reproduced in R. Jakobson & L. Waugh, *The sound shape of language*. Bloomington: Indiana University Press, 1979.

Janda, R. D. (1979). Double-cross in phonology: Why word boundary (often) acts like a consonant. In *Proceedings of the Fifth Annual Meeting of the Berkeley Linguistics Society*. University of California, Berkeley.

Javkin, H. R. (1979a). *Phonetic universals and phonological change*. Report of the Phonology Laboratory, 4, University of California, Berkeley.

Javkin, H. R. (1979b). Phonetic explanations for the devoicing of high vowels. In *Proceedings of the Fifth Annual Meeting of the Berkeley Linguistics Society*. University of California, Berkeley.

Jeffers, R. J., & Lehiste, I. (1979). *Principles and methods for historical linguistics*. Cambridge, Mass.: MIT Press.

Jenkins, J. J., Foss, D. J., & Greenberg, J. H. (1968). Phonological distinctive features as cues in learning. *Journal of Experimental Psychology, 77,* 200–205.

Jespersen, O. (1964). *Language: Its nature, development, and origin*. New York: W. W. Norton. (Originally published, 1922).

Johns, D. F., & Darley, F. L. (1970). Phonemic variability in apraxia of speech. *Journal of Speech and Hearing Research, 13,* 556–583.

Johnston, C. (1896). The world's baby-talk, and the expressiveness of speech. *Fortnightly Review, 60,* 494–505.

Juilland, A. (1965). *Dictionnaire inverse de la langue Francaise*. The Hague: Mouton.

Kagan, J., Kearsley, R. B., & Zelazo, P. R. (1978). *Infancy: Its place in human development*. Cambridge, Mass.: Harvard University Press.

Keating, P. A. (1979). *A phonetic study of a voicing contrast in Polish*. Unpublished doctoral dissertation, Brown University.

Kelkar, A. R. (1964). Marathi baby talk. *Word, 20,* 40–54.

Kent, R. D. (1980a). Articulatory and acoustic perspectives on speech development. In A. P. Reilly (Ed.), *The communication game: Perspectives on the development of speech, language and nonverbal communication skills.* Johnson and Johnson Baby Products Company Pediatric Round Table Series, Skillman, New Jersey.

Kent, R. D. (1980b). Motor skill component of speech development. Paper presented at the Meeting of the American Speech–Language–Hearing Association, Detroit, November.

Kent, R. D. (1981). Articulatory–acoustic perspectives on speech development. In R. Stark (Ed.), *Language behavior in infancy and early childhood.* New York: Elsevier North-Holland.

Kent, R. D. (1982). Sensorimotor aspects of speech development. In R. N. Aslin, J. R. Alberts, & M. R. Petersen (Eds.), *Development of perception* (Vol. 1). New York: Academic Press.

Kent, R. D., & Murray, A. D. (1982). Acoustic features of infant vocalic utterances at 3, 6, and 9 months. *Journal of the Acoustical Society of America, 72,* 353–365.

Kessen, W., Levine, J., & Wendrich, K. A. (1979). The imitation of pitch in infants. *Infant Behavior and Development, 2,* 93–99.

Kewley-Port, D., & Preston, M. S. (1974). Early apical stop production: A voice onset time analysis. *Journal of Phonetics, 2,* 195–210.

King, R. D. (1966). On preferred phonemicizations for statistical studies: Phoneme frequencies in German. *Phonetica, 15,* 22–31.

King, R. D. (1967). Functional load and sound change. *Language, 43,* 831–852.

King, R. D. (1969). *Historical linguistics and generative grammar.* Englewood Cliffs, N.J.: Prentice-Hall.

King, R. D. (1976). *The history of final devoicing in Yiddish.* Bloomington: Indiana University Linguistics Club.

Kintsch, W. (1970). *Learning, memory, and conceptual processes.* New York: John Wiley & Sons.

Kiparsky, P. (1968). Linguistic universals and linguistic change. In E. Bach, & R. T. Harms (Eds.), *Universals in linguistic theory.* New York: Holt, Rinehart & Winston.

Kiparsky, P. (1971). Historical linguistics. In W. O. Dingwall (Ed.), *A survey of linguistic science.* College Park: University of Maryland Linguistics Program.

Klatt, D. (1973). Interaction between two factors that influence vowel duration. *Journal of the Acoustical Society of America, 54,* 1102–1104.

Klatt, D. (1975). Voice-onset time, frication and aspiration in word-initial consonant clusters. *Journal of Speech and Hearing Research, 18,* 686–706.

Kleinman, H. H. (1978). The strategy of avoidance in adult second language acquisition. In W. C. Ritchie (Ed.), *Second language acquisition research: Issues and implications.* New York: Academic Press.

Klinger, H. (1962). Imitated English cleft palate speech in a normal Spanish speaking child. *Journal of Speech and Hearing Disorders, 27,* 379–381.

Knab, T., & Knab, L. (1979). Language death in the Valley of Puebla: A socio-geographic approach. In *Proceedings of the Fifth Annual Meeting of the Berkeley Linguistics Society.* University of California, Berkeley.

Kolarič, R. (1959). Slovenski otroski govor. *Jahrbuch der Philosophischen Fakultat in Novi Sad, 4,* 229–258.

Koopmans-van Beinum, F. J., & van der Stelt, J. M. (1980). Early stages in infant speech development. *Proceedings of the Institute of Phonetic Sciences* (University of Amsterdam), *5,* 30–43.

Koopmans-van Beinum, F. J., & van der Stelt, J. M. (1981). De ontwikkeling van de spreekmotoriek in het eerste levensjaar. *Logopedie en Foniatrie, 53,* 320–328.

Krause, S. (1980). *Fundamental frequency as a cue to postvocalic consonant voicing in production: Developmental data.* Paper presented at the 99th Meeting of the Acoustical Society of America, Atlanta. Also in *Research on speech perception, Progress Report No. 6 (1979–1980),* Bloomington: Indiana University.

Krause, S. (1982a). Vowel duration as a perceptual cue to post-vocalic consonant voicing in young children and adults. *Journal of the Acoustical Society of America, 71,* 990–995.

Krause, S. (1982b). Developmental use of vowel duration as a cue to postvocalic stop consonant voicing. *Journal of Speech and Hearing Research, 25,* 388–393.

Krehbiel, T. E. (1940). *Speech sounds of infants: The fourth, fifth, and sixth months.* Unpublished master's thesis, State University of Iowa.

Kroeber, A. L. (1916). The speech of a Zuni child. *American Anthropologist, 18,* 529–534.

Kucera, H., & Monroe, G. K. (1968). *A comparative quantitative phonology of Russian, Czech, and German.* New York: American Elsevier.

Kuhl, P. K., & Meltzoff, A. N. (1982). The bimodal perception of speech in infancy. *Science, 218,* 1138–1141.

Kurath, H., & McDavid, R. I. (1961). *The pronunciation of English in the Atlantic states.* Ann Arbor: University of Michigan Press.

Labov, W. (1964). Stages in the acquisition of Standard English. In R. W. Shuy (Ed.), *Social dialects and language learning.* Champaign, Ill.: National Council of Teachers of English.

Labov, W. (1966). *The social stratification of English in New York City.* Washington, D.C.: Center for Applied Linguistics.

Labov, W. (1981). Resolving the neogrammarian controversy. *Language, 57,* 267–308.

Labov, W., & Labov, T. (1978). The phonetics of *cat* and *mama. Language, 54,* 816–852.

Ladefoged, P. (1980). What are linguistic sounds made of? *Language, 56,* 485–502.

Ladefoged, P. (1983). Cross-linguistic studies of speech production. In P. F. MacNeilage (Ed.), *The production of speech.* New York: Springer-Verlag.

Lasky, R. E., Syrdal-Lasky, A., & Klein, R. E. (1975). VOT discrimination by four to six and a half month old infants from Spanish environments. *Journal of Experimental Child Psychology, 20,* 215–225.

Lass, N. J., & Sandusky, J. C. (1971). A study of the relationship of diadochokinetic rate, speaking rate and reading rate. *Today's Speech, 19,* 49–54.

Laufer, M. Z. (1980). Temporal regularity in prespeech. In T. Murray & J. Murray (Eds.), *Infant communication: Cry and early speech.* San Diego: College-Hill Press.

Lecours, A. R., & Lhermitte, F. (1972). Recherches sur le langage des aphasiques, 4: Analyse d'un corpus de neologismes; notion de paraphasie monemique. *L'Encephale, 4,* 295–315.

Lehiste, I. (1976). Influence of fundamental frequency pattern on perception of duration. *Journal of Phonetics, 4,* 113–117.

Lehiste, I., & Peterson, G. E. (1961). Some basic considerations in the analysis of intonation. *Journal of the Acoustical Society of America, 33,* 419–425.

Lenneberg, E. H. (1964). Speech as a motor skill with special reference to nonaphasic disorders. *Monographs of the Society for Research in Child Development, 29,* 115–127.

Lenneberg, E. H. (1967). *Biological foundations of language.* New York: John Wiley & Sons.

Lenneberg, E. H., Rebelsky, F. G., & Nichols, I. A. (1965). The vocalizations of infants born to deaf and to hearing parents. *Human Development, 8,* 23–37.

Leonard, L. B., Newhoff, M., & Mesalam, L. (1980). Individual differences in early child phonology. *Applied Psycholinguistics, 1,* 7–30.

Leonard, L. B., Schwartz, R. G., Morris, B., & Chapman, K. (1981). Factors influencing early lexical acquisition: Lexical orientation and phonological composition. *Child Development, 52,* 882–887.

Leopold, W. F. (1947). *Speech development of a bilingual child: A linguist's record. Vol. 2: Sound-learning in the first two years.* Evanston, Ill.: Northwestern University Press.

Leopold, W. F. (1949). Original invention in infant language. *Symposium, 3,* 66–75.

Lester, L., & Skousen, R. (1974). The phonology of drunkenness. *Papers from the Parasession on Natural Phonology.* Chicago: Chicago Linguistic Society.

Lewis, M. M. (1936). *Infant speech: A study of the beginnings of language.* New York: Harcourt, Brace.

Lieberman, P. (1963). Some effects of semantic and grammatical context on the production and perception of speech. *Language and Speech, 6,* 172–187.

Linn, S.-C. (1971). Phonetic development of Chinese infants. *Acta Psychologica Taiwanica, 13,* 191–195.

Linell, P. (1979). *Psychological reality in phonology: A theoretical study.* New York: Cambridge University Press.

Lisker, L. (1974). On "explaining" vowel duration variation. *Glossa,* 1974, *8,* 233–246.

Lisker, L., & Abramson, A. S. (1967). Some effects of context on voice onset time in English stops. *Language and Speech, 10,* 1–28.

Locke, J. L. (1968). Oral perception and articulation learning. *Perceptual and Motor Skills, 26,* 1259–1264.

Locke, J. L. (1978). Selective loss of phonetic production and perception: An index to the child's acquisition of phonology. *Journal of National Student Speech and Hearing Association,* 3–11.

Locke, J. L. (1979a). Homonymy and sound change in the child's acquisition of phonology. In N. Lass (Ed.), *Speech and language: Advances in basic research and practice* (Vol. 3). New York: Academic Press.

Locke, J. L. (1979b). The child's processing of phonology. In W. A. Collins (Ed.), *The Minnesota symposia on child psychology* (Vol. 12). Hillsdale, N.J.: Erlbaum.

Locke, J. L. (1980a). The prediction of child speech errors: Implications for a theory of acquisition. In G. Yeni-Komshian, J. F. Kavanagh, & C. Ferguson (Eds.), *Child phonology, vol. 1: Production.* New York: Academic Press.

Locke, J. L. (1980b). Mechanisms of phonological development in children: Maintenance, learning and loss. *Papers from the Sixteenth Regional Meeting of the Chicago Linguistic Society.* Chicago: Chicago Linguistic Society.

Locke, J. L. (1980c). The inference of phoneme perception in the phonologically disordered child, Part 1: A rationale, some criteria, the conventional tests. *Journal of Speech and Hearing Disorders, 45,* 431–444.

Locke, J. L. (1980d). The inference of phoneme perception in the phonologically disordered child, Part 2: Clinically novel procedures, their use, some findings. *Journal of Speech and Hearing Disorders, 45,* 445–468.

Locke, J. L. (1980e). Levels of speech perception analysis. In W. D. Wolfe, & D. J. Goulding (Eds.), *Articulation and learning* (2nd ed.). Springfield, Ill.: Charles C Thomas.

Locke, J. L. (1982a). *Historical and developmental phonology.* First Forum Lecture, 50th Linguistic Institute, College Park, Md.

Locke, J. L. (1982b). *Lexical avoidance in adults.* Paper presented to the American Speech–Language–Hearing Association, Toronto. November.

Locke, J. L. (submitted). *The role of phonetic factors in parent reference.*

Locke, J. L., & Fehr, F. S. (1971). Subvocal rehearsal as a form of speech. *Journal of Verbal Learning and Verbal Behavior, 9,* 495–498.

Locke, J. L., & Ohala, J. (1980). Phonological universals and the child's phonological development: Unified phonetic view. A shortcourse presented to the American Speech–Language–Hearing Association, Detroit, November.

Locke, J. L., & Yakov, D. H. (1982). Speech as perception: Some contextual effects on phonological segments. *Seminars in Speech, Language and Hearing, 3,* 162–171.

Lubker, J. F., & Parris, P. J. (1970). Simultaneous measurements of intraoral pressure, force of labial contact, and electromyographic activity during production of the stop consonant cognates /p/ and /b/. *Journal of the Acoustical Society of America, 47,* 625–633.

McCarthy, D. (1929). Note on the vocal sounds of a blind–deaf girl. *Journal of Genetic Psychology, 36,* 482–484.

McCarthy, D. (1952). Organismic interpretation of infant vocalizations. *Child Development, 23,* 273–280.

McDavid, R. I. (1950). Our initial consonant 'H'. *College English, 11,* 458–459.

McDavid, R. I., & McDavid, V. I. (1952). H before semivowels in the Eastern United States. *Language, 28,* 41–62.

McGuigan, F. J., & Rodier, W. I. (1968). Effects of auditory stimulation on covert oral behavior during silent reading. *Journal of Experimental Psychology, 76,* 649–655.

MacKain, K. S. (1982). Assessing the role of experience on infants' speech discrimination. *Journal of Child Language, 9,* 527–542.

MacKain, K. S., Best, C. T., & Strange, W. (1981). Categorical perception of English /r/ and /l/ by Japanese bilinguals. *Applied Psycholinguistics, 2,* 369–390.

MacKain, K. S. & Stern, D. N. (1982). The concept of experience in speech development. In K. E. Nelson (Ed.), *Children's language* (Vol. 6). New York: Gardner Press.

MacKain, K. S., Studdert-Kennedy, M., Spieker, S., & Stern, D. (1983). Infant intermodal speech perception is a left hemisphere function. *Science, 219,* 1347–1349.

Macken, M. A., & Barton, D. (1980a). The acquisition of the voicing contrast in Spanish: A phonetic and phonological study of word-initial stop consonants. *Journal of Child Language, 7,* 433–458.

Macken, M. A., & Barton, D. (1980b). The acquisition of the voicing contrast in English: A study of voice onset time in word-initial stop consonants. *Journal of Child Language, 7,* 41–74.

MacNeilage, P. F. (1982). Speech production mechanisms in aphasia. In S. Grillner, B. Lindblom, J. Lubker, & A. Persson (Eds.), *Speech motor control.* New York: Pergamon Press.

Maddieson, I. (1980). Phonological generalizations from the UCLA Phonological Segment Inventory Database (UPSID). *UCLA Working Papers in Phonetics, 50,* 57–68.

Maddieson, I., & Gandour, J. (1975). Vowel length before aspirated consonant. *Indian Linguistics, 38,* 6–11.

Magnusson, E. (1983). The phonology of language disordered children: Production, perception, and awareness. *Travaux de 'institut de linguistique de Lund, XVII.* Lund: CWK Gleerup (Liber förlag Lund).

Malécot, A. (1958). The role of releases in the identification of released final stops. *Language, 34,* 370–380.

Malécot, A. (1960). Vowel nasality as a distinctive feature in American English. *Language, 36,* 222–229.

Malécot, A. (1970). The lenis–fortis opposition: Its physiological parameters. *Journal of the Acoustical Society of America, 47,* 1588–1592.

Malécot, A. (1974). Frequency of occurrence of French phonemes and consonant clusters. *Phonetica, 29,* 158–170.

Malécot, A. (1975). The glottal stop in French. *Phonetica, 29,* 51–63.

Malkiel, Y. (1964). Economie phonologique et perte lexicale. *Melanges de linguistique romane et de philogie medievale offorts a M. Maurice Delbouille,* Gembloux: J. Duculot.

Malsheen, B. J. (1980). Two hypotheses for phonetic clarification in the speech of mothers to children. In G. H. Yeni-Komshian, J. F. Kavanagh, & C. A. Ferguson (Eds.), *Child phonology, vol. 2: Perception.* New York: Academic Press.

Mattingly, I. (1976). Phonetic prerequisites for first-language acquisition. In W. von Raffler-Engel, & Y. Lebrun (Eds.), *Baby talk and infant speech.* Amsterdam: Swets & Zeitlinger.

Mavilya, M. P. (1969). *Spontaneous vocalization and babbling in hearing impaired infants.* Unpublished doctoral dissertation, Teachers College, Columbia University.

Maxwell, E. M. (1981). *A study of misarticulation from a linguistic perspective.* Unpublished doctoral dissertation, Indiana University.

Meader, C. L., & Muyskens, J. H. (1950). *Handbook of biolinguistics: The structure and processes of expression.* Toledo, Ohio: Herbert C. Weller.

Mehler, J. (1971). Comments at a conference held in 1968 and reported in R. Huxley, & E. Ingram (Eds.), *Language acquisition: Models and methods.* New York: Academic Press.

Meltzoff, A. N., & Borton, R. W. (1979). Inter modal matching by human neonates. *Nature, 282,* 403–404.

Meltzoff, A. N., & Moore, M. K. (1977). Imitation of facial and manual gestures by human neonates. *Science, 198,* 75–78.

Menn, L. (1971). Phonotactic rules in beginning speech: A study in the development of English discourse. *Lingua, 26,* 225–251.

Menn, L. (1976). *Pattern, control, and contrast in beginning speech: A case study in the development of word form and word function.* Unpublished doctoral dissertation, University of Illinois.

Miller, W. R. (1971). The death of language, or serendipity among the Shoshoni. *Anthropological Linguistics, 13,* 114–120.

Milner, E. (1976). CNS maturation and language acquisition. In H. Whitaker & H. A. Whitaker (Eds.), *Studies in neurolinguistics* (Vol. 1). New York: Academic Press.

Mines, M. A., Hanson, B. F., & Shoup, J. E. (1978). Frequency of occurrence of phonemes in conversational English. *Language and Speech, 21,* 221–241.

Miyawaki, K., Strange, W., Verbrugge, R., Liberman, A. M., Jenkins, J. J., & Fujimura, O. (1975). An effect of linguistic experience: The discrimination of [r] and [l] by native speakers of Japanese and English. *Perception and Psychophysics, 18,* 331–340.

Möhring, H. (1938). Lautbildungsschwierigkeit im Deutschen. *Zeitschrift für Kinderforschung, 47,* 185–235.

Moser, H. (1969). *One-syllable words.* Columbus, Ohio: Charles E. Merrill.

Moskowitz, A. I. (1970). The two-year-old stage in the acquisition of English phonology. *Language, 46,* 426–441.

Moskowitz, B. A. (1980). Idioms in phonology acquisition and phonological change. *Journal of Phonetics, 8,* 69–83.

Motley, M. T. (1967). *Glossolalia: Analysis of selected aspects of phonology and morphology.* Unpublished master's thesis, University of Texas.

Motley, M. T. (1975). *Selected linguistic analyses of glossolalia.* Paper presented at the Meeting of the Speech Communication Association, Houston.

Murai, J. (1964). The sounds of infants: Their phonemicization and symbolization. *Studia Phonologica, 3,* 17–34.

Murdock, G. P. (1959). Cross-language parallels in parental kin terms. *Anthropological Linguistics, 1,* 1–5.

Naeser, M. A. (1970). *The American child's acquisition of differential vowel duration* (Tech. Rep. 144). Madison: Wisconsin Research and Development Center for Cognitive Learning.

Nakazima, S. (1962). A comparative study of the speech developments of Japanese and American English in childhood, 1: A comparison of the developments of voices at the prelinguistc period. *Studia Phonologica, 2,* 27–46.

Nakazima, S. (1970). A comparative study of the speech developments of Japanese and American English in childhood, 3: The re-organization process of babbling articulation mechanisms. *Studia Phonologica, 5,* 20–35.

Neas, B. J. (1953). *A study of the spontaneous babblings of three- and four-year-old deaf children.* Unpublished master's thesis, University of Kansas.

Netsell, R. (1981). The acquisition of speech motor control: A perspective with directions for research. In R. Stark (Ed.), *Language behavior in infancy and early childhood.* New York: Elsevier/North-Holland.

Neu, H. (1980). Ranking of constraints on /t,d/ deletion in American English: A statistical analysis. In W. Labov (Ed.), *Locating language in time and space.* New York: Academic Press.

Nishimura, B. (1980). Emergence of functional articulation disorders. In *Proceedings of the First International Congress for the Study of Child Language*. Lanham, Md.: University Press of America.

Noble, E. (1888). Child speech, and the law of mispronunciation. *Education, 9*, 44–52, 117–121, 188–194.

Nooteboom, S. G. (1969). The tongue slips into patterns. In A. G. Sciarene, A. J. van Essen, & A. A. Raad (Eds.), *Leyden studies in linguistics and phonetics*. The Hague: Mouton. Reprinted in V. A. Fromkin, 1973, *Speech errors as linguistic evidence*, The Hague: Mouton.

Norris, M., Harden, J. R., & Bell, D. M. (1980). Listener agreement on articulation errors of four- and five-year-old children. *Journal of Speech and Hearing Disorders, 45*, 378–389.

Ohala, J. J. (1975). Phonetic explanations for nasal sound patterns. In C. A. Ferguson, L. M. Hyman, & J. J. Ohala (Eds.), *NASALFEST: Papers from a symposium on nasals and nasalization*. Stanford: Language Universals Project.

Ohala, J. J. (1980). The application of phonological universals in speech pathology. In N. Lass (Ed.), *Speech and language: Advances in basic research and practice* (Vol. 3). New York: Academic Press.

Ohala, J. J. (1983). The origin of sound patterns in vocal tract constraints. In P. F. MacNeilage (Ed.), *The production of speech*. New York: Springer-Verlag.

Ohala, J. J., & Riordan, C. J. (1979). Passive vocal tract enlargement during voiced stops. In J. J. Wolf, & D. H. Klatt (Eds.), *Speech communication papers*. New York: Acoustical Society of America.

Oller, D. K. (1980). The emergence of the sounds of speech in infancy. In G. H. Yeni-Komshian, J. F. Kavanagh, & C. A. Ferguson (Eds.), *Child phonology, vol. 1: Production*. New York: Academic Press.

Oller, D. K. (1981). Infant vocalizations: Exploration and reflexivity. In R. Stark (Ed.), *Language behavior in infancy and early childhood*. New York: Elsevier/North-Holland.

Oller, D. K., & Eilers, R. E. (1982). Similarity of babbling in Spanish- and English-learning babies. *Journal of Child Language, 9*, 565–577.

Oller, D. K., & Eilers, R. E. (1983). Speech identification in Spanish and English-learning 2-year-olds. *Journal of Speech and Hearing Research, 26*, 50–53.

Oller, D. K., & Smith, B. L. (1977). Effect of final-syllable position on vowel duration in infant babbling. *Journal of the Acoustical Society of America, 62*, 994–997.

Oller, D. K., Weiman, L. A., Doyle, W. J., & Ross, C. (1976). Infant babbling and speech. *Journal of Child Language, 3*, 1–11.

Olmsted, D. L. (1971). *Out of the mouth of babes: Earliest stages in language learning*. The Hague: Mouton.

Olney, R. L., & Scholnick, E. K. (1976). Adult judgments of age and linguistic differences in infant vocalization. *Journal of Child Language, 3*, 145–155.

Olstuscewski, W. (1897). *Die Geistige und Sprachliche entwicklung des Kindes*. In M. M. Lewis, 1936, *Infant speech*, New York: Harcourt, Brace.

Omar, M. K. (1973). *The acquisition of Egyptian Arabic as a native language*. The Hague: Mouton.

Osgood, C. E. (1953). *Method and theory in experimental psychology*. New York: Oxford University Press.

Pačesova, J. (1968). *The development of vocabulary in the child*. Brno: Universita J. E. Purkyne.

Pačesova, J. (1976). Some notes on developmental universals in Czech-speaking children. In W. von Raffler-Engel & Y. Lebrun (Eds.), *Baby talk and infant speech*. Amsterdam: Swets & Zeitlinger.

Paradis, M. (1979). Baby talk in French and Quebecois. In W. Wolck (Ed.), *The Fifth LACUS Forum*. Columbia: Hornbeam Press.

Parker, F. (1974). The coarticulation of vowels and stop consonants. *Journal of Phonetics, 2*, 211–221.

Parrucci, R. (1983). *Effects of vowel height on final stop voicing.* Unpublished master's thesis, University of Maryland.

Perecman, E., & Brown, J. W. (1981). Phonemic jargon: A case report. In J. W. Brown (Ed.), *Jargonaphasia.* New York: Academic Press.

Peters, A. M. (1974). University of Hawaii study of the beginning of speech. *Working Papers in Linguistics, 6,* University of Hawaii, Honolulu.

Peters, A. M. (1981). Language typology and the segmentation problem in early child language acquisition. In *Proceedings of the Seventh Annual Meeting of the Berkeley Linguistics Society.* Berkeley: Berkeley Linguistics Society.

Peters, A. M. (1983). *The units of language acquisition.* New York: Cambridge University Press.

Peterson, G. E., & Lehiste, I. (1960). Duration of syllable nuclei in English. *Journal of the Acoustical Society of America, 32,* 693–703.

Piaget, J. (1962). *Play, dreams and imitations in childhood.* New York: W. W. Norton.

Pienaar, P. de V., & Hooper, A. G. (1948). *An Afrikaans–English phonetic reader.* Johannesburg: Witwatersrand University Press.

Pierce, J. E., & Hanna, I. V. (1974). *The development of a phonological system in English speaking American children.* Portland, Oregon: HaPi Press.

Platt, L. J., Andrews, G., & Howie, P. M. (1980). Dysarthria of adult cerebral palsy, II: Phonemic analysis of articulation errors. *Journal of Speech and Hearing Research, 23,* 41–55.

Platt, L. J., Andrews, G., Young, M., & Quinn, P. (1980). Dysarthria of adult cerebral palsy, I: Intelligibility and articulatory impairment. *Journal of Speech and Hearing Research, 23,* 28–40.

Plevyak, T. (1982). *Vocalic effect on children's final stop voicing.* Unpublished master's thesis, University of Maryland.

Poplack, S. (1980a). Deletion and disambiguation in Puerto Rican Spanish. *Language, 56,* 371–385.

Poplack, S. (1980b). The notion of the plural in Puerto Rican Spanish: Competing constraints on (s) deletion. In W. Labov (Ed.), *Locating language in time and space.* New York: Academic Press.

Port, R. F., & Rotunno, R. (1979). Relation between voice-onset time and vowel duration. *Journal of the Acoustical Society of America, 66,* 654–662.

Posner, M. I., Goldsmith, R., & Welton, K. E. (1967). Perceived distance and the classification of distorted pattern. *Journal of Experimental Psychology, 73,* 28–38.

Posner, M. I., & Keele, S. W. (1968). On the genesis of abstract ideas. *Journal of Experimental Psychology, 77,* 353–363.

Posner, M. I., & Keele, S. W. (1970). Retention of abstract ideas. *Journal of Experimental Psychology, 83,* 304–308.

Prather, E. M., Hedrick, D. L., & Kern, C. A. (1975). Articulation development in children aged two to four years. *Journal of Speech and Hearing Disorders, 40,* 179–191.

Preston, M. S., Yeni-Komshian, G. H., Stark, R. E., & Port, D. K. (1969). *Certain aspects of the development of speech production and perception in children.* Paper presented at the 77th Meeting of the Acoustical Society of America, April.

Raphael, L. J. (1972). Preceding vowel duration as a cue to the perception of the voicing characteristic of word-final consonants in American English. *Journal of the Acoustical Society of America, 51,* 1296–1303.

Read, C. (1975). *Children's categorizations of speech sounds in English* (Research Rep. 17). Urbana, Ill.: National Council of Teachers of English.

Ristinen, E. K. (1960). An East Cheremis phonology. *American Studies in Uralic Linguistics, 1,* 249–287.

Roberts, A. H. (1965). *A statistical linguistic analysis of American English.* The Hague: Mouton.

Rositzke, H. A. (1939). Vowel-length in General American speech. *Language, 15,* 99–109.

Rositzke, H. A. (1943). The articulation of final stops in General American speech. *American Speech, 18,* 39–42.

Rozin, P. (1976). The evolution of intelligence and access to the cognitive unconscious. *Progress in Psychobiology and Physiological Psychology, 6*, 245–280.

Rudegeair, R. E. (1970). *The effect of contextual influence on children's discrimination of initial consonants.* Unpublished doctoral dissertation, University of Wisconsin.

Ruhlen, M. (1976). *A guide to the languages of the world.* Stanford, Calif.: Language Universals Project, Stanford University.

Ruhlen, M. (1978). Nasal vowels. In J. H. Greenberg (Ed.), *Universals of human language, vol. 2: Phonology.* Stanford, Calif.: Stanford University Press.

Rūķe-Draviņa, V. (1965). The process of acquisition of apical /r/ and uvular /R/ in the speech of children. *Linguistics, 17*, 58–68.

Rūķe-Draviņa, V. (1976). 'Mama' and 'papa' in child language. *Journal of Child Language, 3*, 157–166.

Rūķe-Draviņa, V. (1982). *No pieciem ménésiem līdz pieciem gadiem* [From 5 months to 5 years]. Stockholm: Baltic Scientific Institute in Scandinavia.

Russ, C. V. (1978). *Historical German phonology and morphology.* Oxford: Clarendon Press.

Sapir, E. (1933). La realite psychologique des phonemes. *Journal de Psychologie Normale et Pathologique, 30*, 247–265. Reprinted in English in E. G. Mandelbam (Ed.), *Selected writings of Edward Sapir in language, culture and personality.* Berkeley: University of California Press, 1963.

Scharf, D. (1962). Duration of post-stress intervocalic stops and preceding vowels. *Language and Speech, 5*, 26–30.

Scharf, D. (1964). Vowel duration in whispered and in normal speech. *Language and Speech, 7*, 89–97.

Schieffelin, B. B. (1979). Getting it together: An ethnographic approach to the study of the development of communicative competence. In E. Ochs & B. B. Schieffelin (Eds.), *Developmental pragmatics.* New York: Academic Press.

Schlanger, B., & Gottsleben, R. H. (1957). Analysis of speech defects among the institutionalized mentally retarded. *Journal of Speech and Hearing Disorders, 22*, 98–103.

Schwartz, M. F. (1972). Bilabial closure durations for /p/, /b/, and /m/ in voiced and whispered vowel environments. *Journal of the Acoustical Society of America, 51*, 2025–2029.

Scollon, R. (1976). *Conversations with a one year old.* Honolulu: University Press of Hawaii.

Selinker, L. (1972). Interlanguage. *International Review of Applied Linguistics, 10*, 209–231.

Shattuck-Hufnagel, S. (1975). *Speech errors and sentence production.* Unpublished doctoral dissertation, Massachusetts Institute of Technology.

Shattuck-Hufnagel, S., & Klatt, D. H. (1979). The limited use of distinctive features and markedness in speech production: Evidence from speech error data. *Journal of Verbal Learning and Verbal Behavior, 18*, 41–55.

Sherrill, J. L. (1964). *They speak with other tongues.* New York: McGraw-Hill.

Shibamoto, J. S., & Olmsted, D. L. (1978). Lexical and syllabic patterns in phonological acquisition. *Journal of Child Language, 5*, 417–446.

Shockey, L. (1973). *Phonetic and phonological properties of connected speech.* Unpublished doctoral dissertation, Ohio State University.

Shockey, L. (1977). Perceptual test of a phonological rule. *Haskins Laboratories Status Report on Speech Research, SR-50*, 147–150.

Shockey, L., & Bond, Z. S. (1980). Phonological processes in speech addressed to children. *Phonetica, 37*, 267–274.

Shriberg, L. D. (1980). Developmental phonological disorders. In T. J. Hixon, L. D. Shriberg, & J. H. Saxman (Eds.), *Introduction to communication disorders.* Englewood Cliffs, N.J.: Prentice-Hall.

Shvachkin, N. K. (1973). The development of phonemic speech perception in early childhood. In C. A. Ferguson & D. I. Slobin (Eds.), *Studies of child language development*. New York: Holt, Rinehart and Winston. (Originally published 1948.)

Sigurd, B. (1968). Rank–frequency distributions for phonemes. *Phonetica, 18*, 1–15.

Simon, C. (1978). *Stop voicing in English and French monolinguals: Some developmental issues and experimental results.* Paper presented to the NICHD conference ''Child Phonology: Perception, Production and Deviation,'' Bethesda, Md.

Skousen, R. (1975). *Substantive evidence in phonology: The evidence from Finnish and French.* The Hague: Mouton.

Slis, I. H., & Cohen, A. (1969). On the complex regulating the voiced–voiceless distinction, I. *Language and Speech, 12*, 80–102.

Slobin, D. I. (1977). Language change in childhood and in history. In J. Macnamara (Ed.), *Language learning and thought*. New York: Academic Press.

Smit, A., & Bernthal, J. (1983). Voicing contrasts in the speech of articulation-disordered children and their phonological implications. *Journal of Speech and Hearing Research, 26*.

Smith, B. L. (1978a). Effects of place of articulation and vowel environment on 'voiced' stop consonant production. *Glossa, 12*, 163–175.

Smith, B. L. (1978b). Temporal aspects of English segment duration: A developmental perspective. *Journal of Phonetics, 6*, 37–67.

Smith, B. L. (1979). A phonetic analysis of consonantal devoicing in children's speech. *Journal of Child Language, 6*, 19–28.

Smith, B. L. (1982). Some observations concerning pre-meaningful vocalizations of hearing-impaired infants. *Journal of Speech and Hearing Disorders, 47*, 439–442.

Smith, B. L., & Oller, D. K. (1981). A comparative study of pre-meaningful vocalizations produced by normally developing and Down's syndrome infants. *Journal of Speech and Hearing Disorders, 46*, 46–51.

Smith, F., & Miller, G. A. (1966). *The genesis of language*. Cambridge, Mass.: MIT Press.

Smith, N. V. (1973). *The acquisition of phonology: A case study*. Cambridge: Cambridge University Press.

Snow, C. E., & Ferguson, C. A. (Eds.). (1977). *Talking to children: Language input and acquisition*. New York: Cambridge University Press.

Snow, K. (1960). *A descriptive and comparative study of the articulation of first grade children*. Unpublished doctoral dissertation, Indiana University.

Snow, K. (1963). A detailed analysis of articulation responses of 'normal' first grade children. *Journal of Speech and Hearing Research, 6*, 277–290.

Srivastava, G. P. (1974). A child's acquisition of Hindi consonants. *Indian Linguistics, 35*, 112–118.

Stampe, D. L. (1969). The acquisition of phonetic representation. *Papers from the 5th Regional Meeting of the Chicago Linguistic Society*. Chicago: Chicago Linguistic Society.

Stampe, D. L. (1973). *A dissertation on natural phonology*. Unpublished doctoral dissertation, University of Chicago.

Stark, R. E. (1972). Some features of the vocalizations of young deaf children. In J. F. Bosma (Ed.), *Third symposium on oral sensation and perception: The mouth of the infant*. Springfield, Ill.: Charles C Thomas.

Stein, D. (1981). Language acquisition and historical change. *Journal of Child Language, 8*, 177–192.

Stockman, I. J., Woods, D. R., & Tishman, A. (1981). Listener agreement on phonetic segments in early infant vocalizations. *Journal of Psycholinguistic Research, 10*, 593–617.

Stoel-Gammon, C., & Cooper, J. A. (1981). *Patterns of early lexical and phonological development*. Paper presented at the Second International Congress for the Study of Child Language, Vancouver, August.

Straight, H. S. (1976). *The acquisition of Maya phonology: Variation in Yucatec child language.* New York: Garland Publishing, Inc.

Streeter, L. A. (1974). *The effect of linguistic experience on phonetic perception.* Unpublished doctoral dissertation, Columbia University.

Subtelny, J., Worth, J. H., & Sakunda, M. (1966). Intraoral pressure and rate of flow during speech. *Journal of Speech and Hearing Research, 2,* 498–518.

Sully, J. (1896). *Studies of childhood.* New York: D. Appleton.

Swadesh, M. (1948). Sociologic notes on obsolescent languages. *International Journal of American Linguistics, 14,* 226–235.

Sweet, H. (1888). *A history of English sounds.* Oxford: Clarendon Press.

Sykes, J. L. (1940). A study of the spontaneous vocalizations of young deaf children. *Psychological Monographs, 52,* 104–123.

Taine, H. (1877). Acquisition of language by children. *Mind, 2,* 252–259. Reprinted in W. F. Leopold & A. Bar-Adon, *Child language: A book of readings.* Englewood Cliffs, N.J.: Prentice-Hall, 1971.

Taymans, L. M. (1976). *The development of English phonology before the age of two: A structural description of single word utterances and early word combination.* Unpublished doctoral dissertation, Northwestern University.

Templin, M. C. (1957). *Certain language skills in children.* Minneapolis: University of Minnesota Press.

Tent, J., & Clark, J. E. (1980). An experimental investigation into the perception of slips of the tongue. *Journal of Phonetics, 8,* 317–325.

Timm, L. A. (1977). A child's acquisition of Russian phonology. *Journal of Child Language, 4,* 329–339.

Tranel, B. (1981). *Concreteness in generative phonology: Evidence from French.* Berkeley: University of California Press.

Trnka, B. (1968). *A phonological analysis of present-day standard English.* University: University of Alabama Press.

Trost, J., & Canter, G. (1974). Apraxia of speech in patients with Broca's aphasia: A study of phoneme production accuracy and error patterns. *Brain and Language, 1,* 63–80.

Tuaycharoen, P. (1977). *The phonetic and phonological development of a Thai baby: From early communicative interaction to speech.* Unpublished doctoral dissertation, University of London.

Tuaycharoen, P. (1979). An account of speech development of a Thai child: From babbling to speech. In T. L. Thongkum, V. Panupong, P. Kullavanijaya, & M. R. K. Tingsabadh (Eds.), *Studies in Thai and Mon-Khmer phonetics and phonology: In Honor of Eugenie J. A. Henderson.* Bangkok: Chulalongkorn University Press.

Uber, D. R. (1982). *Perception and production of -s and -n in Puerto Rican Spanish.* Paper presented at the summer meeting of the Linguistic Society of America, College Park, Md.

UCLA Phonological Segment Inventory Database: Data and Index (1981). *UCLA Working Papers in Phonetics, 53,* 1–242.

Uzgiris, I. C., & Hunt, J. McV. (1975). *Assessment in infancy: Ordinal scales of psychological development.* Urbana: University of Illinois Press.

van den Broecke, M. P. R., & Goldstein, L. (1980). Consonant features in speech errors. In V. A. Fromkin (Ed.), *Errors in linguistic performance: Slips of the tongue, ear, pen, and hand.* New York: Academic Press.

Vanvik, A. (1971). The phonetic–phonemic development of a Norwegian child. *Norsk Tidsskrift Sprogvienskap, 24,* 269–325.

Velten, H. V. (1943). The growth of phonemic and lexical patterns in infant language. *Language, 19,* 281–292.

Vihman, M. (1971). On the acquisition of Estonian. *Papers and Reports on Child Language Development, 3,* 51–94.

Vihman, M. (1976). From pre-speech to speech: On early phonology. *Papers and Reports on Child Language Development, 12,* 230–243.

Vihman, M. (1978). Consonant harmony: Its scope and function in child language. In J. H. Greenberg (Ed.), *Universals of human language, vol. 2: Phonology.* Stanford, Calif.: Stanford University Press.

Vihman, M. (1979). Sound change and child language. In E. C. Traugott, R. Labrum & S. Shepherd (Eds.), *Amsterdam studies in the theory and history of linguistic science, 4. Current issues in linguistic theory, 14.* Papers presented at the 4th International Conference on Historical Linguistics. Amsterdam: John Benjamins.

Vihman, M. (1982). Formulas in first and second language acquisition. In L. K. Obler & L. Menn (Eds.), *Exceptional language and linguistics.* New York: Academic Press.

Vihman, M., Macken, M., Miller, R., & Simmons, H. (1981). *From babbling to speech: A reassessment of the continuity issue.* Paper presented at the Winter Meeting of the Linguistic Society of America, New York, December.

Walsh, T., & Parker, F. (1981). Vowel termination as a cue to voicing in post-vocalic stops. *Journal of Phonetics, 9,* 105–108.

Wang, M. D., & Bilger, R. C. (1973). Consonant confusions in noise: A study of perceptual features. *Journal of the Acoustical Society of America, 54,* 1248–1266.

Wang, W. S.-Y. (1978). The three scales of diachrony. In B. B. Kachru (Ed.), *Linguistics in the seventies: Directions and prospects.* Urbana: Department of Linguistics, University of Illinois.

Waterson, N. (1971). Child phonology: A prosodic view. *Journal of Linguistics, 7,* 179–211.

Webster, R. L. (1969). Selective suppression of infants' vocal responses by classes of phonemic stimulation. *Developmental Psychology, 1,* 410–414.

Weiner, F. F. (1983). The phonologic system: Assessment and treatment of the unintelligible child from a phonologic process approach. In J. Costello (Ed.), *Recent advances: Speech disorders.* San Diego, Cal.: College-Hill Press.

Weir, R. W. (1966). Some questions on the child's learning of phonology. In F. Smith & G. A. Miller (Eds.), *The genesis of language.* Cambridge, Mass.: MIT Press.

Weismer, G. (1979). Sensitivity of voice-onset time (VOT) measures to certain segmental features in speech production. *Journal of Phonetics, 7,* 197–204.

Werker, J. F., Gilbert, J. H., Humphrey, K., & Tees, R. C. (1981). Developmental aspects of cross-language speech perception. *Child Development, 52,* 349–355.

Westbury, J. R. (1979). Aspects of the temporal control of voicing in consonant clusters in English. *Texas Linguistic Forum, 14.*

Whitaker, H. A. (1976). Neurobiology of language. In E. L. Carterette & M. P. Friedman (Eds.), *Handbook of perception, vol. 7: Language and speech.* New York: Academic Press.

Wickelgren, W. (1979). *Cognitive psychology.* Englewood Cliffs, N.J.: Prentice-Hall.

Winitz, H., LaRiviere, C., & Herriman, E. (1975). Variations in VOT for English initial stops. *Journal of Phonetics, 3,* 41–52.

Wolf, C. G. (1978). Voicing cues in English final stops. *Journal of Phonetics, 6,* 299–309.

Wolfram, W., & Fasold, R. W. (1974). *The study of social dialects in American English.* Englewood Cliffs, N.J.: Prentice-Hall.

Yasuda, A. (1970). Articulatory skills in three-year-old children. *Studia Phonologica, 5,* 52–71.

Yegerlehner, J., & Voegelin, F. M. (1957). Frequencies and inventories of phonemes from nine languages. *International Journal of American Linguistics, 23,* 85–93.

Zimmerman, S. A., & Sapon, S. M. (1958). Note on vowel duration seen cross-linguistically. *Journal of the Acoustical Society of America, 30,* 152–153.

Zlatin, M. A., & Koenigsknecht, R. A. (1976). Development of the voicing contrast: A comparison of voice onset time in stop perception and production. *Journal of Speech and Hearing Research, 19,* 93–111.

Zwicky, A. M. (1972). Note on a phonological hierarchy in English. In R. P. Stockwell & R. K. S. Macaulay (Eds.), *Linguistic change and generative theory.* Bloomington: Indiana University Press.

Language Index

Subject Index

260